Baker James Cauthen
A Man for All Nations

Jesse C. Fletcher

BROADMAN PRESS
Nashville, Tennessee

4272-19

All photographs except the one on page 271 are from the Foreign Mission Board.
Photographers are: page 33, Rex Ray; page 100, Fon H. Scofield, Jr.; page 123, Lawrence
Snedden; page 143, H. Cornell Goerner; page 166, Mrs. Baker J. Cauthen; page 187,
Lawrence Snedden; page 231, Warren Johnson; page 251, James E. Legg. The photograph on page 271 is from Southwestern Baptist Theological Seminary.

ISBN: 0-8054-7219-3
Library of Congress catalog card number: 77-80941
Dewey Decimal classification: 266.092
Subject headings: CAUTHEN, BAKER JAMES // MISSIONS, FOREIGN
Printed in the United States of America

To
Genevieve Greer
Editor Extraordinary

Preface

The motivation that underwrites the beginning of a book often erodes under the pressures of research and interpretation. In this project, the very opposite has been true. The process of discovery and delineation has only enhanced the author's initial conviction that the life and ministry of Baker James Cauthen need to be defined and shared.

On the surface such a need emerges from the reality that, in the eyes of many, he is the most important figure in world missions since William Carey. This judgment arises from the fact that he has led in the building of the largest evangelical missionary enterprise in Christian history. For missiologists, the formative dimensions of his life, his missionary experience, the catalytic events which shaped his missionary methods, his leadership through the years, and further evolution of his missionary strategies call for critique and analysis.

It is this author's conviction, however, that the major contribution of Baker James Cauthen has emerged around far more personal dimensions. It's the man's life that speaks most clearly, and it offers a model of dedication for every Christian. Any follower of Jesus Christ who seeks to know what single-minded dedication can yield in the way of fruitfulness and effectiveness will find it in the life of Baker James Cauthen. People seeking the possibilities of warm and mutually satisfying family life through Christian principles will find it in his relationship to his beloved Eloise. Preachers seeking the secret of "preaching fresh" will find it in the study habits and devotional life of this prophetic spokesman. Christians seeking more effective prayer life will find a noble example. Baker James Cauthen has built a deep dependence upon his Lord through prayer.

Within the course of his Christian pilgrimage, others will find a modus operandi for living creatively in crises and for functioning victoriously in trials.

Of course, such material can quickly cross an invisible line into maudlin and unrealistic eulogizing, as an alarming number of biographical works emerging every year clearly testify. Has the author successfully skirted that line? Have the flaws and weaknesses of the principal been allowed to find their way onto a canvas dominated by achievement and strength in a way that reveals true character? Has the conflict in Cauthen's life been told honestly? The reader, the critic, the inevitable further studies will undoubtedly have their definite opinions. The author's only defense is that he tried to tell an honest story from the disadvantage point of his own friendship with and obvious admiration for the Cauthens. The author's hope is that the prayers that flowed forth during the process, not only from his heart but from the hearts of many supportive friends, make possible a contribution to the history of missions and the lives of readers.

JESSE C. FLETCHER

Acknowledgments

Perhaps as in no previous work, this author finds himself indebted beyond his ability to express either descriptively or numerically. Despite this antecedent assurance of failure, however, such expressions must be attempted.

First, the project depended upon the goodwill, patience, and humility of Baker James Cauthen and Eloise Glass Cauthen. Their abdication of self-interest and right of personal interpretation has been dramatic. It has helped alleviate the obvious drawbacks to biographical efforts of living persons. More, the author is indebted to these two people for personal friendship and Christian example.

But the project itself has grown upon the exemplary commitment of many others. The author's family, for instance, will have to be given significant credit for making it happen. They, more than anyone else, gave up the time and energies of a husband and father to make this project possible in the midst of burgeoning pastoral responsibilities. The First Baptist Church of Knoxville, Tennessee, also deserves credit, not only for explicit permission to attempt such an effort, but for prayerful support and patience in the course of it. Cauthen anecdotes and wisdom have been a part of their sermon diet for two years.

But many individuals have played indispensable roles. First and foremost would be Gaynell Seale, who has typed and retyped, commented and encouraged. Her husband and the author's associate, Jerry, has not only been a reactor but a patient courier. This has been Gaynell's first manuscript, but she has gone at it with the professionalism of a veteran.

Several researchers rendered invaluable contributions. Howard Bramlette, now of the Sunday School Board, skillfully researched background in Nashville and in Cauthen country in East Texas.

Nell Stanley did the same in the Jenkins Library and Archives at the Foreign Mission Board in Richmond, Virginia, as did Inez Tuggle and Elizabeth Minshew in Cauthen's personal files. Doris Kelley performed a similar function in the press files of the Foreign Mission Board.

Others must be mentioned for definitive roles as informants. They include Robert Bausum, Ralph Cauthen, W. A. Criswell, Charles Culpepper, Sidney Goldfinch, Cal Guy, W. L. Howse, John Jeter Hurt, Gladys Thompson Keer, Rush Loving, Albert McClellan, Carolyn Cauthen Mathews, Frank Means, Buford Nichols, Porter Routh, Franklin Segler, Lucy Smith, W. O. Vaught, and Elmer S. West.

Yet informants and contributors are far too numerous to name in these brief paragraphs. In many cases their contributions are acknowledged in the book itself. Some are anonymous, both there and here, but they know who they are; and they know my appreciation.

And once again, as the dedication indicates, the author leaned heavily on the skills of Genevieve Greer, former book editor of the Foreign Mission Board, now retired in Edmond, Oklahoma, for editorial guidance. This is the seventh book Genevieve Greer has helped the author complete. She not only did important research in Richmond; she also gave invaluable suggestions in the writing process itself. She is direct, accurate, and remarkably patient.

Appreciation must also be expressed to a special committee of the Foreign Mission Board created to help the author facilitate this effort. M. Hunter Riggins, J. Roy Clifford, and the late E. Hermond Westmoreland provided sincere guidance and encouragement.

But the Cauthens, the clerical and editorial support, the informants, and the encouragers cannot accept responsibility for the oversights, errors, or problems in perception that such a manuscript is bound to include. The author himself must assume responsibility for these and so acknowledge. But even that risk was worth it.

JESSE C. FLETCHER
Knoxville, Tennessee

Contents

PART 1, *THE FORGE*

1.	Alloy of Life	13
2.	The Shape of the Man	19
3.	The Student Preacher	26
4.	In Pursuit of Excellence	42
5.	The School of the Prophets	49
6.	Eloise	64
7.	The Pastor-Teacher	76
8.	The Missionary Question	81

PART 2, *THE FURNACE*

1.	Journey of Obedience	101
2.	Unsettling the Settled	114
3.	Evacuation	119
4.	Inland Bound	127
5.	The Caves of Kweilin	134
6.	Tested	144
7.	Odyssey Home	155

PART 3, *THE FRAY*

1.	Destined for Leadership	167
2.	Return to the Orient	175
3.	Disregarding the Clouds	182
4.	The Red Tide	192
5.	A New Diaspora	205
6.	The Mantle of Leadership	216
7.	Another Man's Dream	227
8.	Dreaming a New Dream	240
9.	Preacher, Husband, Father	254
10.	The Final Challenge	264

Part 1

**The Forge
1909-1939**

*The forge in which any man is formed involves
genetics, models, influence, and circumstances.
But for people who are committed to the grand
notion that God was in Christ, life is purposeful;
and the above ingredients become, in his hands, the
stuff of divine process.*

Young missionaries Dr. and Mrs. Baker James Cauthen with children, Carolyn and Ralph, and Chinese Christian leaders

CHAPTER ONE

The Alloy of Life

The twentieth century was just nine years into its explosive pilgrimage when Baker James Cauthen entered the world in the small East Texas town of Huntsville on a cold night on the twentieth of December. Huntsville was primarily known for its state penitentiary and a teachers' college named after the Texas hero Sam Houston. Usually only a prison break drew notice to the town, and the town itself took very little notice of anything else. Certainly it would hardly have been aware of the small drama unfolding in the modest rented house where James Sylvester Cauthen had ensconced his pregnant wife and small son.

James Cauthen's wife, fiercely completing her labor under the watchful eye of a doctor and a neighbor, had been a student at the college when Cauthen had wooed and married her four years before. They had moved to San Angelo, Texas, where he worked for a time in a clothing store. But neither the job nor the barren West Texas horizon did much for either of them, though their elder son, Joe B. (J. B., as he was known), had been born there. J. B., a perplexed toddler, sat next to the slight and nervous figure of his father, trying to make sense out of the muffled sounds from his mother's bedroom. The next day, December 21, would be his third birthday; and Mother had promised him a very special birthday present. Could this situation have anything to do with it?

A small, slender, and pretty woman with a strong will and a firm way about her, Maude Baker Cauthen was going about her second childbearing experience with the kind of determination that she employed in every task. As the baby appeared, the neighbor let out an exclamation. "My gosh, he's tiny!" The doctor didn't say anything, however, until he had the small infant cleansed and wrapped and the mother cared for and resting. Then he called the father into the room. The three-year-old followed, holding and peering from behind his father's leg.

"He only weighs three and a half pounds, Mr. Cauthen. He may not make it."

"He'll make it." They were both surprised by the strength of the voice from the bed.

Maude Baker repeated, "He'll make it. He belongs to the Lord. I've given him to the Lord. I'll take care of him. He'll make it."

The infant whose tiny face could be covered with a silver dollar, as Grandfather Baker would remind him, was named Baker, his mother's maiden name, and James, his father's first name. His parents thought about calling him James Baker but decided to reverse the names since they already had one J. B. in the family. Baker James quickly became "Bake" to the adoring family who granted added respect to the mother as the child hung on and slowly began to grow—just as she said he would—though often, it seemed, only by the force of her will.

Maude Baker had been fighting odds all her life. Born in the small town of Madisonville, Texas, where her mother died when she was still a girl, she had fallen into the hands of a godly grand-mother who came to live with the family and instilled in her a fierce independence and a deep faith. When it came time to attend college, she moved from Madisonville to Huntsville. Though a Methodist by background, she boarded with a Baptist deacon's family named Morse who had a girl her age. The Morses were not too sure about the young shop clerk who in 1905 courted and married Maude, thus ending their ward's college career. But Maude Baker was sure about him. She added his name to her own and took great pride in doing so.

However, it was years before the Cauthen family gained any understanding of the background of either their name or their family. The name was spelled "Cawthorn" when their forebears settled in Virginia in 1680, having immigrated there from London. The new world attracted them from an old world where their name had existed before the Norman conquest as that of a small town-ship in Yorkshire.

Some of the men who emerged from that Virginia family of Cawthorns fought in the Revolutionary War with General Nathanael Greene when he carried the fight for freedom into

North Carolina. They remained there in Warren County. Later a group moved down to Lancaster, South Carolina. Sometime in this period, they changed the name to the Cauthen spelling. It was the spelling Baker James Cauthen's forebears were using when they moved to Crenshaw County, Alabama, after the Civil War.

Lina Cauthen gave birth to Baker James Cauthen's father, James Sylvester, in Lavaca County, Texas, in 1879. She and her husband had moved there to seek greener pastures than the post-Civil War deep South provided. There would be five boys in the family, including Baker's father, James Sylvester.

A tough constitution was a family trait. Baker's paternal grandfather became something of a patriarch, living to be ninety and setting a trend for the whole family. In the Cauthen home, however, his status was rivaled by Maude Cauthen's father, T. R. Baker, who helped her grandmother raise her. He loved the woods—hunting and trapping—though that wasn't the daughter's favorite place. Nor was it to be her son's.

Baker James Cauthen, still sickly from his rocky start, was less than six months old when his father moved the little family seventy miles up state highway 94 to the Piney Woods town of Lufkin. A new job opportunity in a store seemed to offer more security for the family-minded man.

From Maude Baker Cauthen's point of view, however, the security was questionable. Lufkin had three grocery stores and seventeen saloons when they moved there. It was a long time before the mother would go out after dark, much less let her children, because of the boisterous living that surrounded the saloons in the predominantly mill-town population. Except for the family's eighteen-month sojourn in Nacogdoches not long after his birth, Lufkin was to be in every way Baker James Cauthen's hometown.

Lufkin, Texas, seemed an unlikely nurturing place for a young man who would have an international influence. According to its own historians, Lufkin's birth came in 1881 as a result of an altercation between railroad men and the town constable in a place called Homer, five miles away. The Southern Pacific Railroad was being built through Angelina County and through the county seat of Homer. But when the town constable threw some of the location crew into jail after a Saturday night drinking spree, their supervisor, after he finally secured his men's release, angrily declared that he would reroute the railroad. As good as his word, he went back to the Neches River and ran a new line to miss Homer. The town of Lufkin, named after the railroad builder, resulted.

In addition to the saloons, there were "two large sawmills, two cleaning mills, one iron foundry and machine shop, one ice factory, one canning factory, one steam bottling plant, one confectionary shop, one laundry, one bakery, two cotton gins, two grist mills, two jewelers, one boot and shoe shop, two tailors, one saddler shop, three stationery houses, and one sheetiron works." Two hotels, the Smith Hotel and the Shotwell House, offered rest to travelers.

When the Cauthens moved to Lufkin, the main section of town was called Cotton Square and was dominated by the fire department building, which had two two-wheeled fire carts and five hundred feet of hose with two nozzles.

Other buildings were spread around the hard-packed dirt of the square, whose starkness was relieved by a few pine trees. Buggies and horses were hitched to hitching rails or hitching posts scattered around the square. Four years later, the first Model-T Fords made their appearance with drivers in linen dusters and goggles to panic the horses and awe the citizens.

As the first decade of twentieth century came to an end, Lufkinites, like most Americans, gave little attention to President William Howard Taft and efforts to impose tariffs that would further protect America from an increasingly tumultuous old world. There was little if any awareness of the deliverance of Chinese government from Manchu hands, the bargaining between Germany and France over Morocco, a revolution in Turkey involving the capture of Constantinople, the efforts of Indians to get some voice in their British-ruled country, the overthrow of the Shah of Persia, rioting in Spain, the murder of Prince Eto in Japan by a Korean fanatic, a revolution in Venezuela, or the civil war in Honduras.

In fact, all eyes in Lufkin were on the town women's battle against the local liquor traffic, which they claimed with increasing boldness made their town an unfit place in which to live. Emboldened by the churches, the women took to the streets to voice their outrage. Baker took it all in from the buggy his mother pushed in one of the demonstrations.

Due to the enterprising recruiting of a pastor named Mahan, James Sylvester Cauthen and Maude Baker Cauthen became active in the life of First Baptist Church of Lufkin almost immediately after they moved there.

Any fears or trepidations the pastor and his colleagues had about the aggressiveness of the women in their midst were more than offset by approval of their crusades.

In 1912 Maude Baker Cauthen and her cohorts won their battle, and Lufkin voted dry. It has remained so.

By the time Baker James started to school, the family identity was deeply rooted in the fertile soil of the East Texas milling town. Maude Cauthen taught a women's Sunday School class at First Baptist Church, and James S. Cauthen was elected a deacon and served as secretary of the Sunday School. He made a comfortable living as a clothing salesman.

Despite the three-year difference in their ages, J. B. and his brother "Bake" were very close. Yet from early days the solemn, smallish, and skinny younger son was the more aggressive brother. In some ways, according to Joe B., he had to be. His mother dressed him a bit girlishly and let his hair grow in long curls. Joe B. warned his parents that Bake would never survive the fights if he started to school looking that way. He had already had his share in the neighborhood. Finally, Maude relented and tearfully cut Bake's hair before he started to school. Joe B. was greatly relieved. Baker didn't take much off of anybody; and J. B. feared that no bigger than he was, he might not live through that first year.

At the time Cauthen started to school, the United States was sensing the full potential of the twentieth century. Its growing number of Model-T Fords and widening newspaper coverage reflected the progressive spirit abroad in the world. The year Cauthen was born, research began in genetics; Richard Perry reached the North Pole; Louis Bleriott crossed the English Channel in a monoplane; and Henry Ford manufactured his first automobile.

Yet Baker Cauthen's horizons, even in those early years, turned within rather than without. Undoubtedly the piety of his soft-spoken, exemplary father was significant, but the deep religious convictions of his mother were probably most definitive in guiding him along spiritual lines.

Even before starting to school, Baker developed strong affinities for religious matters and a strong tie with his mother. One day he watched her at work in a closet that she was cleaning in a bedroom adjacent to their living room. On a sudden impulse, he rushed into the closet, closed the door behind him, and hugged her tightly. Whether she interpreted the hug as spontaneous affection or spontaneous mischievousness, she was more preoccuped with the fact that the snap lock on the door had engaged. She couldn't get it open. With the door closed, she was beginning to feel the heat from the fire on the other side and became worried about passing out. Bake, sensing his mother's concern, reassured her. "Don't worry, Mother. I'll pray, and God will open it." She left him to his devices, and she commenced hers with a mop handle. When the door popped open, Bake stepped out brightly and told his exasperated mother, "See. I told you God would open the door." Years later, she enjoyed telling that incident to friends and admirers who visited the Cauthen homeplace.

Besides his mother and father, Cauthen had another model by the time he was six years of age. It was R. L. Cole, who became pastor of the First Baptist Church in Lufkin in 1914. Cole, a most effective minister, had a partial facial paralysis that caused him to speak from the side of his mouth. Cauthen was impressed by his pastor. He would cajole his brother into playing church with him, and he would make J. B. be the song leader. Cauthen would then preach, twisting his mouth around so that he could speak like Cole.

J. B. remembers the overwhelming effect of that effort at the funeral for a cat over which his younger brother presided.

The smallish Baker hated to admit his age. At five he wanted to begin school; and when his mother and father objected because they would have to pay tuition for him to begin a year early, he shed copious tears while berating his parents. "You don't want me to grow up to be a know-nothing, do you?" His desire to be and act more mature than his age marked him from his earliest years.

CHAPTER TWO

The Shape of the Man

The Lufkin newspapers in 1916 were full of stories of the war in Europe. The Russians opened an offensive in Galatia. The Germans made their first zeppelin bombing raid on Paris. A small group of political ideologist called Communists formed a cell in Berlin. Germany declared war on Portugal. The United States objected to German attacks on unarmed merchant ships. Bulgaria declared war on Romania, and the Central Powers proclaimed the kingdom of Poland.

America resisted fiercely any efforts to be made more than simply interested in Europe. Teddy Roosevelt declined the nomination of the Progressive Republicans for President as Woodrow Wilson was renominated by the Democrats. Wilson was reelected on November 7 of that year over Charles E. Hughes while the Senate was passing the famous Immigration Bill and trying to get used to its first woman member of Congress.

Baker James Cauthen and his family were more concerned with a revival being held at First Baptist Church. Their pastor, R. L. Cole, was preaching. The Cauthen boys were both stirred to think of their own salvation. J. B. was nine, and nobody really questioned his readiness, although the parents had asked the pastor to come by and visit him. As he did, Bake indicated that he was ready, too. Cole looked at the smallish youngster and realized that he might be as spiritually knowledgeable as the older brother.

"Why do you want to be baptized, Bake?" he asked.

"To show the world I love Jesus," the youngster replied.

Cole, speaking from the side of his mouth in his characteristic way, said, "Let him come."

The parents were not sure. They took the salvation experience very seriously, and they wanted no premature decisions.

That night in the service, young J. B. launched out into the aisle as soon as the invitation hymn began to be sung and walked down the oak-floored sanctuary to the front. He wasn't really surprised when he found young Bake right behind him. Nor did the younger Cauthen son seem perturbed when some of the folk who were convinced he was too young proceeded to grill him on spiritual matters. As it turned out, the young backyard preacher, veteran of "our gang" type congregations and pet funerals, was more than equal to the questioning of the most knowledgeable of the Lufkin laymen. Bake and J. B. were baptized into the membership of the First Baptist Church that April.

A significant moment for both boys, it was a natural extension of early religious notions for the younger. Whether that which had commenced spiritually in his life began earlier or in that moment of decision will be revealed only by God, but that it had begun was evidenced in every facet of the youngster's life.

Not that he did not have a sense of his own tendency to rebel against God. His potential for selfishness and sin had already emerged in many ways. During the previous year when an American Expeditionary Force marched into Mexico, Baker and his brother were caught up in the strong feelings against Mexicans. Bake walked up to a little Mexican boy on the sidewalk, said, "I don't like you," and pushed him off into the mud. He got away with it as far as the Mexican was concerned, but in his heart he was chagrined by the kind of meanness of which he was capable.

The boys were forbidden to go into the downtown area during their childhood; but in one of his preschool days, Baker slipped away. He wandered for some time before he began to worry about how he was going to get back home without incurring the inevitable mother-administered whipping. He hatched a plan. Going to the grocery store where the family traded, he bought a broom on credit. When he got home, his mother was not impressed. She whipped him and then gave him another trip to town, this time to return the broom. He stood in the doorway of the store, threw the broom inside, and shouted, "There's your broom."

Though only six, Cauthen was aware of man's sinful capacity; and in his backyard sermons, he was capable of excoriating it. His profession proved he was capable of repenting of it.

From that day on, the center of the two boys' lives revolved around their tightly run, well-disciplined home, the various odd jobs held during out-of-school hours until they were grown, and the First Baptist Church of Lufkin.

It was the church more than newspapers with their emphasis on European affairs that brought a larger world into the youngest Cauthen's vision. His mother took him to Woman's Missionary meetings, where stories of missionaries enthralled him. He announced once to his older brother that undoubtedly he would end up "preaching the gospel to the heathen in China."

This interest increased his appetite for knowledge. He read the newspapers avidly and was aware of the events that pulled the United States into the European war in 1917.

In early 1917, eight-year-old Baker James Cauthen and his closest friend, his brother J. B., began to realize that the war in Europe about which they had heard vague things was sounding more personal. German submarines were sinking American ships. Bake's father came home from the shop on April 6 with news that America had declared war against the Central Powers. American troops would soon be joining the fighting. On the streets of Lufkin, they heard talk that the war would soon be over when the American boys got on to the scene.

Bake and J. B. took to marching around the backyard with shouldered sticks for weapons.

When the first soldiers left Lufkin for basic training in San Antonio at Fort Sam Houston, there was a big parade. All Lufkin was a part of it. The Hoo Hoo Band, for years Lufkin's major entertainment organization, played at all parades, public gatherings, and even changed character from time to time to become the Lufkin Opera House Orchestra. It and the soldiers gave the boys a thrill.

The Cauthen house on North First Street was not far from the Southern Railway tracks where trains often switched. In the summer of 1917, Bake and J. B. often went down to the tracks to see the soldiers. Most of the time they stood at a safe distance, listening to the confident and sometimes raucous soldiers chattering with well-wishing Lufkinites; but at other times, they ventured closer. Once a soldier reached down and gave young Bake a small New Testament. The boy carried it through the years and occasionally worried about having it when that soldier probably needed it before the war was over.

Boys wore knickers in those days. When the Cauthen boys turned out for special events, it was with big bow ties, black Buster Brown shoes, patent-leather belts, sailor collars, and sagging stockings.

That same summer, at the beautiful lake outside of Lufkin, Mrs. Cauthen's Sunday School class gave a picnic in honor of the soldiers about to depart for Europe. Cauthen, still small for his size but getting scrappier all the time to make up for it, was determined to learn to swim that afternoon. He followed the other kids piling into the water for relief from the heat. His efforts began to reward him with some ease in swimming, but he didn't like to open his eyes. Without a sense of direction, he was soon in deep water. When he opened his eyes and saw his problem, he panicked and began to thrash about. A soldier named Dick Philan jumped in, fully clothed in his Sunday best, to grab the terrified boy and pull him to safety. Cauthen always remembers his debt to the man.

Summer days were spent working. Both of the Cauthen boys took any kind of job they could get and purchased bicycles with money they saved. Occasionally they joined in neighborhood games with other kids—usually a game called "shinny with a stick" or another called "wolf over the river."

They caught a lot of guidance from their mother, but a lot of example from their father. He was a good listener and by his listening could elicit the problems and confidence of others. Maude and James Cauthen were very close, a closeness never more obvious than in the winter of 1918 when the young father came down with the flu. Many Lufkinites had already died from the dreaded respiratory and intestinal malady, and rumor had it that hundreds of thousands of people in the nation were dying from it. The boys had been inoculated against smallpox earlier that year by the family physician, but there was no inoculation for the flu.

Both were old enough to be sobered by danger. Their father was special to them. On Saturday nights the boys often went to a picture show, and later Bake worked at the show taking tickets, sweeping out, and selling popcorn. After the show they would come by the store, where their father worked until nearly midnight on Saturday, and go home with him. Other times they waited up with their mother until their father arrived, jumping from behind the door to scare him. He never failed to act scared. A neighbor said, "There's an awful lot of love in that family."

As the flu epidemic worsened, only Mrs. Cauthen was allowed into her husband's room, and she took elaborate precautions. Every time she touched her husband's bedpost she washed her hands in carbolic acid. Bake and J. B. could go to the door and peek in, but they were not allowed to enter. Every now and then their father rewarded their vigilance with a turn of his head—his eyes feverish, his skin sallow looking—and a weak smile.

The boys got uneasy when their grandfather, T. R. Baker, showed up. Their mother would not allow her father into the house. "If you get the flu, it will kill you," she said. Bake wasn't sure. Granddad Baker, his namesake in a way, was no ordinary man, he knew. The old man loved the woods; and when his wife had died many years ago, he had become a trapper and a hunter. No flu bug could bother him.

Finally, as the new year of 1919 dawned, the little family's crisis was over. It was obvious that Dad Cauthen wasn't going to be one of the thousands and thousands who became victims of the flu during the winter of 1918.

The flu epidemic almost overshadowed the fact that the war was over in Europe, with the armistice signed on November 11. There were some celebrations, but a lot of people were afraid to be in groups of people. There was one exception: The Cauthens always went to church.

After the war, Mrs. Cauthen began working sixty hours a week at a local store for fifteen dollars. "You boys are going to college," she announced to J. B. and Bake when they began to complain of her absence. The whole industrious family was at work.

The father trained both boys to value money. J. B.'s first job involved Bake. Their father offered J. B. ten cents a load to move fertilizer in his wagon from across the street to their yard. J. B. loaded up the wagon, and Bake crawled on top. One trip of that was all J. B. could manage. On the next trip, he put in about two shovels full of fertilizer before Bake. After a while, their father came out and asked J. B. how many loads he had taken. Despite the pitifully small pile of fertilizer in the Cauthen yard, J. B. had made quite a few trips. The father explained why it wasn't going to work that way: "Two shovels full and Bake don't make a load of fertilizer."

Soon Bake was picking up similar jobs and showing zest for work. He got his first steady job in 1921 at the local movie house as ticket taker and popcorn salesman. He was twelve years old. Bake worked there at nights during the school year of 1921-22 and all summer. His heavy schedule trimmed what little weight he had sported in his fifth-grade picture. At that time, he had been full-faced and looked right spiffy in his belted and pocketed wool coat with his hair parted almost in the middle—the way he wore it until just before he was married.

Bake used the money he made to buy his own clothes. When he was twelve, he opened his own bank account with five dollars his grandfather gave him earlier. He planned to save the money and buy a watch with it someday. His father used to say to friends, "Bake still has the first dime he ever made." Bake tithed faithfully and saved everything else that he didn't use for his own clothes. "Don't spend money for anything that is not worthwhile and that you don't need," his mother would caution him.

Despite his smallness and his trailing around after an older brother, Bake was outspoken. His older brother said that quality first showed when they visited a Methodist church in Nacogdoches and watched a Methodist "sprinkling." Young Bake stood up on his pew and said, "That's not the way Jesus was baptized." A Baptist preacher who heard about it said, "God may call that boy to preach."

The year that World War I broke out, the same year that the soldier gave him the New Testament, Cauthen had some feelings about that himself. It really came about with his discomfort regarding profanity. He had quite a temper and felt greatly tempted to use some of the profane words he heard, but decided he didn't want that kind of thing to have an upper hand in his life. Praying for victory over the temptation, he asked God what he would have him do. "I replied audibly to my own question," he declared. "I said, 'I ought to work for God.'"

By the time he entered high school in 1922, he was quite articulate. Active in the Lufkin High School Hi-Y, he participated in programs with speaking parts and entered speech-making contests. On Hi-Y days, he spoke in several churches in the county with a sermon about the YMCA triangle of body, mind, and spirit.

The realization that he was going to devote his life to work for God matured in young Bake Cauthen to the point where he knew he was to prepare himself for the gospel ministry. In 1926, when he was still sixteen, he graduated from Lufkin High School as president of his class, with enough money saved from years of working after school and in the summers to buy an automobile. He planned to commute each day to Stephen F. Austin College in Nacogdoches, Texas, beginning in September. He lined up three other riders who would pay the cost of gasoline and provide company for the hour's drive each way. His plans were to get a good foundation in the form of a liberal arts program and then go on to seminary to prepare himself to preach.

As it turned out, he was going to have to prepare while he preached.

CHAPTER THREE

The Student Preacher

From Baker Cauthen's earliest years, he though of himself as older than he actually was. Perhaps the challenge of an older brother admitted him to a peer relationship from the very beginning. Perhaps the encouragement and ambitions of his mother gave him an older outlook. Possibly his slight size had something to do with the way he was. Most likely, his formidable intellectual skills and ability to express himself added to his stature. Whatever the cause, when he graduated from high school in the summer of 1926, he considered himself grown. He carried himself in a way that caused others, including peers, to give him credit for maturity beyond his sixteen years.

When young Cauthen spoke, his gifts were obvious. His calling was fully established in his own mind and in the eyes of others. Now was the time for further education, and he was eager for it. His ambitions were intense. He wanted the best possible preparation for Christian service. Although Baylor University in Waco was his choice, he realized the financial demands were beyond his family's resources. He didn't mind working, but he didn't want to compromise the studying opportunity.

The answer was Stephen F. Austin College in Nacogdoches, Texas. The twenty-five-mile distance made necessary the automobile purchased with money frugally earned and put aside during his high school years. His three passagers were all girls and all fellow students. One, Gladys Thompson, was the nearest thing he had to a girl friend. While he enjoyed social life, he did not let himself become too involved. Within a few months after he started to college, he began to date another girl who interested him. But when he saw that his math grade dropped as a result, he backed away quickly. His pragmatism was total. Nothing was going to get in the way of his preparation.

The scope of his efforts was evident in a letter to his mother on Mother's Day the next spring. His letters to her, always affectionate, reflected both the idealism of the age and the intimate relationship between them. He wrote:

"Mothers have always had a share in the training of great men. Moses was trained by his mother; Walter Scott by his father. Scott's mother was a lover of poetry and painting; Byron's mother was his worst enemy; the mother of Napoleon was of a deep piety and a superior mind. The mother of Patrick Henry was noted for her superior conversational powers. But *my* mother is noted for her deep piety, intellect, leadership, love of poetry, and appreciation of the noble things of life. If I am ever to become a man of any accounts, can you not see the part you will play?"

Two months after he began school, an opportunity came which sealed the direction of his life. Though he was committed to Christian ministry, his opportunities had been limited to youth programs, Hi-Y programs, and Sunday School responsibilities. Cauthen at this time was five feet, ten and one-half inches tall, but weighed only 110 pounds. Slightness of build make his piercing eyes and precise oratory even more dramatic.

One Friday night in November he was in the store where his father worked. A young man who was already a minister and friend of Cauthen's came in.

"Hi, Bake. How are things at Stephen F. Austin?"

"Fine. It's a good school, and I'm studying hard."

"I bet you are. Are you speaking anywhere this weekend?"

"No."

"You know where the Providence Church is?" Bake had passed the small, one-room structure on several occasions.

"Yes."

"How about speaking down there Saturday night? They don't have a pastor. I agreed to try to help get them someone, and I just haven't been able to do it." Bake looked at his dad. There was no question about what he felt he should do.

"I think you ought to go," his father said.

"I'll be glad to." Cauthen grinned at his friend as his mind started turning over sermon ideas.

"Good. It's all settled," he said.

The Providence Church, seven miles down highway 94 from Lufkin toward Groveton, had forty-eight members. It was what Baptists call a "quarter-time" church. That is, it met once a month. When Cauthen got through preaching that Saturday night, November 10, 1926, the chairman of the deacons said, "How about coming back tomorrow morning, son?" He confessed later that when they saw his youth, they had decided to hear him before they asked him back. "I'll be glad to," Cauthen said. After that service, the same deacon prevailed on him to return the next Wednesday night for a service.

On Wednesday night, Baker had barely enough time to get back from Stephen F. Austin, deliver his passengers, and get cleaned up before his mother had a meal on the table for him to eat prior to journeying the seven miles to Providence. His father came in from the store about that time and said, "I'd like to go with you." Bake looked up, surprised and pleased. "I wish you would."

To Bake's surprise, after he finished his devotional message, the deacon who had spoken to him on Sunday night called the church into business session; and they proceeded to call him to be their preacher. Cauthen stood up and said, "But I have not even been licensed to preach." The deacon replied, "I feel sure that can be taken care of." Cauthen's father was asked by the presiding officer if he had anything to say. He stood and looked at his son, then at the group a minute, and said, "I have confidence in Bake to serve the Lord effectively." Early the next morning, the elder Cauthen contacted the pastor of the First Baptist Church in Lufkin, at that time J. R. Nutt, about his son's call and the matter of a license. On the following Sunday, the First Baptist Church of Lufkin voted to license Baker James Cauthen to preach so that he could be installed as pastor of the Providence congregation when it met again the following month.

Two weeks after Cauthen became pastor of the Providence Baptist Church, the wife of the oldest deacon passed away, and the young pastor was called upon to preach his first funeral. He was a week shy of his seventeenth birthday, but not one bit shy of the sense of responsibility and stature necessary to perform the task. Family members indicated that he was of great comfort to them.

That spring, the seventeen-year-old pastor and college commuter was ordained to the gospel ministry by the First Baptist Church of Lufkin. R. L. Cole, at this time associational missionary, J. R. Nutt, pastor of the church, and a former pastor, James T. McNew, led in the service. The whole church, who had watched the youngster's spiritual experience deepen and grow steadily through the years, felt an investment in his ministry.

His fellow commuter, Gladys Thompson, attended the ordination service and assured Baker that he was going to be something very special. "You can't miss with parents like yours," she said, noting the pride and support that came from Maude and James Cauthen.

That summer Cauthen enrolled for additional courses at Stephen F. Austin and kept commuting. No need to slow down now that he saw his direction clearly! In the spring, he persuaded the Providence Church to meet twice instead of once a month. They also responded to a suggestion that they invite R. L. Cole to preach a summer revival. Cauthen and Cole, his model preacher from his earliest years, worked well together that summer. When the revival meeting was over, thirty candidates awaited baptism.

On a Sunday afternoon in July, the 110-pound Cauthen waded into the Neches River and began baptizing those who had received Christ and made a public profession of their faith during the week's revival services.

The baptism went smoothy until Cauthen came to a man named "Red" Conditt, the future county sheriff, who weighed well over two hundred pounds. Standing with his hands folded, he towered above Cauthen. With no outward anxiety or any hint of inadequacy, Cauthen proceeded to baptize the man.

His brother, not at all hesitant to tell him the way things really appeared, later said, "What Bake did was climb on that man and sink him and then let him get out the best way he could." Whatever humor was attached to that, it did not rob the people of a sense of spiritual significance.

A neighbor, W. E. Lawrence, remembered the event nearly fifty years later as the highest spiritual moment of his life. He and his wife brought Baker's young friend, Gladys Thompson, to the service. (The Lawrences' daughter Margaret later married Winston Crawley, who was to become an able colleague of Cauthen at the Foreign Mission Board.)

Cauthen quickly earned a reputation as an effective personal witness. During that first summer he witnessed to Wayne Lovett, a big farm boy just a little older than he was. Cauthen asked Lovett to wait after church one Sunday night, then dealt with him earnestly about Christ's claims on his life. After a time the two men went outside the church and knelt in the shadow of the building, which was outlined by a full moon. There Wayne made his profession of faith and the next Sunday made it public before the church. He was one of those Cauthen baptized in the Neches River.

A few weeks later, a message that Lovett was in the hospital awaited Baker when he arrived home from Stephen F. Austin. Cauthen found the man near death with a ruptured appendix; and as he waited with the family, Lovett died. The family's appreciation for his concern about the boy's spiritual well-being and the church's appreciation for his handling of the family's grief were profound. No one questioned the seventeen-year-old's abilities anymore. He was their pastor.

Another pivotal event took place twelve miles northwest of Lufkin that same summer in a little country church at Pollock. In the spring of 1927, this little community asked him to come up on one of his off Sundays from Providence and preach for them on Sunday afternoon. He did so and agreed to continue on Sunday afternoons twice a month. They called him as their pastor, too.

After the Providence revival, Cauthen went to Pollock to hold a week-long meeting. Something happened there, significant even beyond his ability to recognize it at the time.

Good crowds gathered in the little frame church at Pollock on the first Sunday evening of the revival. The intense, incredibly slender, wavy-haired, handsome—even a bit pretty—young man almost immediately took charge of the crowd with the fervency of his evangelistic preaching. One lady said years later, "I looked up there and saw this slip of a boy facing a crowd including so many big, burly men, and I immediately felt sorry for him. But as he began to preach, my pity was redirected. I began to feel sorry for *me*. The force of his words and the slashing finger with which he punctuated his remarks brought me under deep conviction."

But the catalytic event came for Cauthen when he extended an invitation for people to trust Christ. To his surprise, people immediately began to leave their seats and publicly confess faith in Jesus Christ. Others came to rededicate lives that had strayed from

God's purpose. Several people united with the struggling little church by transfer of membership. On the second, third, and fourth nights, this phenomenon continued. As the crowd built each night, the tension mounted toward the invitation. Cauthen skillfully stated the invitation. As the people began to sing, the results were repeated. People who had never been moved and who had never been prone to respond to invitations, emotional or rational, immediately came forth. Grown men wept; women were contrite; and youngsters came forward pale and trembling under their conviction.

As Cauthen looks back on it now, he marks that revival as his first recognition of a very special gift for what preachers through the years have called "drawing the net." It also made sure that he would not run out of preaching opportunities. For years he had as much work as he could handle in the Unity Baptist Association.

With these demands for his kind of preaching and his continuing college work, Cauthen had his hands full. But by single-mindedness and hard driving, he kept it all on track.

Baker James Cauthen went through his second full year of college with the same speed and incredibly busy schedule. The responsibility of commuting back and forth to Nacogdoches from Lufkin each day continued. Pastoring both the Providence and Pollock churches brought an increasing number of spin-off demands as part of a dynamic ministry. With all this, Cauthen kept up an amazingly active college life.

In high school, Baker had been a member of the debate team and the dramatic group. He had had a part in the senior play. At Stephen F. Austin he continued his debate work, added the coeditorship of the *Pine Log,* which was the school paper, and continued his dramatics.

He especially enjoyed the debate club, where he was without peer in articulating his thoughts and grasping issues. His ability to see the various facets of a matter and spot implications before almost anyone else soon made him a respected and a winning debater.

In addition, his ability to express that verbal skill on paper led him to work on the school newspaper. That was the basis for his making his first major trip: he went to Canyon, Texas, in the spring of 1928 for a journalism meeting. He specifically remembers meeting a young man named Joe Burton there. Their paths were to cross often as Burton became a leading figure in the Southern Baptist Convention publishing scene at its Sunday School Board in Nashville.

Cauthen went through the summer of 1928 the way he had the previous one, holding revivals in various churches in the Unity Association and helping his own small churches have their traditional revival meetings. But he also kept going to school. Consequently, when he enrolled in the fall of 1928 for what should have been his junior year, he was a senior. And he was admired and respected enough, despite his commuting status, to be elected senior class president.

Cauthen was then only eighteen years of age. However, his fellow seniors not only accepted him as their peer but, in that far simpler day, judged his particular skills as so ideal and his life-style as so disciplined that they held him in near awe. They elected him most popular boy and named him coeditor of the *Pine Log*.

Cauthen also played the male lead in the senior class play, "Deirdre." Enthusiastically received, the play opened up still another facet of the young man whose total seriousness about his calling could hide neither the spark of his wit nor the spontaneity of his humor.

Nor did his college involvements seem to hamper his ministry. In fact, Cauthen saw his ministry as a significant balance to what was happening in college. Most colleges in the fall of 1928 were places of lively debate about world affairs, including the controversial Bolshevik movement, and about religion, especially with reference to evolution. The Scopes trial in Dayton, Tennessee, fueled collegiate debates all over the country; and Nacogdoches was no exception. Doubt abounded as humanistic notions gained strength. The country was prospering. It was on a binge of "onward and upward" declarations. World War II had revealed on a worldwide scale what earlier America had discovered continentally—a manifest destiny.

The country elected Herbert Hoover as president in the fall of 1928 and idolized Captain Charles Lindbergh, "The Lone Eagle," who only a little over a year before had electrified the world with his solo flight across the Atlantic in thirty-three hours and thirty minutes. Lucky Lindy was not only the stuff of sermon illustrations for young preachers like Baker James Cauthen; he was also an

Baker James Cauthen and M. Theron Rankin confer with three Chinese evangelists in Wuchow (1946).

example of the drive that infused so many young collegians. J. Edgar Hoover and his FBI, in their fight against organized crime and the illegal liquor traffic, furnished another set of heroes.

Cauthen, with his determination to prepare himself for the highest place in which the Lord might want to use him, his disciplined life, and his wide range of accomplishments, typified the spirit of the age.

Such industry seemed to be self-rewarding. In the fall of 1928, Cauthen exchanged the Providence and Pollock pastorates for two others. The larger one was the Sulphur Springs Church, an open country church that met two Sundays a month and that was a bit larger than Providence Church. Seventy-five to one hundred people attended on a given Sunday. It was at this church that Cauthen really began to get into his pastoral role, spending the night in the community, which he reached by going twenty-five miles directly east of Lufkin to the little town of Zavala and then twelve more miles south. He was appreciated by all the people, especially so by a grand old deacon named Barge, whose house was always open to Cauthen. The country atmosphere wasn't much different from Lufkin. The bathroom was still located at the end of the path.

At almost the same time Cauthen resigned the Pollock Church, where he had continued to preach on the Sunday afternoons when he wasn't at Providence, and accepted the Burke Church eight miles directly south of Lufkin. He found sentimental identity in the Burke Church in that its pews had been purchased from the First Baptist Church in Lufkin when the latter built a new building in 1926. Cauthen enjoyed telling his little congregation at Burke that they were sitting in seats that he had "slept on for many an hour." Then he would add belatedly, "as a baby."

Just prior to his nineteenth birthday, Cauthen agreed to hold a revival in Zavala. It was the most remarkable of the young man's new career. He preached earnestly, his driving intensity moving the crowd with his reason and obvious intellectual prowess on one hand and his ability to reach them emotionally with a carefully developed story on the other. By the middle of the week the church was packed full every night, and there were many professions of faith and dramatic experiences. One night a family who had been involved in a triangle romance out of which murder had been committed came forward one by one, confessing their sins before the whole group. Cauthen led them in an emotional reconciliation. The event electrified the whole church and turned them toward spiritual things as nothing had before.

Cauthen still laughs over an incident that followed. On a cold morning right after the revival, a group was talking about the spiritual fire in the church. They had more of a fire than they knew. One happened to look up to the ceiling and discover that the church was on fire. Fortunately, they were able to put it out without much damage.

Despite such events day by day, school went on in Nacogdoches. Cauthen was driving a carload of young women who were picking up the cost of driving the car. There was Bessie West, Florence Boone, Gladys Thompson, and her younger sister. Cauthen and Gladys were dating some, but there was nothing serious on the part of either.

That summer Carney and Cauthen started a Mexican mission together at the nearby lumber mill. Some Lufkin Baptist young people helped under Cauthen's leadership. Several of them were honored by one large Mexican family, the Villarreals, who named each new child after one of their newfound friends at the Mexican mission. Baker James Villarreal reappeared much later in Cauthen's life when one of the Southwestern Seminary missions professors, Dr. Cal Guy, was preaching in New Mexico. He was approached by a fine Mexican Christian who identified himself as Baker James Villarreal. Guy, knowing Cauthen well, pursued the background of the name and then informed Cauthen about his namesake.

Despite Cauthen's drive, intensity, and total ambition in this period, he had a delightful sense of humor. When the school annual at Stephen F. Austin was threatened with cancellation due to the lack of subscriptions, the student leaders asked Cauthen to speak at a rally to raise subscriptions. Cheerleaders were there to lead a response to each statement he made. Soon he was caught up in the swing of it. He would make a telling statement about the need of the student body to subscribe to the annual and then pause as the cheerleaders would lead the crowd in a response.

Soon they were all caught up in the excitement and delight of it. "Don't you want your mug in the annual?" Cauthen would say. The crowd would roar a delighted "Yes!" When it was all over, the annual was saved, and Cauthen's versatility was further established.

But Cauthen's life wasn't all success stories, revival meetings, and extracurricular achievement. He was also locked into serious intellectual struggle in his heart and mind.

Cauthen was to say later, "Through my years of preaching, I could not identify with the profligate, for I had never been one. I could not identify with the drunkard, for from my earliest years I formed convictions about alcohol that left me without any desire even to experiment. I could not identify with the adulterer or embezzler or ne'er-do-well because my own path had been so early determined by Christ's claims on my life and the influence of my family and the discipline of my profession. But I could and can identify with anyone struggling with intellectual problems related to the faith. I understand intellectual doubt all too well."

Cauthen's intellectual stresses came as his sharp, inquisitive mind was led by such key teachers as D. R. Hodgin and the college president, A. W. Birdwell. It was the heyday of psychological approaches to behavior and religion. James Harvey Robinson's book *Why We Behave Like Human Beings* precipitated a sharp examination of religious experience. Cauthen struggled with the simplicities he was trying to preach on Sunday against the complexities with which he was confronted on Monday.

Hodgin, who had a Quaker background and had been greatly influenced by the philosopher Spinoza, was especially challenging. He was philosophical in his teaching and was drawn to Cauthen's sharp mind. They talked at length about what Hodgin liked to call the "Sturm und Drang," which means the strom and stress of mind. His was a probing approach with Cauthen. Many times it left the young preacher silent on the drive back to Lufkin as he struggled with his doubts about some of the very tenets that he preached so fiercely and forcefully.

Cauthen would ask himself, "What's the main beam of the Christian faith? If I were driven to the last line of defense, what would it be?" He decided that the deity of Christ was that main beam, that last line. His decision was based on the fact that God was in Christ. Cauthen thought that was the answer to the main question: Has God really manifested himself in the world? "If he has, I decided, I can believe in miracles and the resurrection and the atoning work of Jesus Christ. If God was in Christ, not only is this not difficult to believe, but it follows."

Cauthen also decided not to overplay his own understanding of things. "I don't know much yet. It would be foolish to feel I need to answer everything now. I will make mistakes in my ignorance if I try to do it, so I will learn to pigeonhole things that I cannot answer and act on what affirmations of faith I have." The problems that cropped up on the edges of his affirmation he called "brush-fire issues."

A most stabilizing influence on Cauthen was the college president, A. W. Birdwell. He was a man of firm faith who recognized Cauthen's potential as well as his struggle and gave him some guidelines in grounding his own faith. Birdwell helped him to develop the technique of pigeonholing problems that he couldn't solve until he had more information. "Don't feel that you have to resolve every issue on the information in hand," Birdwell would urge him. "Time and additional data and understanding will resolve many of these things for you and will save you premature resolution which could put you on the wrong track." Cauthen found it a useful tool then and later.

Did he preach even more forcefully as if to overcome his doubts? Probably. But Cauthen, in retrospect, feels that his preaching experience was every bit as helpful in stabilizing him through those years of intellectual awakening. As he went out to preach, he noticed that his congregation wasn't concerned with the intellectual problems that concerned him. They were struggling with the ongoing predicaments of life. The first tremors that were to lead to the Great Depression were already being felt. In contrast, there was the excitement of the oil boom in East Texas and the reality of big money beginning to flow into several areas that had been pockets of poverty.

Cauthen decided to preach what he knew. He leaned firmly and strongly on the answers he already had. He refused to be paralyzed by the questions that remained. Thus preaching affirmatively, he found his faith growing. He took heart from his ability to minister to people who were becoming increasingly insecure. The turmoil of the world and the impact of information that began to flow into that world through radio and newspaper troubled the isolation within which they had previously been able to keep a fragile bal-

37

ance.

Cauthen gives credit to Birdwell and the demands of his ministry with helping him bridge his period of intellectual stress and strain. Years later he said, "I still have feelings of great tenderness for a person in intellectual struggle, for the person who, badly troubled in his heart, asks, 'What can a person in integrity believe?' "

Cauthen, in his preaching, made unusual friends. A preacher and bachelor named T. R. Morris was the Unity associational missionary in 1929. He had replaced Cole, who had moved on to other responsibilities. Morris preached in a meeting for Cauthen at Sulphur Springs. Later when he met and courted Myrtle Behannon, a longtime friend of the Cauthen family, he asked Cauthen to perform the wedding ceremony. Cauthen did so in his parents' home. It wasn't his first ceremony, but he remembers it with great warmth; and he followed the family for many years.

Also at the Sulphur Springs Church, Cauthen befriended Ashby Grimes, a man with a very rugged background. Grimes had become a Christian under Cauthen's preaching. He was already a legend in the Sulphur Springs area for having shot Will Craven, an ex-con with a Dodge City-type reputation. Craven had lived, but he vowed eternal hatred and sure revenge for Grimes.

One Sunday following Cauthen's efforts to preach on the importance of reconciliation, Ashby Grimes was deeply convicted. Tearfully he said to Cauthen, "Preacher, I've got to straighten out this matter with Will Craven." Moved by Grimes' response, Cauthen replied, "If God has laid that on your heart, by all means, you must do it." Grimes looked up expectantly and asked, "Will you go with me?" The 110-pound nineteen-year-old swallowed hard and said, "Yes." The next weekend Cauthen, a deacon named Cammack, and Ashby Grimes climbed into Cauthen's car to drive deep into the piney woods to the isolated cabin where Will Craven was reported to be living. Cammack said Craven once hauled a mule up to the Southern Pacific Railroad, tied it, let a train hit it, and then made the company pay for it. He'd gotten away with that. The local sheriff had nailed him for bootlegging, however, and he had spent time in the penitentiary. Out now, he was "up to no good," people had told Cauthen.

As they drove up to Craven's cabin, Grimes said to Cauthen, "You go in first if you don't mind, Preacher." Praying hard,

Cauthen went to the cabin and knocked hesitantly on the rickety screen. The big, rough-hewn, unshaven man who answered seemed bigger even than rumors had indicated. Cauthen introduced himself as the local preacher, and Craven responded respectfully. Then, looking over Cauthen's shoulder, he said, "Who's that?" Craven had vowed to kill Grimes if he ever saw him again. Cauthen said quickly, "That's Ashby Grimes. He's been converted to Jesus Christ, and he wants to talk to you. May we come in?" Craven turned and went in, and Cauthen motioned for the others to come. The uneasy crowd sat down in the sparse and worn chairs in Craven's cabin and alternated silence with chitchat.

Trying to think of something to say, Cauthen asked Craven about life in the penitentiary and then, finally, brought up the subject of Grimes. Craven refused to talk to Grimes. "I won't talk to him," he said. "I'll talk to you, but I'm not going to talk to that man." None of Cauthen's already highly developed persuasiveness could move the man. He was like a stone wall. Cauthen led in prayer, and they retreated to the car, the two shielding Grimes with their own bodies as they walked away. All the way to town, Cauthen reassured Grimes that he had done all he could. Grimes never forgot Cauthen's willingness to tackle such a difficult task.

In such moments, and in the restatements of his faith in his preaching, Baker James Cauthen not only settled his intellectual questions but firmly fixed his mind on the pastoral ministry. There had been times he had thought a bit about teaching, and other times he had even thought about being a missionary. But his experiences in preaching and in pastoring convinced him that this was who he was to be. His driving ambition was so channeled. He felt he had to prepare himself for the biggest kind of responsibility, in case God so entrusted him.

It was A. W. Birdwell who helped Cauthen fix his direction for further preparation. Birdwell convinced him that he needed credentials within Baptist life and that he should go to Baylor. He convinced him that too many preachers were not intellectually prepared for their task even when they were theologically prepared. It was decided that Cauthen should enter Baylor University to secure a Master's degree in English and history to complete his liberal arts background. Then he would go to the seminary for his theological training.

Although Cauthen did not know it, Birdwell wrote to J. B. Tidwell, one of the leading preachers in Texas and a Bible professor at Baylor, and to the university's president, S. P. Brooks. "Get ready for this young man," Birdwell wrote. "He has unlimited potential. He's already a better preacher than most men in Texas, and he just turned nineteen. Don't let his size or his youthful looks fool you. Judge him by the set of his jaw, the fire in his eyes, the persuasiveness of his tongue, and the sharpness of his mind."

Cauthen finished his undergraduate work with a deep belief in the gospel's ability to change men and an abiding confidence in the Scriptures as the Word of God, inspired by God himself.

"If God can hold the magnificence of the heavens in his hands, not only having conceived it but continuing to sustain it, he can give a reliable record of his efforts to reveal himself to man and of his desire to reconcile man unto himself through his own Son Jesus Christ." A concept of inspiration gave him a whole Bible and no need to enter the nitpicking controversies that divided so much of Christendom into the polemic camps called fundamental and modernist.

In the spring of 1929, just prior to his graduation from Stephen F. Austin College with a Bachelor of Arts degree featuring a major in English and a minor in history and education, Cauthen accepted his fifth church. It was at a place called Manning, a mill town twenty-one miles southeast of Lufkin. Cauthen would travel fifteen miles on the road toward Zavala and then turn south six miles to Manning. The one church building there belonged to the mill. Both Methodists and Baptists met there, the Methodists on one Sunday and the Baptist on the next. Cauthen resigned his church at Burke and pastored Manning and Sulphur Springs through the summer. He spent Saturday nights there and sometimes Sunday nights.

In the summer of 1929, the first time he had not been in school since the fall of 1926, Cauthen preached in revivals all over Unity Association. His hectic schedule was something he took for granted, though everybody else worried. "He's too frail to do that," the women in the church would protest. Even the men were perplexed. How could somebody who looked that frail do so much? Cauthen approached his task with the discipline of an athlete. He would preach all week and sometimes spend all day Saturday in bed getting ready for Sunday. And then he would spend all day Monday in bed trying to recover before he started another revival that night. It was almost a relief when he started to Baylor University in the fall of 1929. Reluctantly, he resigned the Sulphur Springs Church, leaving him with only the Manning Church. That way, he would come back only every other weekend. He felt it absolutely imperative that he acquit himself well at Baylor.

CHAPTER FOUR

In Pursuit of Excellence

In the fall of 1929, when Baker James Cauthen fulfilled his long-standing dream to enroll in Baylor University, Herbert Hoover was reassuring a jittery America that there was nothing to fear, that the economy was on a solid base, and that unparalleled growth was just ahead.

Cauthen had wanted to go to Baylor as far back as he had been able to define his educational needs and goals. But the tuition of a private school such as Baylor and the need to earn his way, which his pastorates allowed him to do, kept him living in Lufkin and commuting to Stephen F. Austin, a state school. Careful planning, fortuitous events, and frugal habits—his life-style—now made Baylor possible.

His riders going back and forth to Stephen F. Austin had defrayed his transportation expenses. He had paid his tuition, bought his books, purchased his meals, bought his clothes, and even managed to lay a bit aside from the modest salaries his little churches paid him and the revival honorariums. Finally, those savings made Baylor a reality.

Through Birdwell-guided correspondence and the assistance of Dr. and Mrs. J. M. Dawson of First Baptist Church, Waco, he arranged to live near Baylor in the home of Dr. and Mrs. L. E. Finney. Dr. Finney was director of development for Baylor. The Finneys had a room upstairs facing Speight Street that was ideal for Cauthen's need. He entered the front door into an entrance hall, proceeded up steps directly ahead to a landing, and turned left into his room. It had a gas stove he could light on chilled mornings, a bed, a desk, lamp, and a small wardrobe in which to hang his clothes.

Soon he was settled in his quarters and had completed get-acquainted sessions with the Finneys. "That man's going somewhere. Mark my word," Dr. Finney told his wife. Then Cauthen proceeded to the campus to meet Dr. A. J. Armstrong, the famous Browning scholar under whom he would take his Master's degree in English. The young student and the renowned professor hit it off immediately. Cauthen shared Armstrong's love for Robert Browning, whom the professor recognized as a poet of faith and affirmation without peer.

Armstrong was a man of high ideals and strong convictions. People either liked him very much or thoroughly disliked him. He was hard-driving, could be sharp or even sarcastic, and left his students either wounded detractors or dedicated devotees.

In his very first conference with Armstrong, Cauthen was struck with a picture of Mozart hanging in the professor's lecture room. An ethereal kind of picture, it was expressive of the musician's vision of what he was trying to get into his work. Cauthen found that it stimulated his own idealism. He told Armstrong that he saw in it the picture of a man catching ideas and translating them into something he could communicate. Such a picture, he said, inspired him as a preacher. Armstrong was evidently inspired by Cauthen's interest because later he gave it to the young man as a wedding gift.

The next man Cauthen set about to know was the famed Bible teacher and preacher J. B. Tidwell. A man of great faith, Tidwell was dedicated to discovering and developing young preachers of promise. Dr. Birdwell had written him and told him Baker James Cauthen was just such a man. Tidwell sized up the promising student, decided Birdwell was exactly right, and began to open a myriad of doors for the young preacher. On the Sundays Cauthen did not journey back to Manning (every other Sunday), he often preached in churches where Tidwell arranged for him to supply.

As Cauthen continued his Birdwell-arranged rounds, he proceeded next to Dr. W. W. Melton, pastor of the Seventh and James Baptist Church. He listened to either him or J. M. Dawson preach on the rare Sundays he was neither at Manning nor following assignments arranged for him by Tidwell. Melton later became executive secretary of the Baptist General Convention of Texas, and Cauthen maintained a friendship with him through the years, as he did with the others. With each of them he shared his seriousness, his goals, and his desire to learn. Though not a flatterer,

Cauthen found it easy to convey to men of stature his appreciation for them and his desire to learn from them. Men responded to his efforts not only then but in the years that followed.

Once his initial contacts were made, Cauthen buckled down to the course of study Armstrong outlined for him. He came to the campus early, either to classes or the library. Early in the afternoon, he would walk to the Finney house with a load of books that seemed too heavy for his slight frame.

The young preacher, skinny to the point of being eye-catching but attractive enough to capitalize on that, also tried to know some of his fellow students. However, he purposefully laid aside the man-about-campus demeanor that had earned him the senior class presidency and "most popular" designation at Stephen F. Austin. Now selective and purposeful, he wanted to meet pilgrims on his path who were serious and who had promise in and of themselves. A Tidwell-arranged opportunity, in the early weeks after his coming, to speak at the Baylor Religious Hour on Wednesday night opened these kinds of doors.

One young lady with a sharp eye for newcomers to the campus was an attractive daughter of missionaries to China. Eloise Glass first noticed the slender Cauthen at a get-acquainted Training Union party at Seventh and James Baptist Church. Later, when it was advertised that he would preach at Baylor Religious Hour, she was struck by the fact that anyone so young should get such a prestigious opportunity. And she was fascinated by his name. The "Bake Cauthen" of Stephen F. Austin and Unity Association was Baker James Cauthen, graduate student, at Baylor.

Eloise Glass introduced Cauthen to a regular luncheon group at the school cafeteria. They took him in and provided him with his first and, as it turned out, lifelong circle of Baylor friends. Meal after meal provided Cauthen an opportunity to get to know not only the ebullient and attractive Eloise but also her quiet, unassuming sister Lois. Also among the group were Robert Fling, an outgoing young man with a broad smile, the studious Ray Roselle, a young preacher named Harrall Hall, and a friend of the Glass sisters named Dorcas Meadows.

Especially important to Cauthen among the luncheon group were two young preachers who, by virture of their skills and their roles as pastors of two of the better student churches, were already special on the campus. One was a bombastic junior named W. A. Criswell, and the other an ambitious, intense, but obviously gifted senior named Kermit Melugin. After the Baylor Religious Hour episode, they made Cauthen one of their own.

The men addressed each other by their last names. "Hello, Criswell." "Hello, Cauthen. Put your tray down and tell us what Browning was really like." The big laugh would be answered by a shy grin and then countered with some serious inquiry into preaching texts, Baptist politics, or other career-related subjects. Cauthen became even closer to all of these people when he was inducted into the honorary English society, Sigma Tau Delta. Cauthen and Criswell became mutual admirers and also subliminally competitive. Their birthdays were one day apart, Criswell being a day older.

Efforts to draw Cauthen into the social activities of the group met with only minimal success. His thesis on Browning was to be entitled "The Mind of Robert Browning"; and his mentor and champion, A. J. Armstrong, had already asked his classes to write one- and two-page interpretations to aid and abet the young graduate student. The latter fact certainly impressed Eloise Glass. She took even deeper note of the intense young man.

Every other weekend, either Friday afternoon or Saturday morning, Cauthen would leave the campus in his Nash car for the church at Manning. Sometimes he would spend the night there; sometimes he would spend the night in Lufkin and drive down to his church the next morning.

Cauthen had already developed the habit of allowing himself no idle time. All moments of reflection were spent working on problems or sermons or directions or actions. Only later in life would he learn the skills of distraction, recreation, and reflection. He did join the Glass sisters in some activities of the Volunteer Band weekends when he was not on preaching assignments.

Cauthen was keenly aware that he was away from home for the first time. He missed his father and his brother, who continued to be his good friend and companion. But based on correspondence still extant, he missed his proud, dedicated, and single-minded mother most. His admiration showed in a belated birthday letter.

He first apologized, saying, "You are so very, very dear to me, and you are so extremely unselfish while I seem to think only of making something of myself." Later in the same letter, he said:

"Mother, I am proud of you. It has not been your lot to have the world shower you with praises and with things of outward show, but nevertheless you have gone about doing good, even in the spirit of the Master. Behind you are many, many redeemed souls you have been able to bring to the Savior. In our town are numerous people whom you've encouraged and inspired by your kind words and your optimism. It is somewhat strange about you. You have troubles of your own, and they bear upon you; but when you come in contact with other people who are oppressed by cares, you forget your own heartaches and seek to encourage them. When I have been discouraged, you have never met me with anything but confidence and inspiration. How I do appreciate it."

Elsewhere he said, "You have never been enthusiastic about your children's occupying a place of worldly prestige, but you have always cared that we might render service."

He went on to say:

"How well do I remember that years ago you used to pray that God would let you live until your children might become large enough to do for themselves.

"And how dear you've been since God has put me into his ministry. Every encouragement which was possible, you've thrown it my way. You have been heart and soul behind every scheme which would equip me for usefulness. It is said that every great man has either a wonderful mother or a wonderful wife. I have had the mother; that much is certain. Gladys said to me, 'Bake, you can't keep from making good with that mother and father of yours behind you . . . .' I shall never be in too large a place but that I shall be able to point proudly to you and say, 'See, there is *my* mother.'"

In a later letter he confessed:

"Mother, I do not know what God has in store for me. He may want me somewhere in the great battle of life filling a great place. In my heart I believe that he does. Or he may on the other hand want me as a mudsill in the great edifice which we Christians are trying to build, but you may know that wherever I am or whatsoever may be my fortune, you will hold a place in my heart that no one can supplant. There is a little place in my heart which is all yours; the deeds are made out and properly signed, and there is a notice on it which reads, 'This place is not for sale.'"

That these two letters were especially precious to the proud mother is best evidenced by the fact that they are the only two passed down from that whole period. The ongoing contact during those years was maintained by visits instead of letters.

The reference to Gladys Thompson in the earlier letter is significant. Aside from the Stephen F. Austin girl he had dated as a freshman until his math course suffered, Gladys Thompson had been his main female friend. She was the only person he took out and in whom he confided. Yet as they both were to confess then and later, "We were just good friends."

Given Cauthen's single-minded determination to prepare himself for what in his heart he felt would be a great place in the kingdom, a very restricted social life was understandable. That he allowed himself significant and promising friends could be interpreted either as the work of an opportunist or the careful commitment of a man to relate every contact and every activity to the central purpose of his life.

Cauthen's pastor heart continued to expand with his work at Manning. Sometimes on Saturday night, he would go out from Manning for preaching missions. In a little town called Saron, he held Saturday night and Sunday afternoon preaching for a time in the winter of 1930. After a meeting at Christmas, he baptized converts one cold day in a nearby stream. One of the converts was a crippled man. Cauthen had two other men put him in a chair and carry him into the water. Then he rocked the chair back in the water until the man was immersed. Onlookers considered it a tender and moving scene.

A close friend of Cauthen's was a teacher at Manning at that time. They had gone to Stephen F. Austin together. Cauthen confided to him, "This is the best Christmas I've ever had." The teacher-friend was perplexed. He said, "I don't understand that. All you've done is preach." Cauthen smiled. He had already discovered that preaching was not only his gift but his joy.

His contacts as a young pastor furthered his ability to relate to people in every station of life. A deacon, Mr. Luther, who had a good job in the nearby mill, was one of his favorite hosts. Living in the home were a married daughter, a son, and a child with some birth defects who was named Lindy after the airman.

As the end of the year began to roll around, Cauthen looked

north toward Fort Worth and Southwestern Baptist Theological Seminary. This precipitated many discussions among the luncheon group in the cafeteria. W. A. Criswell talked to him long and hard about going to Southern Seminary. "That's where the scholarship is," he confided to Cauthen, who countered with his faith in Southwestern men like W. T. Conner and Lee Scarborough, both of whom he had heard in Baptist meetings.

Actually, he didn't have an option. Keeping the Manning Church was absolutely necessary to his financial structure. But Cauthen liked Criswell, and his skills were undeniable. The White Mound Church that Criswell pastored in Coryell County was one of the better student churches. Cauthen saw that for himself when he went with the mission band, including Eloise Glass, to White Mound for a special week of services. But if he was impressed with Criswell's opportunity, he had to be even more impressed with the word that Kermit Melugin had been called to the large Polytechnic Baptist Church in Fort Worth and would be pastoring there while attending seminary. Now that was a student church!

Soon the year was over, and Cauthen bade his friends farewell. They assured each other that their paths would cross often. He returned to Lufkin, his Manning responsibilities, and a summer of revivals up and down Unity Association. Gladys went with him sometimes, and his mother, father, and brother were nearly always in attendance. His mother and father would lead small supportive prayer groups prior to the preaching services and were especially good at personal witnessing. The results of their efforts were often evident in the response to the invitations Baker extended.

Occasionally he and Gladys attended a movie. They also had long talks. She remembers his clear-cut drive to achieve. His convictions were deep; his defense of them was persuasive. He couldn't be easily convinced that he was wrong. The range of his preaching grew. He could be very hard on the congregation in one minute and bring tears from them with a well-told story in the next. He was committed to evangelism as the center of his ministry. And Gladys was convinced that he was going to be one of the outstanding leaders among Baptists.

CHAPTER FIVE

The School of the Prophets

Baker James Cauthen moved into Southwestern Seminary's Fort Worth Hall in September of 1930. The great four-story building provided not only dormitory space but faculty offices, some classrooms, and a cafeteria. Its columned portico, looking north across the city, stood at Fort Worth's highest point. While the view from the high spot of an essentially flat area is not spectacular, the building's altitude became obvious when a Texas blue norther would blow in. The dormitory door became either the stepping-off place for a bitterly cold walk to one of the other two buildings or the threshold of a haven of warmth, fellowship, and poverty.

The Great Depression, as it would later be called, was not quite one year old when Cauthen entered Southwestern. The financial disaster that marked its beginning, the stock market collapse, had occurred in October of 1929. Though he would later become an astute observer and interpreter of national and world events, he had taken little notice of that event. The Baylor year was too heady and heavy. Life in Angelina County was not calculated to give one an economic world view. Only economists were worried about the breakthroughs in mass production following World War I, which raised American output of goods sharply without a corresponding rise in consumers' buying power. Even economists took little note of the supersalesmen who emerged in the 1920s, selling Americans things they not only had been able to get along without before, but things they weren't sure what to do with when they got them.

Americans are a speculative people—the legacy of pioneering. Put supersalesmen with superspeculators, and you soon have a mountain of credit. When the tab finally came in, millions couldn't pay what they had contracted to pay. Notes that could not be paid were called, and goods that could not be sold stacked up. A financial collapse was the result. The economic system couldn't cope with the panic that followed. Beginning in the highly industrialized cities of the north and east, its rippling effect was being felt everywhere by the fall of 1930.

Of necessity, people all over the United States began to practice the kind of frugality that Cauthen had grown up with. It didn't alter his life-style one iota. He had always gotten by on as little as possible, saved as much as possible, and kept his personal overhead low. But his own frugality did not blind him to the way people were hurting.

Students were dropping out of seminary that fall because they were unable to support themselves. A grapefruit diet at Southwestern Seminary in the fall of 1930 was not a fancy way to lose weight: it was a singular way of keeping what little weight you had. There were no Hoovervilles (cardboard-box shanty towns) near Seminary Hill, but the trains that passed along the western perimeter of the campus sometimes had more passengers underneath on the rods than in pullman accommodations. Thousands of Americans were on the move, looking for a place where the depression hadn't hit or where somebody just like them might be needed. Only, when they got there, hundreds of people "just like them" were already congregating on the edge of town in hobo villages.

President Hoover's administration tried to build confidence. Someone coined the slogan "Wasn't the depression terrible?" But most people, Baker James Cauthen included, had yet to find out how really terrible it could be.

Political extremists were blamed for the country's problems. However, many people who had neglected religious thoughts during the postwar era of affluence and giddiness did manifest new interest in the church. The seminarians decided that opportunity was building in the winds of difficulty that were blowing everywhere. Many of them, however, had the problem of trying to figure out a way to buy up the opportunity in terms of fees and staying alive while at seminary. In a day when the catch phrase was "Brother, can you spare a dime?" not too many could.

Most who came to the seminary came on the wings of faith and grew in the process. A few faltered. Baker James Cauthen roomed first with a man who found the demands of studying and the temper of the times too heavy a combination. He left before the

Dr. Baker James Cauthen, Mrs. Cauthen, Mrs. Charles Culpepper, two unidentified women, and Missionaries Lucy Smith and Rex Ray, back row; Missionary Mary Gould, a Chinese secretary, and Carolyn and Ralph Cauthen, front row; in front of the temporary headquarters in Hong Kong year was out with the equivalent of a nervous breakdown. The next year his roommate was Robert Fling, who became a lifelong friend.

Cauthen continued to pastor the Manning Church. In the spring of 1931 he secured a railroad clergy pass. After that he took the train to Lufkin on weekends, keeping his automobile there for pastoral use. His flock realized that his considerable preaching skills were being sharpened and refined by the inspiration of theological study.

At first Cauthen was disappointed in the seminary. The four-day week instead of the six days he had been used to at college was a sharp change. Too, the seminary was oriented more to practice than to theory. Once the young student adjusted to a professional approach to learning, he became committed to its value. From undergraduate days, he had planned to earn not only his Master of Theology degree but to continue on and take his Doctor of Theology degree (an additional two years).

Cauthen's dedication and quick mind soon attracted the attention of the venerable Dr. W. T. Conner. By virtue of his intellect, homespun humor, and incredibly broad grasp of the theological spectrum, Conner was already legendary. He liked Cauthen. Some of his colleagues reserved judgment, however. Despite Cauthen's disarming smile and forthright way of relating to those with whom he came in contact, he could be seen from afar as overly serious and intense. Obviously, he was set on "going places" in his chosen profession.

In the summer of 1931 Cauthen returned to Angelina County, the Manning Church, and the revival circuit for June and July. In August he was contacted by the White Mound Church of Coryell County. Having graduated from Baylor University, Criswell was going to Southern Seminary in Louisville and would resign the White Mound Church. Ambitious and aggressive, he had decided that his "holy-roller preaching image" might be balanced by the studious climate of the Louisville campus. Southwestern campus was noted more for its evangelistic spirit and piety among young theologues.

Criswell proved both his respect for his friend and his love for the church by nominating Cauthen to succeed him. The White Mound Church felt fortunate to get another strong preacher, for they had seen leaner days in years gone by. They soon compared the two preachers by saying that Criswell was called to preach the power of the gospel, but Cauthen was called to preach the beauty of it. Both men had a tremendous gift for moving an audience to deep emotion, but they came at it quite differently.

Criswell wasn't the only Cauthen friend to graduate from Baylor that spring. Eloise Glass also graduated, and she broke with family tradition to attend Southwestern. She, too, had considered Southern Seminary, but a spring meeting of Sigma Tau Delta had brought Baker James Cauthen back on the scene. He talked with her earnestly about Southwestern and such professors as W. T. Conner. She decided she could get what she wanted there despite the fact her own father had attended Southern Seminary and despite Criswell's admonitions that Southern was the only place to go.

However, she saw the busy young Cauthen during her first year at seminary in 1931-32 only at a distance and in brief greetings. He continued single-mindedly in his studies. Between those and traveling alternately to Manning and to White Mound, he had little time for socializing. Providence did bring them together in the summer of 1932 during a summer revival at White Mound.

The church deacons asked Cauthen to preach the annual brush-arbor revival and a young man, Fred Swank, to lead the music. One of the deacons, Quince Davidson, and his wife decided to invite Eloise Glass to work with the young people. They had met her earlier when Criswell brought her to White Mound during a mission emphasis and had been much impressed by the vivacious China-born girl.

Because she was part of the revival team, she was invited to accompany Cauthen and Swank as they went from home to home for meals. It was here that she really began to know and appreciate the curly-haired young preacher.

This revival was typical for the era and the area. The arbor had been built at a much earlier date. A large wooden roof was supported by cedar columns, and sawdust was generously sprinkled underneath for a floor. Rows of benches, constructed for the purpose, looked toward a large platform that could handle a good-sized choir and assorted speakers and musicians. Kerosene and Coleman lanterns were hung around the edge of the tabernacle for light.

As time for the service drew near in the evening, cars began driving up around the tabernacle. Many faced in close to the arbor to allow older and infirm people to stay in their cars and hear. Some people spread blankets in front of the cars at the edge of the tabernacle and put younger kids to sleep, sometimes even before the preacher began to do it.

Swank, good-natured and ebullient, would soon have the crowd singing enthusiastically. He always had them ready for the preacher. "Bake," as the team called him, would get up, roll up his sleeves, take off his tie in symbolic identification with the crowd, and "go after it." Soon he would be dripping wet, but that only seemed to fire his intensity. The altar call invariably was answered by numbers of people responding to Cauthen's clear, emotional invitation.

Eloise Glass began to think it would be a beautiful thing if God would call Baker James Cauthen to China. Surprised at herself and a little bit frustrated with her feelings, she wouldn't let herself think anything else since she was deeply committed to returning to China. This was the third year of her friendship with Cauthen, and they shared mutual respect—nothing more. She had written him a couple of times after he left Baylor, and he had answered politely but initiated nothing more. He wasn't dating much, she knew— "not even the girl from Lufkin," Mrs. Davidson had confided to her. "But," she sighed as the White Mound revival closed and the team broke up, "I'm willing to go to China single."

Cauthen received his Master of Theology degree in May, 1933, writing his thesis on the subject of demonology. Southwestern Seminary evidently did not cherish his effort, as it has long since been either discarded or lost.

He enrolled immediately in the doctoral program, majoring in theology under W. T. Conner. The new level of study excited him especially because it allowed him a more significant relationship with the man he admired so much. It also provided opportunity to apply his agile mind intensely again as he had enjoyed doing during his Master's year at Baylor.

The year 1932 was later regarded as the very depth of the depression. That fall, as Cauthen continued his seminary work and his ministry at White Mound and Manning, the national elections brought Franklin Roosevelt to the helm of the United States, promising better things—"Happy days are here again."

Of more significance to Cauthen's life and career than F. D. R. was the fact that his Baylor friend Kermit Melugin, who had become the prodigy pastor of Polytechnic Baptist Church in Fort Worth, had resigned that church to accept a call across town to the North Fort Worth Baptist Church. Cauthen's old friend and sponsor, Dr. J. B. Tidwell, was called as the interim pastor at Polytechnic and convinced the committee they needed to hear Baker James Cauthen.

Early in December of 1932, as a lame-duck President was preparing to leave the White House, with millions of people out of work, millions hungry, and the rest leery of the future, Cauthen did preach at Polytechnic. He was introduced by a man named Cloyd Dunn, who did the job succinctly: "Our speaker today is Rev. Baker James Cauthen. Rev. Cauthen will now speak."

Despite any defense for his presence, Cauthen's abilities led the church to warm toward him, and the committee sat down to talk very seriously with him. Since they had already successfully tried a young man, Melugin, they were not opposed to Cauthen's youth. But the fact that he was single was something else. After they heard him preach, they decided that wasn't as big a problem as they had thought. He made his plans for graduate studies very clear to them, and the committee accepted the fact that his time was limited. A young man getting ahead was to be admired. Though very few of the Polytechnic people had as much as a college education, they believed everyone ought to try for one.

In 1932 only one young person in eight between eighteen and twenty-two years of age was in college, and only four in eight had even gone to high school. Cauthen, with his Bachelor's degree, his Master's degree in English, and near completion of his Master's in theology, was already an educated giant despite his tender age. He turned twenty-three a few days after the Polytechnic Church voted to call him. They called despite the fact that when they asked him about his plans for marriage, he simply said he had "no marriage plans."

Cauthen resigned the churches at Manning and White Mound and began his pastorate at Polytechnic on New Year's Day, 1933. The people at his former churches were not surprised. They knew their young pastor was on his way, and the step up to the

Polytechnic Church, running nearly five hundred in Sunday School, was only confirmation of their own convictions.

But the job Cauthen faced was anything but easy. The church was composed mostly of blue-collar workers, many of whom had lost their jobs; and it was deeply in debt. At the height of the optimism of the twenties, they had built an educational building. Now they not only were not paying on the principal but were unable to pay even the interest. Their indebtedness was approximately $73,000, at that time a staggering sum. In addition, they owed a local store for pianos, the Sunday School Board for literature, and various merchants for chairs and other items. While appreciating Melugin's eloquent discourses and obvious oratorical gifts, the people were not motivated to any kind of sacrifice for the church. They were making enough sacrifice for themselves.

Shortly after the new year, Cauthen wrote his mother and dad about his feelings as he prepared to assume the responsibility of the Polytechnic Church:

"I realize that I am facing the most serious thing of my life. None of the little and small must characterize my actions if I would serve Christ acceptably. Were it not that I feel the Lord had brought about my going to this church, I would not go. But I do not dare turn it down. I feel thoroughly incompetent to face the issue as I now know my weaknesses in an acute fashion. I am no giant; I am no big preacher; I am no wonder. I am just a little fellow in a job that is a million times too large for him—unless the Lord lays his hand upon me in power. If I did not feel that the Lord would do so, I would not dare go to Polytechnic. It would be the height of foolishness. Only the power of God can move to victory."

Cauthen's verbal humility was not altogether appreciated by his peers. Many people misinterpreted his confidence in God and his willingness to tackle anything as cocksureness and even pretentiousness. But Cauthen was now well across the treacherous stream of self-understanding without falling off either to the side of being overly impressed with himself or to the side of loss of confidence. He early accepted the notion that a man ought not to think too highly of himself, and he reminded himself of that even when his emotions were flush with confidence.

He saw other men getting ahead faster than himself, and he accepted that. Criswell was already making a name for himself in

Kentucky, and of course Kermit Melugin's success was fabled. But Cauthen had accepted whatever place God would allow him. He was paying the price for honing his skills. He had been faithful to each opportunity. He had taken care of his health like a long-distance runner. He was ready for the task. He affirmed that God had called him, and he believed firmly that God would make him equal to the situation.

In the same letter to his parents, he tried to express his appreciation for his family, revealing an awareness that his own competence was in no little way a legacy from them:

"Surely in these important months ahead of me and the years lying on beyond, you will not fail to pray for me. Many a time when I am hard pressed and feeling despondent, I will be encouraged in my heart by saying, 'Mother and Dad are praying for me now.' Many a time just before I preach on Sunday morning or on Sunday night, I will doubtless turn my mind back to the home church in Lufkin and will see you sitting there ready for the service, yet breathing a prayer for your preacher boy. You don't know how much confidence I have in your prayers. Somehow I feel as though if Mother and Dad are praying about a thing it's bound to come out all right. God has answered your prayers in the past, and I know that he will do so again."

Deciding to move from the seminary to the "Poly" neighborhood, he arranged for a room in the home of a widow and her nineteen-year-old son. He had his own bathroom, a private living room with a southeast front, and a large bedroom with three windows. They would agree to serve him breakfast and supper in the deal. For this, he was to pay the sum of $25 a month. Since the Polytechnic Church had agreed to pay him $125 a month, he had enough left to handle the cost of driving his Chevy coupe back and forth between Poly and the seminary (gas was only nine cents a gallon), get an occasional new preaching suit, and add to his library. He could ask for no more.

A week before he took over at Polytechnic, Cauthen's schedule was overwhelming. He had agreed to preach at a Tarrant County Workers' Conference and a week later at a Sunday School rally. One was to be at Travis Avenue Church and the other at Broadway Church, Fort Worth's largest Southern Baptist churches. The young preacher was coming up in the world.

The Tuesday before he preached his first sermon, he wrote his parents and confessed some fears:

"I'm not blue about going into this new task, but I do feel my tremendous weakness. It makes me quake sometimes as I think of what is ahead of me. It has been a time of searching my own heart. I had to decide whether I would be a John Mark or a Jonah running from a job, or whether I would be like Isaiah and like Andrew and John following the Lord. As never before in my entire life, I am looking to God to help me. I feel, yes, I know that he is going to stand by me. If I didn't believe it, I never would have accepted this call. It is a foregone conclusion that if the Lord does not help me, I am whipped before I begin. I know that God loves me, and I know as well as I know I am alive that he's heard my prayer in times past. Surely God would not let me come to this crucial hour in my experience when I am honestly trying to know his will and then let me be led astray and be trampled down into the dirt a crushed, ruined, broken failure for life. No, God is going to go with me. The same one who said, 'Go,' also said, 'And lo, I am with you alway even unto the end.' So—I go."

Herein Cauthen most nearly revealed his own heart. His insecurities related not so much to not being up to the situation but to his somehow failing God. His confidence was not so much in his gifts as in the work of God in his life.

People at the Polytechnic Church were not waiting passively for Baker James Cauthen. They planned an elaborate welcome Sunday for January 22, 1933, which from their point of view attracted more attention than President Roosevelt's inauguration a few days earlier in Washington, D.C.

Banners and buttons were distributed bearing the slogan "I Believe in Baker James Cauthen." A beautiful brochure with Cauthen's picture on it said, "Polytechnic Baptist Welcomes Rev. Baker James Cauthen as Their Pastor." Members planned a Sunday School service with 700 present, morning worship with every seat filled, a lunch-hour fellowship and social period, followed by Training Union at 6:30 P.M. with 225 present, and a special musical program with Cauthen's message at the evening service. A flattering biographical sketch was sent to newspapers along with Cauthen's picture. The brochure featured dozens of testimonials solicited from friends commending the pastor to the church. They reveal how Cauthen was seen at this point in his life.

J. R. Nutt, his former pastor at First Baptist Church, Lufkin, wrote: "It's been my deep joy and the joy of our people to watch the growth and development of this fine young man. He is a young man with a well-trained mind, splendidly educated, and thoroughly consecrated to his call and work."

Dr. A. J. Armstrong wrote: "I knew him intimately while he was at Baylor, and I can say most sincerely that he's one of the finest young men I have ever taught. He is a consecrated, earnest, and intelligent man with a saving grace of common sense."

A near literary gem came from the Rev. R. E. Day, pastor of the First Baptist Church in Big Springs, Texas, who said: "Because of Brother Cauthen's ability as a speaker, you will listen when he talks. Because of his shepherd's heart, you will follow him. Because of his clean life and consecration, you will love him. Because of his soul-winning power and ability to lead the church in Kingdom affairs, you will hold on to him."

Dr. Conner, Cauthen's favorite professor, mentor, and sponsor, said, "I consider Brother Cauthen one of the brightest, most promising young men we have had in the seminary."

Quince Davidson from the White Mound Baptist Church wrote: "I find him to be one of the most spiritual, consecrated Christian gentlemen I have ever had the pleasure of knowing. I feel sure the future holds great possibilities for him and that he will make one of the outstanding leaders in the Baptist denomination."

Cauthen's old sponsor J. B. Tidwell, probably the man most responsible for his going to the Polytechnic Church, wrote, "I think he may be counted as one of the fine leaders in our younger ministry."

Cauthen's pastor at the time he was baptized, R. L. Cole, wrote, "He is easily among the greatest young preachers of the state."

Dr. Albert Venting, who was a professor at Southwestern Seminary also and who, along with his wife, lived in Fort Worth Hall at the time Cauthen was there, said, "Your church is indeed fortunate . . . ."

A. W. Birdwell, the president of the state teachers' college at Nacogdoches who had urged Cauthen to go to Baylor before going to the seminary, wrote, "It is my deliberate opinion that Baker James Cauthen will, in the next dozen years, be one of a half-dozen of the state's most outstanding preachers."

Dr. E. D. Head, pastor of First Baptist Church, Houston, and destined to become president of Southwestern Seminary, wrote, "He is a young man of rare culture, of scholarly interests and achievements, of winsome personality, of marked gifts as a preacher of the gospel of Christ, of deep consecreation and humility of spirit."

While serving as president of the Ministerial Alliance at Southwestern Seminary, Cauthen had impressed his fellow student W. I. McClung with his "ability as an executive and a leader in this office." In addition, McClung said, "In all respect to those noble men in the ministry, it's my candid opinion you have chosen God's man to lead."

A former member from Cauthen's church in Manning said: "He stands as a stone wall for Christ. Words can't express the love I have for him. His character is without flaw, his mind well developed beyond his years."

Members of the church also wrote of their expectations and their enthusiasm. There were such phrases as "I am looking forward to the leadership of Baker James Cauthen . . . . We need a great church at Poly, and under Baker James Cauthen, we will have it . . . . I pledge to prove my belief in our new pastor by striving to go forward with him . . . . In Cauthen we have the best example of culture, spirituality, friendliness, and perseverance that can be found among men . . . . The adult department believes in Cauthen . . . . The young people's department believes that Cauthen loves the Lord and is called by the heavenly Father to preach the words of Jesus Christ . . . . I am prayerfully awaiting our pastor's coming . . . . I believe in Brother Cauthen because of his inspiring faith, because of his sincere desire, because early in life he heard and answered God's call, because we feel that God has called him to be our pastor . . . . a life of great power and promise . . . I think we have the best . . . . deep spirituality and intense earnestness . . . consecrated . . . eager to join him . . . his passion for lost souls . . . Hello, Brother Cauthen. We are for you, with you, and ready to go."

While the Sunday did not measure up to its goals, it was beyond anything the church had enjoyed for years. They counted 640 in Sunday School and 215 in their training session, and they did fill the auditorium. Three people made professions of faith, and two more joined the church by letter. That afternoon Cauthen spoke at a Sunday School rally, and the audience broke into applause afterward, a rather uncommon thing in that day.

Plunging into his pastorate with great zest, one of Cauthen's first challenges was to build a staff. He had only a secretary and a janitor when he began. Since part of his key battle would be fought in rebuilding the Sunday School and the church training program, he needed an able man to be his minister of education. He approached W. L. Howse, a fellow student at Baylor and now teaching religious education at the seminary. The Howses had lived in Fort Worth Hall when Cauthen was there. Cauthen asked Howse to become his educational director, adding that work to his teaching responsibilities. He offered him fifty dollars a month as salary if his wife Genevieve would come to work as the office secretary as part of the deal.

Howse was making only thirty dollars a month as a teacher at the seminary, plus whatever grapefruit he could get from seminary property in the valley and whatever pecans they could pick up from the trees behind Fort Worth Hall. So the fifty dollars looked pretty good. He said yes; and the church, willing to give their young pastor a free hand in all things, called Howse.

The two men together began to visit the church members systematically. Cauthen would see ten to twelve people in an afternoon. He worked hard all week doing his seminary work, his visitation, and his staff work, and he reserved Saturday to get ready to preach. Saturday morning he would go into the office, and Genevieve Howse would hold all calls, allowing him to work all morning. Then he would come out for lunch; and if he wasn't finished, he would go back again. But according to Howse, he never went into the pulpit unprepared. Nor did he fail to communicate with people of all ages. The congregation responded enthusiastically, and the offerings began to reflect it.

At this point, Cauthen revealed another facet of himself. The leaders of the church knew they were getting a talented preacher and a man of deep spirituality, but they had not known of his sharp business sense. Cauthen and Howse journeyed to Waco, Texas, where Cauthen boldly set up an interview with the president of the insurance company that held the mortgage on their church building. There he proposed that the company refinance the loan in such a way that the church could handle the interest payments and begin a gradual reduction of the principal.

Based on what the church was evidencing under Cauthen's leadership, it seemed the best deal the insurance company could strike, so it was accepted. In preparation for the conference, Cauthen consulted a businessman he had not met before, but the man was known for his faith in Baptist causes. It was that businessman, Carr Collins, who gave him the clues he needed to sway the insurance company. After Cauthen's visit to Collins' office, the people of the Polytechnic Church were not the only ones "believing in Baker James Cauthen."

During Cauthen's early ministry at Poly, many young families rallied to his side. One of these was the Sherman family. John Sherman was the son of a man who had pastored the Polytechnic Church until he died of a heart attack in 1921. The man who had followed Sherman's father led the church into what was subsequently called modernism. Though Melugin had tried to put the church back together again, he did not have the leadership qualities needed. When Cauthen came, John Sherman responded immediately to what he called Cauthen's "firm and very straightforward leadership."

Cecil Sherman, one of John's sons, now pastor of the First Baptist Church in Asheville, North Carolina, said his father saw Cauthen as the kind of man who would say, "The bear's up that tree; let's go get it." One day when Cauthen visited the Shermans, John Sherman took him back to where his father's library was housed and said, "Take what you want." Cauthen took several of the books, including Matthew Henry's commentaries, which he subsequently lost in China. This fact never bothered John Sherman, though both of his sons became preachers and would have loved to have those books. He never stopped "believing in Baker James Cauthen."

In the summer of 1933, Cauthen, Bill Howse, and his wife Genevieve took an automobile trip to New Mexico and Colorado. The three of them became even closer, and their respect for each other deepened. Cauthen came back impressed with the Howses' marriage and wondering whether it was best to be single in the Lord's work.

That fall he taught a course in Southwestern Seminary's theology department while beginning his doctoral study. It gave him a chance to touch base again with his old friend Eloise Glass. He saw her one day walking along the campus—lithe, enthusiastic, and beautiful. The thought occurred to him, *She's a good friend, but how would I feel if some fellow came along and married her?* His feelings intensified when he asked her to go somewhere with him on the one weekend that Eloise had a visit from an out-of-town friend. He was the son of a lady whom Eloise had nursed an entire summer. The incident took Cauthen aback. *She may not always be there,* he thought.

CHAPTER SIX

Eloise

Eloise Glass turned twenty-four the September Baker James Cauthen began to wonder how he would feel if someone else claimed her. Eloise had been born in Hwanghsien in the Shantung Province of North China on September 10, 1909, the fourth child of missionaries Wiley B. Glass and Eunice Taylor Glass. Her parents had been in China just under six years when she was born. The first Glass child was a boy who died in infancy. The second was also a boy, Bentley, a little over three and one-half years of age; and a third, a sister Lois, was not quite two when Eloise was born.

Her parents had already weathered the rigors of several North China winters, the repercussions of the Japanese-Russian War, terrible famine, and disease that had already taken an infant and had almost taken the life of Eunice Glass. Within months after Eloise's birth, the whole family was on the high seas for their first furlough in the States. Almost as soon as they returned to China, while Eloise was still too young to have memories, they were caught up in a frenzied revolution in relationship to the work of Sun Yat-sen. It was to change the face of China forever. But the toddler's main memory was of the loss of a baby brother, young Wiley B.

That memory, however, quickly receded before another. Her mother, whom she barely remembers, fell critically ill with tuberculosis. Despite gentle and tender care by a missionary nurse who served in Hwanghsien, she died in the spring of 1913 when Eloise was four and one-half years of age.

For several months she had been kept away from her mother. She remembers looking across the room from the bedroom door and seeing her mother's hair spread across the pillow. A dim memory prevails of a time before that when her mother would put

Eloise and her sister Lois to bed, sit on the side of their bed, and sing to them, "I think when I read that sweet story of old . . . thousands and thousands who wander and fall have never heard . . . but Jesus has bade them to come." Her mother had a passion for missions. She had been called to missions even before she met her husband and had expressed hopes that her children would take up the same calling.

Another memory clusters with these for Eloise. She can remember standing and holding onto the skirts of a missionary woman outside of a Chinese church where the Chinese had the funeral for her mother. Then she remembers being taken away from those skirts and placed in a mule litter that trailed other mules carrying her mother's coffin as they made their way in a solemn cortege to the coastal city of Chefoo. They buried her there in an international cemetery. The grieving missionary father and his three small children stayed for a time while some of the missionary women made clothes for the children before he took them back to Hwanghsien.

In January of 1914, as all Europe was teetering on the brink of what soon would be called a World War, Eloise's sister Lois had to start going to Chefoo to boarding school. The father reluctantly decided that the younger child should not be left at home alone; so when Eloise was barely five, he took his girls to Chefoo. With his heart nearly breaking, he left them crying and pleading for him not to leave. Only when the housekeeper of the school went and brought the older Bentley, who had already been at the school for a couple of years, could the girls could be quieted.

Except for vacations and, when she was in the fifth grade, a furlough year with her father and stepmother, Eloise Glass lived at the missionary school sponsored by the China Inland Mission for thirteen years.

The school followed the British system, with a lower school and an upper school, which were in turn divided into the girls' school and the boys' school. Three months out of the year, usually August and then December through February 1, the children were out of school and could go home. That is, they could go home if they were lucky enough to live close by. Eloise and Lois Glass were among the lucky, as Hwanghsien was only sixty miles away. Some of the China Inland Mission kids got home only once a year, and others saw their parents only when the missionaries came out from the interior.

Eloise's best friends were two sisters from Szechwan Province. The whole class of girls, nine in number, have kept up with each other with a round robin letter through the years since.

While the girls were at school a half-sister named Gertrude, now known as "Trudy," was born. Because she was ill and stayed home that year, Lois grew very close to Trudy. Eloise became a bit jealous of their special relationship.

Eloise liked books and hated chores. The patient Lois was always willing to do whatever was required of her, so Eloise often let her sister take the brunt of things. But her respect for Lois, who later became a missionary and returned to China, was and is without bounds.

In 1926 the girls finished school and returned to Hwanghsien to work with their parents while they awaited furlough. Then, in 1927, they all went to America together. When they arrived in the States, the girls found that their new clothes were hopelessly out of style. It really didn't matter to them. After all, from the girls' perspective, style in the late twenties was part of a worldly and unspiritual environment.

W. B. Glass spent his furlough in Waco that year in order to be with his girls as they started in Baylor University. He left them the next year ensconced in an apartment, well adjusted to the Baylor campus, and doing well in school, social life, and church involvement.

The summer he left for China, the enterprising Eloise moved to Houston to promote the circulation of the Texas Baptist newspaper, the *Baptist Standard,* on a commission basis. With her father's help and some letters of recommendation, she went before any church that would have her, promoting the *Standard* and taking individual subscriptions. "I did right well, too," she remembers.

Eloise Glass was a junior when Baker James Cauthen arrived in Waco in the fall of 1929. By this time the attractive coed felt quite at home in her environment. Members of the Seventh and James Baptist Church, she and Lois were involved in a welcome party that the church gave for new students. With no steady beau, Eloise was "always looking out for interesting new students." She decided that Baker James Cauthen, "a stringbean with auburn curls he couldn't control and beautiful brown eyes," was just such a person.

She tried to be careful about her aggressiveness, however. In her first year in Waco, a revivalist was warming up a group of students at Seventh and James and asked if there was anybody there who wasn't married but wanted to be. She was too fresh out of China to understand the kidding involved, and she stood up. Realizing she was the only one standing, she stood out even more with her furious blushing.

She was a little more wise to the ways of collegiate culture, however, when she met Cauthen. To her delight, he joined the cafeteria table that the girls frequented. She thought Baker James Cauthen an intriguing name. When he spoke at the Wednesday night Baylor Religious Hour, she went to hear him out of curiosity and came away convinced that, despite his youth, he was among the best preachers she had ever heard.

During Cauthen's Baylor year, they were named to the honorary English society, Sigma Tau Delta. Though he was a Master's student and she an undergraduate, she was his grader in one undergraduate course he had to take. His superior scholarship impressed her there. They also saw each other sometimes in the Volunteer Band. As she confessed later, she also watched him as he walked down Speight Street with a load of books checked out from the library to study in his apartment. In China, her father often had told her to be sure and bring back a man. She could not help wondering if that man might be someone like Cauthen.

Probably not, she reasoned with herself. He had a girl back in Lufkin, and she knew from chance comments that he was deeply committed to a pastoral ministry. When he left to go to Southwestern, they talked about writing. When he didn't, she wrote him twice. He answered, but not in a way that would encourage the correspondence.

Eloise got back to the task of finishing her third year with as high a gradepoint average as possible. As an M.K. (missionary kid), she received free tuition, along with a Woman's Missionary Union stipend of $150 a year from what is called the Margaret Fund. In addition, her dad sent her $20 a month. By selling Christmas cards and representing a local beauty parlor—trying, for a commission, to get other Baylor women to frequent the place—she got by quite well. A Baptist association in Florida had adopted her and sent her gifts all during her college years and later even made her several quilts for her wedding.

An unexpected chance to renew acquaintance with Cauthen came to Eloise at a Sigma Tau Delta meeting held at Hillsboro, Texas, when former students from Dallas and Fort Worth were invited to attend. Cauthen came, and they talked about her plans to go to seminary. She had been considering the Woman's Missionary Union Training School at Louisville, Kentucky, since her father had attended Southern Seminary there. However, she wanted a theological degree rather than the degree in religious education offered at the Training School. She longed to study philosophy of religion, church history, New Testament, and even preaching. As she talked with him, Cauthen said, "Why not Southwestern? The scholarship is as good as you'll find anywhere." Since Eloise was impressed with his scholarly abilities, Baker's remark carried a lot of weight with her.

Cauthen was glad to see Eloise when she got to Southwestern the next fall but seemed preoccupied with his studies and his churches at Manning and White Mound. After some initial conversations, their lives went separate ways again.

Pondering over his preoccupation, she remembered his interest in her summer activities. He had been entranced by her adventuresomeness. She had gone to New York, found a job on the New Jersey coast, worked in a boardwalk confectioner's in the evenings, and explored New York on weekends when she had saved enough to make the trip. She was strictly on her own, knowing only the young woman with whom she had traveled in the beginning (and that one had married and stayed in New York City). But Eloise made friends rapidly.

That summer gave her a better perspective on life, she thought, when she checked into Southwestern Seminary in September and persuaded them to enroll her as one of only two women to be admitted along with the men into the Master of Theology course. She had complete confidence that she could work toe to toe with any of the men in any theological area except preaching, and maybe even in that.

Eloise had a good first year. The next summer she accepted a position in Oklahoma, traveling from association to association as missionary speaker on a team promoting Sunday School and Training Union work. In August she received an intriguing invitation. When the Quince Davidsons invited her to come to White Mound and lead the young people's prayer meetings in connection with a summer revival in which their new pastor, young Baker James Cauthen, would preach, she was thrilled. Would she do it? Of course she would.

It was a delightful week for Eloise. She felt comfortable with her task and picked up her friendship with Baker right where it had left off. Only, this time, she sensed that something was happening she wished she could stop. She was losing her heart to the fervent and gifted young preacher, and the feeling seemed completely one-sided. Eloise led prayer groups before the evening services and counseled with young people who made decisions. When the team visited prospects for the church or young people who had not yet made a decision to trust Christ, she was often brought into the counseling task.

Despite the effectiveness of the messages, her thoughts often wandered. Kerosene lanterns flickering around the brush arbor, children crying in the background, packed crowds, music—all made her aware that no matter how comfortable she felt in this life and how much she liked the young man behind the pulpit, God had called her to China. It was equally evident that God had not called him. What could she do with the feelings that welled up inside her each time she saw him? God had called her; God would have to handle that.

When she came back from her Christmas vacation with relatives in January of 1933, Eloise Glass was not surprised to learn that Baker James Cauthen had been called as pastor of the Polytechnic Baptist Church. For a man of his age, it was quite an honor despite the fact that Kermit Melugin had already been there. Around campus, most people agreed that Cauthen, Criswell, and Melugin were probably the three best young preachers anywhere. But Eloise also heard others saying, "He's too young. He's biting off too much too soon. He's too cocksure. When he tangles with that debt-ridden, depression-battered, controversy-torn church, he will find out that ministry has not been served up on a silver platter. He'll see!"

"They'll see!" she said. She had no doubt that her young friend was up to the task. But just in case, she spent a considerable part of her intercessory quiet time holding him up before the Lord. As word came back of his effectiveness and enthusiastic reception, she quietly thanked God.

From time to time that spring, she saw him on campus. Some people said he "drove like Jehu" in his Chevy coupe between the Polytechnic Church and Southwestern campus, barely meeting his schedules. Some were impressed at how well he balanced his teaching at the seminary, pastoring the rebounding Polytechnic Church, and pursuing his own doctoral study. She enjoyed his success and struggled to console herself with the promises of the God who called her back to China.

When she returned to the campus from summer camp in Arkansas in 1933, Cauthen saw her and strode across the lawn in front of Fort Worth Hall to walk with her. "Say," he said, "I'm going to speak at the orientation session here for new students next week, and some friends of mine tell me there is a young lady there I should meet." He mentioned her name. "Do you know her?" Eloise didn't and was not sure she would tell him if she did. But she smiled as sweetly as she knew how—and she knew how to smile very sweetly—and promised to look out for the girl. "Thanks, Eloise. I appreciate that," he said as he stopped off to turn into his classroom. She was too preoccupied with her own frustrations to notice that he turned to give her a second glance as she walked off.

Eloise had no way of knowing that some of his deacons and the kindly mothers of the church took every opportunity to tell Baker that he really ought to find some lovely young lady at the seminary and marry her, that every preacher needed a wife. In fact, some had daughters they were perfectly glad to pair with Bake. His intense attitude and ninety-mile-an-hour schedule, however, held off most of those efforts.

Even so, Eloise was surprised when Baker called her the next week and asked her to go to a Sunday School rally with him at one of the local churches. "I can't," she said, more frustrated than she had ever been. "Raleigh Dawson is coming to town. You've heard me speak of Raleigh?" Yes, he had, but that didn't make him feel any better. Raleigh was the handsome son of an invalid lady for whom Eloise had cared one summer, and the thought bothered him. In fact, it bothered him so much that the next week he tried again. No, Raleigh was gone. She was free.

Baker James Cauthen speaks at the ground-breaking ceremony of a Baptist church in Hong Kong (1951).

"Fine," he said.

"What are we going to do?" she asked.

"Well, we're going to run Arthur DeLoach up to a church meeting and then . . . well . . . let's let it be a surprise."

The surprise was an airplane ride from Meecham Field on the north side of Fort Worth. Cauthen was fascinated with airplanes. He and W. L. Howse had flown in a Ford trimotor on an afternoon excursion a few weeks before, but this was an open cockpit biplane. As the two of them crowded into the passenger's seat, it was hard to tell which one was more excited. He loved the speed and exhilaration and the thrill of it, and it was obvious she was game for anything. The next week they tried again. Only this time, it was a speedboat on Lake Worth. "You really do like things like this," she said.

"Well, don't you?" he teased.

"You know I do," she laughed.

She wasn't quite so sure about the speed with which he drove his automobile, but God seemed to be watching over him in every other way. After that, he surprised her by asking her if she would give him a picture. She said yes, if he would give her one in return. She put his picture up in her dormitory room and was slightly chagrined to find that he kept hers in his desk drawer at the church. People coming into her room would ask her about Bake's picture. She would assure them, "Oh yes, we've been good friends a long time."

In the meanwhile, she struggled. She knew that she could go back to China single, that her father's disappointment was not nearly as important as obedience to her heavenly Father. Finally, God gave her the victory. She would go single.

It was fully settled in her mind when Baker picked her up one day in October and took her in his car up to Inspiration Point in Fort Worth. She was staying with the Shamburger family over the weekend and was exempted from the chaperone rule. As president of the dorm council, she had helped get it changed that year. Instead of an approved chaperone, another seminary couple sufficed. Josephine Harris, who later became a missionary to Hawaii, was vice-president of the dorm council and co-conspirator with Eloise in liberalizing the rules.

As his car pulled up to a stop on Inspiration Point that day,

Cauthen turned to her and proposed. It wasn't dramatic, but it was articulate. She listened with pounding heart as he told her of his feeling that their friendship of already four years was deep and healthy, that he believed God had brought them together, and that it was his will that they marry. He didn't know how God was going to use him, but he felt that he was going to use him. And he wanted her alongside him.

Eloise gasped for breath. She had known for quite a while that she loved him. But now, when he was asking her the very thing she had longed for him to ask, she couldn't reply. Deliberately, she told him of her call and surrender to missions. She had told him before, but now she told him in terms of what he was asking. At the same time, she confessed her deep feeling for him. They prayed together. She agreed that she would give him an answer later.

A month later, Eloise still didn't know what to do. Baker was being very patient—ever thoughtful, never pressing.

One day she was in her room ironing. As she often did during such chores, she began to pray. She asked God to rid her heart of any wrong desires and confessed to him that more than anything else she wanted to know his will in the matter of marriage. Suddenly a thought burst upon her consciousness: *Eloise, you don't have to know the whole way that I am going to lead you. You only have to know what's right now.*

She thought, *If I don't have to worry about the whole way, I don't have to think twice about what's right now. I should marry Bake.* Her heart soared as she decided that God had given her the thought and that she indeed had the "go-ahead" to marry Baker—to assume her place alongside him and his pastorate, to trust the future and China, if indeed it was in her future, to God.

Baker's schedule kept them from getting together for several days after that. She told him as they were sitting on the east stone bannister of the steps to Cowden Hall one day after he had finished the class that he was teaching. It didn't surprise her at all that he was not surprised. He had known from the beginning, but she had to know it for herself. "You can't believe how frustrating it was," she said, "to feel our hearts straining toward each other with joy and, because of those students around, finding no way to express it other than by holding hands."

Cauthen found a more appropriate setting to present a ring. He had purchased it while she was in Oklahoma City on a speaking engagement and was carrying it for the day when she would say yes. It never occurred to him that she would say anything else.

The W. L. Howses gave the announcement party. They invited mutual friends from Travis Avenue, from Polytechnic, and from the seminary without telling them what the party was about. Genevieve and Eloise greeted the guests at the door as they arrived. At the refreshment table, their friends were greeted with a cake that announced the engagement.

Baker and Eloise planned their wedding for May, ten days after she received her Master of Theology degree. She would be one of the first women ever to receive the degree—and one of the last for a long time, as the seminary stopped admitting women to the Th.M. program. "I'd hate to think I caused that," she said.

During the interim between their engagement and their marriage, Bake and Eloise worked hard to get around the strict seminary rules without breaking any. She went to the Polytechnic Church on Sundays. They played golf on other days with the Howses and deliberately knocked balls into the rough. In fact, they spent a lot of time in the rough together. Bake became quite adept at hitting the ball into the wooded sections.

On other weekends they went horseback riding in Forest Park. She had access to jodhpurs and boots, and enough vanity survived the China Inland Mission training to allow her to look very smart in such moments.

Since Eloise's parents were in China, and there was no one in the Fort Worth area to do the things parents usually do, Genevieve and W. L. Howse took on most of those responsibilities. Together, Eloise and Baker asked W. T. Conner to perform their wedding ceremony. He was pleased; but when the time came for the ceremony, he was nervous beyond belief. According to Howse, Conner was shaking so hard he could not hold his Bible. "That preacher just held onto his Bible for dear life. How he could shake like that and not affect his voice has always been a mystery to me," Howse said.

The wedding was held in the chapel of Cowden Hall. Bentley Glass, Eloise's brother, gave her away, and her sister Lois was a bridesmaid—along with Sybil Leonard, who later married Woodson Armes, and Ardell Watkins, who married Frank Burress. And

W. A. Criswell and Nane Starnes were there to stand with Cauthen.

The church at Polytechnic, of course, responded as if every one of them was a part of the wedding family. They filled Cowden Hall and greeted the newlyweds enthusiastically. Also, they immediately raised Baker's salary from $125 to $175 a month in recognition of his new responsibilities. They enjoyed more than they would ever let him forget their response to a Scripture passage that he had used the Sunday after the engagement was announced. The Scripture read, "Behold, and see if there be any sorrow like unto my sorrow wherewith the Lord hath afflicted me in the day of his fierce anger."

As the wedding drew near, Eloise was both heartened and saddened by the letters and presents that came from China. Her father sent a dress length of white Chinese silk to Mrs. W. T. Conner, who made her wedding dress for her. He wrote Baker, saying that though they had not met, everyone had spoken highly of him. "Anyone my daughter would want to marry has to be a fine man," he said, and added, "My girl has a very affectionate family, and no matter what other attainments and honors you present her, she will need consideration, tenderness, and love more than anything else. Just love her, and she will be happy."

At a seminary function shortly after the wedding, Eloise signed the guest book "Baker and Eloise Glass." Baker has not been quite as forgetful of that as she would like.

CHAPTER SEVEN

The Pastor-Teacher

Cauthen's bride was a welcome, energetic addition to his ministry. She visited with him, became Adult Department superintendent, taught a Sunday School class, worked with the Woman's Missionary Union, and even did some biblical research for him. He handled much ribbing from seminarians and fellow faculty members with good humor. "That Bake's a lucky guy," they teased. "Eloise does all the research. All he has to do is preach it."

As Eloise found out, however, Baker's preparation for preaching was a solo matter between him and the Lord. Having traveled from place to place with denominational workers and having heard them give the same message over and over again, she was immediately impressed that Baker always "preached fresh."

Cauthen's preparation was not traditional. It didn't include the manuscript recommended by the preaching professors; nor did it include a year's planning of projected titles. Each week he went to the Lord to find the Scripture through which God would speak to his congregation. Then he worked long and hard over that passage, developing a detailed outline that he half printed, half wrote on any convenient piece of paper he could tuck in his Bible.

Eloise learned to recognize his writing even from a distance. It was very small and slanted upward from left to right. She also learned that he would rather preach than eat, or do anything else for that matter. Preaching was the essence of life for him, and this fun-loving girl tried to decide what they were going to do for diversion.

She found out early. They would travel. Baker was adventuresome and inquisitive. As they took off on a trip a few months later with Bill and Genevieve Howse, she realized just how adventuresome. On that trip, as she listened to Genevieve and Bill talk, she learned of an incident that provided a significant insight into Baker's character.

During the trip that Cauthen and the Howses took to New Mexico the previous summer, they spent a few days in a small motel near Riodosa. One day they went horseback riding with the notion that they would rent horses again the next day and climb the trail to the top of the twelve-thousand-foot Sierra Blanca Mountain. But when they got up the next morning, they realized they had ridden the horses too long and were too sore. Baker said brightly, "Let's climb the mountain on foot." Genevieve and Bill, anxious to walk off the soreness from the horses, quickly agreed. With Baker leading the way, the three started out, carrying nothing but the clothes on their backs. By lunchtime they were nowhere near the top, but kept pressing on, thinking each crest would reveal it. "Baker was insistent that we reach the top," Howse remembers.

By late afternoon, exhausted and hungry, they encountered two Apache sheepherders who lived in tents on the edge of one of the high meadows. The sheepherders invited them to share their tents. After looking inside, they decided that wasn't exactly for them. Instead, they offered to pay one of the sheepherders to go down to the motel on his horse and bring back some blankets. It was dark when he got back. They built a small fire in an arroyo near the tents and tried to stay warm, not knowing that the wind rushed down the draws from the mountaintop at night, intensifying the cold.

Wrapping up in their blankets as best they could, they sat close together on a big flat rock. When they were ready for sleep, they lay with their heads on the higher part, of course. That allowed the wind to rush right over their heads and under their blankets. They remembered it as the longest night they had ever spent. As Howse recalls, the Indians were singing as their guests tried to go to sleep. When asked what they were singing, they replied that it was an Apache war song. Howse said he wasn't sure but that they were preparing for a scalping party—or at least robbing. Baker didn't seem to be worried. He considered it a grand adventure.

The next morning they could hardly believe their ears when he suggested brightly that they press on to the top. Their hosts roasted a few ears of corn for them on the coals of their fire. After eating the corn and thanking the Indians profusely, they began climbing. At the top the view was spectacular. They could see the white sands of New Mexico off in the distance. To this day, the Howses remember how completely satisfied Baker was at their having attained their goal, no matter how unrealistic it seemed to be in retrospect. "He is like that," Howse laughs.

On the trips that followed, which included Yellowstone Park and the Great Century of Progress Fair in Chicago, Baker learned that his wife was just as energetic and adventuresome as he. It gave him a great sense of strength and camaraderie. Though he tried from the very beginning to practice the advice of the father-in-law he had never met, to treat her with tenderness and give her lots of love, he was always amazed at her strength and spirit.

That fall before their marriage, Baker poured his energies into raising money for foreign missions through the annual Lottie Moon Christmas offering. Despite the stubborn efforts of the Woman's Missionary Union, Polytechnic had in the past done very little for the special offering. Baker suggested that they pray about what they should do. They kept deferring the problem to him. Accepting the responsibility, he said, "I'll tell you what we should do. We should give one thousand dollars."

The amount overwhelmed even the Howses. This church was struggling to pay its debts and meet expenses each week, but Baker was insistent. He dealt patiently with every negative voice from staff to deacon to committee member, and he slowly convinced every one of them. As they saw it through his eyes, it would be the kind of impossible task that would strengthen their faith. If the church would let God help them accomplish this, there was no telling what else they could do.

When it came time to announce the goal to the people of Polytechnic, Bill Howse watched amazed as Cauthen handled it so skillfully and persuasively that they were soon with him. Rising courage was in every face. But then their pastor delivered his punch line—one thousand dollars!

Howse said it was as if a wet towel had been thrown in their faces. Cauthen saw their reaction, immediately backed up, and started another round of leading them to the goal. He talked about Christmas giving and the challenge to give their major gifts at the Christmas season to Christ rather than to each other. Slowly their shock and disbelief collapsed before his faith and persuasiveness. They agreed to try. He urged them to hold their money until a

Sunday morning when all would give it together. But he kept telling them to save, to pray, and to seek God's leadership.

Finally, on a Sunday in December, he asked all to bring their gifts and lay them on the altar in what several remember as the highest hour the church had ever experienced. When they counted the money, the debt-laden church had given over $1,100 for foreign missions. People all over the city heard about it. Howse says it did more to unite the church, to give the members confidence, and to awaken them to the world beyond themselves than anything they had ever done. Howse thought that single event, more than anything else, ignited the church; and it truly began to grow.

Throughout 1935, despite the fact that Cauthen was now teaching missions, winding up his own thesis, and speaking everywhere he was asked, the church prospered. It was only a block away from the campus of a Methodist college, Texas Wesleyan. Because of that, the Polytechnic area was often known as Methodist Hill. As the Polytechnic Baptist Church grew, however, and began to draw significantly from the blue-collar workers in the area, some began to call it Baptist Hill.

Dr. T. L. Holcomb, who had been executive secretary for the Baptist General Convention in Texas, had now become pastor of the First Baptist Church in Oklahoma City. Cauthen, ever looking toward the best, asked Dr. Holcomb to come to Polytechnic to preach for a revival, after discussing the matter with W. L. Howse. To their surprise and delight, Holcomb agreed. Cauthen and Howse worked hard on plans for the meeting for the summer of 1935 and experienced one of the most remarkable revival meetings that either was ever to know. Though Baker would give Howse the credit, Howse said Baker's ability to organize, prepare, and lead that group toward an objective left him no doubt about the man's ability to handle anything that might come to him through the years.

Meanwhile, at Southwestern Seminary, where he served as part-time professor, Cauthen's abilities in the classroom were also attracting attention. That attention was undoubtedly helped by stories that came to the campus of the remarkable response in his church. Since most of the students were looking toward such responsibilities themselves, they felt a ring of authenticity in all that Cauthen said and did.

But they were even more impressed with his preparation and with his earnest delivery in class. His obvious facility for talking knowledgeably on almost any subject witnessed to the wide range of his reading and preparation. Others pointed out that if you could catch him in the midst of his hectic schedule, he would stop and listen to you as earnestly as if you were the only one on the scene. It was a quality to which both students and church members responded enthusiastically.

CHAPTER EIGHT

The Missionary Question

The summer of 1935 brought the Cauthens to a monumental decision. Because they heard regularly from the Glasses and other friends of Eloise in North China, they felt close to events there. An exciting revival in the Shantung Province had enlivened those reports since 1931. Eloise squealed with glee or praised God softly as news came of victory after victory among Chinese Christians she knew. But 1935 was a big year in China for other reasons. The centennial of Baptist missionary effort there, it was a year of visitation by people from all over the world who encouraged the China missionaries and led to dreams of major new steps forward.

One such vision was an All-China Baptist Seminary to be established in Shanghai. Dr. W. B. Glass figured strongly in the planning, and the Foreign Mission Board's new executive secretary, Dr. Charles Maddry, visited Shanghai and talked to missionaries from all over the area with a view to that step. One of the major concerns was who would be brought to the seminary to teach. Partly because the missionaries knew his wife, partly because they knew of his reputation at Southwestern Seminary, Baker James Cauthen's name was prominent in the discussions. While still in China, Maddry dispatched a letter to Cauthen, inviting him to seek appointment as a missionary with a view to helping begin the work of the All-China Seminary.

When the letter came, Eloise was beside herself with joy. God had at last completed her vision. Her sense of direction had been true. She would be going back to China after all.

It was all she could do to mask her disappointment when her husband indicated that he wasn't sure God wanted them in China. He wanted to be open to God's leading. Although he had various missionary interests and had been especially impressed by biographies of Matthew Yates and Adoniram Judson, he had a deepening sense of call to the Polytechnic Church. And he felt especially prepared to work within the combination of communities that were coming into the church. An increasing number of talented and educated people were coming into the church from Texas Wesleyan College and were relating well to the blue-collar workers who had constituted the preponderance of the church before and who were also increasing. Cauthen knew God was blessing his work with the church.

Also, he was scheduled to continue teaching missions at Southwestern that fall. And, in sharp contrast to previous semesters, he was to be on a regular salary. The inherent vote of confidence was more significant than the additional money.

Early after the receipt of Maddry's letter, Cauthen thought for a time that God could be speaking to him through that letter. He drafted a reply, tentatively accepting the offer, and showed it to Eloise. She said, "I'm afraid you are saying what you would like to feel instead of what you really feel." Knowing her deep sense of commitment to China and her long-standing desire to go back, Cauthen was surprised.

He counseled with Dr. Scarborough and with Dr. Tidwell when he came up from Baylor to speak in chapel. "You must stay," Tidwell stated adamantly. "God has obviously laid his hand on you for the place you are now in."

Eloise and Baker talked long and prayed much. "Why don't you talk to Dr. Conner about it?" Eloise asked when she realized that her husband was honestly struggling with an interpretation of the letter from Maddry in relationship to his understanding of God's will. "I believe I will," he replied.

Conner listened thoughtfully as his young protégé talked. He had grown increasingly fond of Cauthen and deeply believed in him.

Early in Cauthen's studies at the seminary, he had taken Conner to Lufkin with him to preach at his church at Manning. The renowned theologian stayed overnight with the elder Cauthens and was much impressed by them. They in turn were all but overwhelmed by having the man about whom they had heard so much actually staying in their home. In a chapel talk a bit later, Conner said, "If Cauthen doesn't amount to much, it is his own fault because he surely came out of the right kind of home."

As Conner preached in the Manning Church, he made a strong statement that really moved the young student, and Cauthen said a firm "Amen!" Conner stopped, looked at him, and then looked back at the congregation. "It looks like Brother Cauthen got that point, so I assume the rest of you did," he said. Needless to say, that amused his hearers.

But now as Cauthen talked to him, Conner struggled with his own sense of priorities. He loved the missionary task and felt deeply committed to it and to his students who had gone to various places around the world. He always tried to keep the missionary imperative before them as he unfolded the theology that clustered around the gospel reality. But as he began to talk to Cauthen, another line of thinking emerged. "Cauthen, if you were to go to China and teach in the seminary there, you would influence many Chinese, and they would influence many others. That's the truth. You would make a good missionary. But if you stay here, you will probably influence many men to go to China, and they will influence many Chinese who will influence many others. In other words, with your pastorate and your teaching opportunities here, you will have an even larger opportunity to influence the work there. It won't seem as immediate, but its long-range realities are there."

Cauthen left the professor's office, pondering his thoughts. Conner didn't realize it, but he had spoken to the young man the very thoughts that had dominated his own thinking but that he had felt were too presumptuous. It was as if they had been confirmed. That night he told Eloise: "With no further light, and despite my deep interest in what's going on in North China and your obvious preparation for the work out there should God call us, I'm not able to interpret this letter as a call. And I am very much aware of a continuing call to Polytechnic and to the seminary. I'm going to have to write Dr. Maddry and tell him that God has not yet called me to China."

Eloise smiled. She knew her man and had no reason to doubt that this was an honest statement. Through him, God must be speaking to her, too, she decided. "Then by all means, do that, Baker," she said. "I'm sure Dr. Maddry will understand. And I'll write my daddy and share your thoughts with him."

After his talk with Conner, Cauthen sat with him listening to another man speak on missions. Cauthen turned to Conner and said, "How does that make you feel?"

"It makes me wish I could go . . . every time," Conner said seriously.

Gradually, Cauthen was able to sort out the difference between his feelings and his sense of leadership. He made his decision and wrote Maddry that he did not yet have God's call to China. Maddry answered, "If at any time before you reach the age limit you do feel you should go, let me know immediately. The door is always open for you."

Cauthen readdressed his energies toward Polytechnic and his role as acting professor of missions at Southwestern. W. L. Howse felt God leading him to the Broadway Baptist Church in Fort Worth and heavier teaching responsibilities at the seminary in the field of religious education. He had completed his doctorate and was becoming one of the leading experts in that burgeoning field of ministry. Cauthen quickly turned to another young man he had met at the seminary, Franklin Segler.

Segler and his wife Fannie May had been in Cauthen's class in missions in the spring, and Cauthen had come to know the young couple. In turn, Cauthen impressed them. Segler said, "His was an attractive personality, and he came across to students as a scintillating mind. He covered voluminous materials in his lectures, which demanded a great deal of note taking by students. His assignments were also demanding, and students had to work hard to make good grades in his classes."

When Cauthen first approached Segler to be his minister of education, Segler pointed out that he had worked for five years in that field before entering the seminary and now felt that God wanted him to be a pastor. He had not planned to continue work in the field of religious education. "Let's call you an associate pastor and give you the privilege of preaching occasionally," Cauthen countered, reasoning that this would help Segler become a pastor later on. His propensity to work out a way to reach mutually complementary goals with people seemingly going in opposite directions was keenly developed at this stage.

Segler soon found that Cauthen gave a great deal of himself and expected the same from everybody working with him. Segler felt if

Dr. Baker J. Cauthen speaking at the Baptist seminary in Taipei

Cauthen had a blind spot, it was his tendency to assume that everybody was as gifted as he. Yet Segler found him approachable, fair, and willing to sit down and talk about expectations and directions.

His new colleague was especially fascinated with Cauthen's preaching. Essentially expository in nature, his sermons always made the Bible come alive with intensely practical application. The obvious charisma in his preaching was gripping and his evangelistic appeal compelling.

Segler testified to friends that there "wasn't a lazy bone in Cauthen's body." He visited the sick and members of his church tirelessly, counseled with young and old alike, and seemed especially able to deal with any tough problem that came up.

Soon after Segler arrived, he and Cauthen learned that one of the couples working with young people was involved in an unhealthy way with another couple working with the same group. Cauthen first counseled with them and then firmly removed them from leadership with youth. His firmness, even adamancy, in doing this shocked his congregation. They and his fellow staff members discovered, however, that his leadership power was overwhelming when he set his mind.

Cauthen was an excellent administrator and leader of the entire church, but Segler sensed the pastor's special commitment to the Sunday School and Woman's Missionary Union. His respect for what the women were able to accomplish with their mission studies, weeks of prayer, and special offerings was profound.

Segler and Cauthen collaborated on one of the latter's rare incidents of pranksterism. They had taken some young people to a retreat at the Tres Rios Encampment. The Seglers and the Cauthens had adjoining cabins a bit apart from the young people. One night they got back from supper, the Seglers found their tennis shoes nailed to the floor, while the Cauthens found their sheets wet and knotted. Until they heard the Cauthens laughing, the Seglers thought they were the only victims. Impressed with Cauthen's ability to laugh, Segler suggested, "We ought to do something to get back at them."

"What can we do?" Cauthen said, his face brightening. The two huddled and decided on their strategy. After the youngsters retired to their cabins and the lights went out, a water hose was turned on from behind an old cart. A firm spray directed toward the screen windows of the cabins where the young people slept was answered with squeals of dismay. When their mission was accomplished, the two parsons, with the cart shielding them, slipped back through the woods to their cabins and locked the doors, almost choking on their laughter. Segler said, "You wouldn't believe how much Baker James enjoyed that. His excitement was unbounded. When the young people found it out, it actually deepened their relationship to their pastor."

One of the young counselors working with the young people that night was Frank Means, another seminary student. He was among those who got soaked. Means was a native Missourian who graduated from Oklahoma Baptist University in 1934. He worked a year before entering Southwestern Seminary in 1935. There, because of a previous friendship with Franklin Segler, he joined Polytechnic Baptist Church. He had already heard about Cauthen, but was shocked at how youthful the man looked. As soon as his new pastor began preaching, Frank understood why he enjoyed the reputation that was already his. "I'd mentally join the church every time he preached."

Means, who was to become a lifelong friend of the Cauthens, remembers the first sermon he heard Cauthen preach. In a most effective way, he was asking a question over and over again in rhetorical style as he was prone to do. The question was, "Do you love Jesus?" After he had repeated it several times, a little child jumped up and said, "Yes, I do love Jesus." Everybody broke up—even Cauthen—and it took him a while to get his message going again. Means was impressed that the preacher was able to enjoy the incident even at his own expense.

A year later, Means was ordained by the Polytechnic Baptist Church, with Dr. W. T. Conner leading the examination and Baker James Cauthen delivering the charge on the subject "The Preacher's Attitude Toward His Task." Means felt strongly that Cauthen was a man of God in every sense of the word. He argued vigorously with those who disparaged Cauthen as an overly ambitious, albeit gifted, preacher. Because of Cauthen's early success in the ministry, that charge was often lodged. Eloise Cauthen, more aware of it than her husband, became a bit sensitive about it.

Years later, when Means introduced Cauthen at Glorieta Baptist

Assembly and said, "He has made quite a name for himself," Mrs. Cauthen remonstrated with Means. "Baker has not made a name for himself. He has tried to be zealous for his Lord." Means laughs. "Seeing her flashing eyes and knowing her deep loyalties to her husband, I wasn't prone to argue the point."

In 1936, Mrs. Cauthen's father came home on furlough from China. Thin and rundown from heavy responsibilities in North China, he was still exuberant over revivals that had been running almost continuously in Shantung Province since 1931. It was Baker's first opportunity to get to know his father-in-law, and he was immediately captivated with the man's insights and wisdom as he and Eloise listened for long hours to the China experiences. Through Glass's eyes, world missions opened up for Cauthen in a way that was dramatic even to his missions students, who noticed the new fervor in his teaching.

Cauthen had Dr. Glass preach at Polytechnic and was greatly impressed when George W. Truett invited Glass to preach at First Baptist Church in Dallas. His son-in-law took Dr. and Mrs. Glass to the Southern Baptist Convention the next year in New Orleans, and they became fast friends. Glass, who had already been reassured by friends and acquaintances that Eloise had married a fine young man, was completely satisfied. And he wasn't at all convinced that the couple wouldn't end up in China after all. "Just give them time," he said to his wife, Jessie, whom he had married a few years after the death of Eloise's mother.

Baker and Eloise grew apprehensive as Dr. and Mrs. Glass prepared to return to China the next year. The Japanese had attacked Shanghai and begun all-out war against China. "Can you go back?" Baker inquired earnestly. "Yes. The United States is not at war with Japan. We can go in through Manchuria," Glass said. Later Baker found out that Dr. and Mrs. Glass had ignored a telegram from the Foreign Mission Board asking them not to proceed. He marveled at the man's commitment to China and questioned his own personal commitment to Christ against this new model.

Meanwhile, Cauthen tried to wind up his own doctoral work, which seemed to drag for an interminable length of time because of the scope of his responsibilities. In 1936 and 1937 he taught a course on Oriental and African missions, one on European and Latin American missions, one on missions in the Bible, and another on comparative religions. The catalogue read, "A study of the living religions of the world will be made and comparisons made between these religions and Christianity. The religions studied will be Hinduism, Jainism, Buddhism, Sikhism, Confucianism, Toaism, Shintoism, Judaism, Zoroastrianism, and Mohammedanism. Especially recommended for pastors and volunteers for the mission field. Two hours per week throughout the first semester."

What the catalogue did not mention was that this was also the subject of Cauthen's thesis. He was making a comparative study of the doctrine of salvation in the various religions.

Late in 1936, Cauthen invited Charles E. Maddry, executive secretary of the Foreign Mission Board, to come and preach. He spent a long time talking with him and again heard Maddry's stated conviction that the door would remain open for Cauthen in case God were to move him toward the mission field.

The year 1936 was big in many ways. Cauthen finally completed his Th.D. degree, which his friend and mentor, Dr. W. T. Conner, celebrated by writing Cauthen's family in Lufkin. He said:

"I do not know whether Baker James had informed you or not, but he stood his examination for his Th.D. degree yesterday and made a very fine grade. In fact, I do not think we have had anybody who has stood a better examination. He stood a good examination in all three of his subjects, and we gave him a grade of 98. I am writing to congratulate you on his making such a fine record.

"Another thing I am very pleased about is that he has decided to stay here and teach at the seminary rather than go to China. I'm saying this not on the ground that I am not interested in China or its mission, but I am saying it on the ground that I think he will count for more in missions by teaching in the seminary than he would by going to China. By his teaching here, his influence will count in all fields where Southern Baptists have mission work. Nothing has happened at the seminary for a good long while that has given me more pleasure than this decision on his part. I believe it is of the Lord and his life will count for much here in the seminary and in the Polytechnic Church. I naturally take it for granted that you are pleased with this too, although I do not think you would object to his going to China if you thought it was the Lord's will. I look forward with great pleasure to the fact that he is to work here as the head of our missions department."

With the degree behind him, the decision about China settled, and his work as pastor and teacher clearly before him, Baker James Cauthen and his bride settled down to the nearest thing they would have to a routine for years to come.

Shortly after Cauthen was called to be pastor of Polytechnic Baptist Church, he was nominated by Southwestern Seminary for a special membership in the Fort Worth Rotary Club. Using the experience as a bridge to other facets of life he would not otherwise reach, Cauthen plunged in wholeheartedly. By 1936 he had been elected a director and vice-president of the club, and the next year the club invited him to speak. Their president was so impressed that he devoted a whole column in the paper to say it was doubtful if any subsequent program that year would match the one brought by Baker James Cauthen. He quoted Cauthen at length and indicated his speech included the best definition of Rotary that he had ever heard.

The splash Cauthen made in a subsequent Rotarian event was even more memorable. When the club sponsored a local fashion show, a program chairman convinced the slender Cauthen and a member on the muscular side to dress up as women and stand at the door, posing as hostesses for the arriving Rotarians. Not a single member sensed the charade, although several, on observing Cauthen, wondered who that attractive woman was.

When the masqueraders lost their tresses and thus their cover at the close of the program, the surprise was dramatic and the joshing that followed seemingly endless. Cauthen, for all of his serious demeanor (some people were convinced that he was unable to take himself any way but seriously), displayed a sense of humor and good nature that won him many new friends. History was blessed with a large picture of the two masqueraders published in the Fort Worth *Star Telegram.*

A few months later, the club expressed its appreciation for Cauthen by voting to visit his church service on Sunday evening to, as their bulletin put it, "show their love and esteem for Baker Cauthen."

Commenting on his youth, the Rotarian editor said, "we believe with Bacon that 'A man that is young in years may be old in hours, if he's lost no time; but that happeneth rarely.' "

When, in 1937, Franklin Segler left to take a pastorate in

Louisiana, Cauthen, true to his word to encourage Segler in his sense of calling, gave him his blessing. Heavily dependent upon and increasingly skillful at working with staff, Cauthen led the church to call Clifford Holcomb to be minister of education and music director.

On April 16, 1937, Cauthen entered his seminary class rumpled and exhausted—unheard of for him since he prepared himself for the classroom like an athlete, both in the amount of sleep he got and in his personal grooming. This was different. In the wee hours of the night, Eloise had awakened him with the word that their baby was ready to deliver. In fact, she wasn't sure but that she might deliver immediately.

Baker got her to the hospital in time for the experts to handle the birth. In late morning, the doctor informed him that he was the father of a baby girl, nineteen inches long and six pounds in weight. She had dark hair and to Cauthen's skilled pastoral eye was unusually cute, even for a baby. They named her Carolyn.

Holcomb says that Cauthen was giddy when he took the pulpit on Sunday morning. Describing a baptismal service he had held in Angelina County in a soapstone-bottomed creek, he laughed and said, "I just got them down and let them get up the best way they could." The thing struck him as so funny that he himself giggled. People were shocked. They had never heard their pastor in such a mood. But after the shock rippled across the room, it was followed by almost uncontrolled laughter. Holcomb remembers that Dr. Conner almost fell out of the pew, laughing at his protégé's demeanor. Holcomb claims that Conner called Cauthen the only student he had ever had who could challenge him intellectually.

Later that year, Baker took Holcomb and his wife Louanah to Columbus, Texas, to hold a revival meeting together and then return home on the following Sunday night. They were to begin early-morning meetings they had planned at Polytechnic for the next day. Their revival honorarium came in the form of a check; so when they started home they pooled their cash and realized they had very little. Halfway to Polytechnic the car broke down, and they had to have it pulled into a garage.

Cauthen put all of their change and bills into a pile, paid the mechanic, and then announced that they had $1.25 left for gasoline and food. "We'll make it," he reassured them with a grin.

"The Lord takes care of those who do his work, regardless of how foolish they are." When they got to Fort Worth and to a station where they were known, they filled up the 16-gallon gas tank. It took 16.1 gallons.

Cauthen read voraciously and reviewed books for Southwestern Seminary's publication. He would often give the reviewed books to the church library or bring one by for Holcomb or one of the other staff people to read. Holcomb remembers one book that Cauthen brought to him, saying, "I think you would enjoy this." A section of it was underlined. Later he heard Cauthen refer in a sermon to the part that he had seen underlined, and it sounded almost verbatim. To check it, Holcomb went back to the book. He knew it had been weeks since Cauthen had read it: yet he had been able to quote the rather lengthy passage exactly. "Have you seen that book recently?" he asked Cauthen. "No. You still have it," Cauthen answered. When Holcomb told him he had quoted the passage verbatim, he just grinned. "I guess it stuck with me."

By them Cauthen was known as something of a benevolent authoritarian in the Polytechnic Church. But there were those who would buck him. A leader in the children's Sunday School department decided they needed new paperback songbooks. He forwarded the request through Holcomb. Cauthen said, "No. We can't afford it." The man came back and said, "We want those books." Cauthen explained to him, "We just can't afford new books." The man stated, "We're going to buy the books with our tithe." Cauthen grinned and said, "Those ought to be real helpful books in your department." He could be very strong, but he also knew how to slide.

The First Baptist Church in Fort Worth was what is called an independent church. Its leader was known not only as authoritarian but as anti-Southern Baptist. However, Cauthen made no distinction between people received from that church and any other. One of the women received into his church from First Baptist was known as a very fine Bible teacher. She informed Cauthen and Holcomb that the Lord had come to her in a vision and told her that all the adult Sunday School classes should be combined into a single class, and she was to teach it. Cauthen questioned her at length, but she was adamant. Cauthen finally said, "So I'm to understand the Lord appeared to you in a vision with this message?" She said, "Yes, that's right. We must do it." Cauthen said, "Well, I'll not argue with you or with anyone about something that came to them in a vision. But since he holds me responsible for shepherding his flock, I feel sure he will also appear to me to confirm this. As soon as he does, I'll get in touch with you."

At an associational meeting one day, two local preachers became angry as they argued their respective positions on an issue. The discussion grew tense. Cauthen asked for the floor and said, "Gentlemen, I have a thought." Succinctly, he summarized the situation with the two points of view and suggested a reconciliation that not only made both men happy but quickly carried.

But he didn't win them all. One day a man obviously troubled came to Cauthen and said, "Pray for me and my family." The man did not ask for a formal conference, but just made his prayer request. Cauthen assured him that he would pray for him and made a mental note to follow up on the matter. The press of time, however, kept him from doing so. A few weeks later, a call came early one morning with the terrible news that the man had turned on the gas in his home and taken his own life and the lives of his whole family. Cauthen fought off depression and a sense of guilt for a long time and then resolved in his heart to make every such request a sober call to deep prayer and to offer any help he could.

He especially came to feel that people who were difficult were often simply crying for help. When one man seemed to be especially contentious, Baker remarked to Holcomb, "That man may just need our help more than the others, and this is the only way he can say so." Holcomb, who knew how much the man had tried their patience, was amazed at Cauthen's spirit.

In the summer of 1938 the church scheduled a major revival with Jewish evangelist Hyman Appleman preaching. Powerful in his impact on a church, Appleman was also definite about what he wanted done. Holcomb was to be in charge of the music. When some question arose about it, Holcomb was deeply grateful that Cauthen clarified the situation with Appleman in tactful but firm terms.

It was a fruitful revival. Not only were there many decisions; but the Applemans' child, the Holcombs' child, and the Cauthens' second child, Ralph Baker, all were born during the week. Needless to say, the revival is remembered to this day more for that than anything else.

As the Japanese expanded the fighting in China and more and more pro-China literature and sentiments were expressed in newspapers in the United States, the Cauthens were kept sharply aware of their heart involvement through Dr. and Mrs. Glass and Eloise's sister Lois. Stationed at Laichowfu in Shantung Province, Lois had to move into Hwanghsien because of the war. Although Hwanghsien, too, expected to be a battlefield in 1937, it was still quiet in late 1938 when the Cauthens prepared to lead Polytechnic in the annual foreign missions emphasis. Because this event in 1934 had become the rallying point for the church's renewal under Cauthen, it continued to be a time of great excitement.

Whether because of the preparation for this emphasis or the impact of his own teaching at Southwestern Seminary, Cauthen came home one day and said to Eloise, "We must reopen the China question in prayer. Let's covenant to pray individually that God will show us what he wants us to do." With two toddlers, the task of keeping a home, and a deep involvement in the church, Eloise was not nearly so much in a position to appreciate that thought as she would have been in 1935. But her conviction had not changed. Her sense that God would someday lead them to China was still there, and she solemnly agreed to pray with him.

The catalytic event came in a Presbyterian church. Cauthen had read a book entitled *The Finality of Jesus Christ,* written by a leader of Presbyterian missions named Robert E. Speer. Learning that Speer was to speak at the Hemphill Presbyterian Church, he went on a November evening and sat in the balcony.

It was not the man's eloquence that moved him, but his line of reasoning. He spoke of the man who, in the twenty-second chapter of Luke, was asked to give his upper room to Jesus and the disciples for the Passover. "The man was called to give the most important thing he had, the very best room in his house," said the gifted theologian. "Afterward, the Lord gave it back to him. It was the same room, but it was different because the Lord had been there." Cauthen was gripped by the idea. That room signified his life. If the Lord wanted it, he wanted to deliver it over to him. He went home, and after the family went to bed he retired to a corner with his Bible. A series of Scripture verses began to fall in place for him, and he wrote them down and studied each one separately:

Matthew 16:25—"For whosoever will save his life shall lose it; and whosoever will lose his life for my sake shall find it."

John 12:24—"Verily, verily, I say unto you, Except a corn of wheat fall into the ground and die, it abideth alone: but if it die, it bringeth forth much fruit."

Mark 8:34—"And when he had called the people unto him with his disciples also, he said unto them, 'Whosoever will come after me, let him deny himself, and take up his cross, and follow me.' "

Luke 14:33—"So likewise, whosoever he be of you that forsaketh not all that he hath, he cannot be my disciple."

Matthew 19:29—"And every one that hath forsaken houses, or brethren, or sisters, or father, or mother, or wife, or children, or lands, for my name's sake, shall receive an hundredfold, and shall inherit everlasting life."

Matthew 10:37–38—"He that loveth father or mother more than me is not worthy of me; and he that loveth son or daughter more than me is not worthy of me. And he that taketh not his cross, and followeth after me is not worthy of me."

Philippians 2:5,8—"Let this mind be in you, which was also in Christ Jesus . . . And being found in fashion as a man, he humbled himself, and became obedient unto death, even the death of the cross."

Carefully, he read those verses over in sequence. He thought again of Speer's remarks about the upper room. Speaking in an audible voice, he said, "Lord, it is clear to me that you are calling me to go to China." Taking his pen, he wrote under those verses in the back of his Bible, "November 1, 1938, 10:20 P.M." He awakened Eloise and shared the decision with her. Nothing had changed. Her resolve was stronger than ever. All she needed was the assurance of God's timing. Baker's call gave her that assurance.

The next week he wrote Charles Maddry, reminding him of their previous conversations and Maddry's statement about an open door. He concluded by saying that he and his wife were volunteering for service in North China.

Next, he faced the difficult task of talking to his old mentor,

W. T. Conner. He prepared himself for several days to answer the arguments that he knew Conner would bring, the same arguments that had been so persuasive in 1935. As Baker sat down and reviewed his experience and culminated it with the events of November 1, Conner looked quietly at him and said simply, "You must go." It was reassuring confirmation.

That Bible with the Scripture verses written in the back has been in Cauthen's hands ever since. It was in the glove compartment of his car in the garage at their home in Fort Worth when the garage caught fire shortly after he answered the call to foreign service. The fire destroyed the car; but when Cauthen pried open the charred glove compartment, he found the Bible intact. He carried it with him for many years, and it has been rebound often. It's now retired and enjoys a cherished place in the Cauthen home.

In the spring of 1939 news from China was forbidding, but their missionary processing through the mails with Richmond, Virginia, proceeded. Cauthen sent letters, including life sketches and clarifying information requested for the appointment procedure, but still did not confide in the church. He did not want to disturb them unduly; nor did he want to "jump the gun." If God closed the door, he'd just as soon they never knew.

One week he and Eloise and the children journeyed to Lufkin to share their decision with his parents. According to Baker's brother J. B., his mother, his spiritual confidante through the years, was distraught. "Bake, if you go to China, I'll just die. I'll just die dead as a doornail." Softly, Baker replied, "Well, Mother, you'll just have to trust the Lord because God's called me to China."

Immediately afterward, Mrs. Cauthen developed some physical problems and had to see a doctor. Baker worried about her. Her doctor replied to his inquiry, "She's all right; she's just worried." He drove back to Lufkin, sat with her in the backyard, and talked it through. "After a while," Baker said, "my mother began to see that the thing that was motivating me was the thing that had been leading me from those earliest days, that it was an extension of the same thing. I could see her faith building and rising to the occasion."

Then word came from Richmond that they were invited to come for final processing and appointment. They arranged to go between Sundays, saying nothing to the church, which was used to having Cauthen away because of his teaching responsibilities and calls for revivals.

Before leaving, Cauthen received one final confirmation, though it came in a negative way. A pulpit committee from one of the largest churches in the country laid before him their conviction that he should be their next pastor. The salary, several times what Cauthen was making, was fabulous for those days. He decided the only way they could understand his declining was to tell them the real reason. "God has called us to China. We will be going very shortly," he said.

One of the members was horrified. "You're not going to take your wife and those children to China where the Japanese are raping and killing everyone in sight, are you?" Cauthen replied, "If that's where God wants us, I have no choice. I'm convinced God can take care of me and my wife and my children."

In Richmond, their processing went smoothly. For medical and psychiatric exams, the Board checked its candidates that year into a local mental hospital for a few days. The candidates teased each other about their situation, but rejoiced together when all were cleared and appointed in a solemn ceremony at the Board's head-quarters.

When they returned to Texas, Cauthen had a missions class to meet; and he met it. He told the class that he had become convicted that God wanted him to go to China, that people in the United States had multiple opportunities to hear the gospel but that there were people in China who had not yet heard the name of Jesus Christ. He was going to leave his pastorate and leave his professor-ship and invest his life in that country. His students were deeply moved, and the news became the talk of "the hill."

On the following Sunday, he shared news of his appointment with his church. There were tears and rededications. It was discussed throughout the area the following week. Some pointed out that Eloise Cauthen had always wanted to go back and said she had finally convinced Baker to go. Others who knew Cauthen's own strong will replied that nothing short of the act of God could make him do anything that he wasn't convinced he should do. The Cauthens were invited to speak at many places but received one of their greatest blessings in a special missionary service at the seminary. After Cauthen gave his testimony, twenty students surrendered to missionary service.

With a reputation already as a gifted preacher, pastor of a large church, and professor at Southwestern, Cauthen became even more of a celebrity following news of his missionary appointment. His church had had approximately a thousand additions during his little more than six years there. Its debt had been substantially reduced, and it had again become one of the significant churches in the area.

Gifts came to the Cauthens from every quarter, including things that people thought they would need in China. He especially cherished the gift of a public address system for preaching and laughed when he received it. "This system will motivate me to learn the language," he said. "It will haunt me until I can preach over it in Chinese."

In June they went to the Southern Baptist Convention in Oklahoma City. On Foreign Missions night, Charles Maddry proudly presented eleven newly appointed missionaries. Sidney Goldfinch, who with his wife Frances had been appointed for Paraguay, remembers Maddry's excitement over the appointment of a man with Cauthen's credentials. Maddry said, after presenting the Cauthens, "We caught a big fish that time, didn't we?"

The Bill Howses will never forget the day that the Cauthens drove by their house to say goodbye, their Ford car loaded to the hilt with provisions they were taking with them to the west coast. There they would ship their car ahead and then board a passenger ship for the trip to China. The public address system was tied on top of the car.

After a time of refreshment and sharing, Bill Howse led them in prayer. As they started out, all four adults close to tears, Cauthen looked at his friends, held his wife's hand, and said, "If we never get to China, if our ship is bombed by the Japanese and sunk before we ever set foot on China's soil, I want you to know now that you're not to feel sorry for us because that will have been the will of God for us. It's under his leadership that we go."

Bill and Genevieve Howse stood in their yard and watched the Ford with Baker and Eloise and the two toddlers go down the street, turn the corner, and disappear from view. Both were too choked to speak. Finally, Bill said, "I believe those are the two happiest people I've ever seen in my life."

Part II

The Furnace
1939-1945

There appears in the life of some men a catalytic period that takes what has been forged already and tempers it. Such a period becomes the furnace in which what has been shaped in the forge is made ready for its ultimate task.

Dr. Baker James Cauthen working at his desk in Richmond at the Foreign Mission Board

CHAPTER ONE

Journey of Obedience

Baker James Cauthen's journey of obedience with his wife and two small children was a segmented odyssey. Somehow, as they followed God's leadership, it flowed as a single story. The trip across the western United States in the heavily loaded Ford was a kaleidoscope of memories. With the back seat converted into a playpen for the children—Carolyn two years old and Ralph not quite one—they marked their journey by cafés where they stopped to get the children's bottles warmed and roadside parks where they made sandwiches from ingredients that Eloise had packed. That part of the story flowed naturally into the next as they watched a great crane lift that same car aboard the ship that would take it on a roundabout journey to Shantung, North China. Their own quarters on the passenger ship that took them across the blue Pacific to the same destination, with stops in Honolulu and Japan, were surprisingly luxurious.

The Cauthens quickly got into the swing of shipboard life. Blessed with balmy weather for the whole trip, they enjoyed themselves immensely. Since the children could be fed early and then cared for by one of the ship's attendants, their parents could come into the dining hall together. The couple's youthful appearance, exuberance, and obvious delight with each other convinced several of their ship companions that they were honeymooners. As they began to appear on the ship's decks during the day with their two small children, this theory broke down; but for Eloise, the trip was "like a honeymoon."

Keeping small children on a leash had always seemed shocking to Eloise when other parents did it. But the ship's rails were such a tempting sight for her own small children that she had to "eat crow" and put them on leashes. As she wrote friends back in Fort

Worth, "Ralph is crawling across the Pacific Ocean."

At supper each evening, the ship's purser read news summaries of world events picked up on the ship's radio. As things heated up in Europe under the provocation of the Fascist alliance led by Adolf Hitler and Benito Mussolini, all the travelers followed the news intently and apprehensively.

The country that the Baker James Cauthens were leaving behind was struggling with contradictory emotions. Jobs were still hard to come by, but more people were working. Franklin Delano Roosevelt was in his second term, and a few very bold voices were talking about the possibility of a third term.

Roosevelt was using radio to reach the country and cause it to back his actions as no other president had been able to do. Over 27,000,000 of the 32,000,00 families in the United States owned radios and regularly tuned into such shows as the "Chase and Sanborn Hour" with Don Ameche, Dorothy Lamour, and ventriloquist Edgar Bergen's popular dummy Charlie McCarthy. But neither Charlie McCarthy nor Roosevelt demonstrated the power of radio quite as well as Orson Welles' "Mercury Hour" with its dramatization of H. G. Wells' "War of the Worlds." Projected on the air as a simulated news broadcast, it caused panic everywhere.

People continued to worry about Communist influence, but drew encouragement from the feats of FBI director J. Edgar Hoover, who warred vigorously against crime of any sort.

Industry was beginning to crank up again, but not in ways that worried Adolf Hitler. America was not then even a third-rate power militarily. The depression had all but stalled its heavy industry. Ford Motor Company, however, did introduce the Mercury—a sign of faith in the future.

The motion picture industry was enjoying super success. Shirley Temple was charming the nation, and Mickey Rooney, Tyrone Power, and Spencer Tracy were bringing laughs, sighs, and gasps with their exploits. A girl named Judy Garland, in a whimsical piece called "The Wizard of Oz," was packing the theaters. So were Gene Autrey, Clark Gable, and Ronald Coleman with their pictures.

Four days before the Cauthens sailed from San Francisco on the twenty-fifth of August, Hitler and Stalin announced a nonaggression pact. Apprehension increased that Hitler would move on Poland even more blatantly than he had taken Czechoslovakia.

Roosevelt and his secretary of state, Cordell Hull, knew that Hitler's ultimate intention was conquest of the whole world. And since Chamberlain's moral surrender at Munich on the Czech question, neither man believed that the British were capable of patrolling the whole world with their navies as they once were. Roosevelt wanted to renounce neutrality in support of the Allies in hopes of deterring Hitler. But he could not bring Congress to back him. The Gallup Poll reported that month that 57 percent of the country wanted neutrality; 51 percent, however, expected war, and 58 percent believed the United States would ultimately be drawn into it; 90 percent said they would fight if America were invaded; only 10 percent said they would fight if America were not invaded.

Charles Lindbergh, pointing out that America had the Atlantic on one side and the Pacific on the other, said the nation need not fear Europe's wars. "Stay out of it," Lindbergh said. He was a man of wide influence.

Two years before the Cauthens sailed, an American gunship, the U.S.S. *Panay*, was sunk by Japanese bombers. Their diplomats made appropriate apologies, and the United States accepted them readily though there was ample intelligence that they had actually meant to test America's nerve. America had failed the test, according to Japanese thinking—and in the opinion of many Americans, also. Other Americans felt that the Japanese could have the Far East; Hitler could have Europe; and they could simply enjoy safe, peaceful America. Wiser men knew it could never happen, but it was the prevailing pipe dream.

This meant that the Cauthens were sailing against the tide of public opinion as they started for China. But then the gospel and individual responses to it have never been matters of public opinion. It meant that the Cauthens, as heroic as they might have seemed in the eyes of a few dedicated souls, seemed foolish in the eyes of the larger body of potential supporters. "Bring them all home," was heard in many a Baptist church regarding missionaries.

After six days at sea, news came to the Cauthens' ship of the German *blitzkrieg* or lightning war on Poland. Every meal on shipboard after that was dominated with news and interpretations. Two days later, Great Britain and France declared war on the Axis powers. Before the new missionaries got to language school, the Russians had entered the conflict against Poland, and Poland fell.

103

The Cauthens' ship docked for a time in Honolulu, where the kids got to play in the surf. They were met by Southern Baptist missionaries, the L. E. Blackmans, who entertained them graciously.

When the ship landed in Yokohama, missionary E. O. Mills met the Cauthens and escorted them to Tokyo for a visit. They could sense the increasing hostility between Japanese and Americans. The fact that the Japanese were already bombing and fighting the people to whom they were going to give their lives in ministry gave the Cauthens an uneasy, almost unreal feeling.

At a restaurant in Tokyo, little Ralph apparently decided to work on international relationships. He reached a chubby finger across the booth behind him. A Japanese businessman, otherwise cold and distant, smiled hesitantly and took the little finger in his hand. It was, Mrs. Cauthen thought, the best piece of international diplomacy she saw accomplished in those mad days.

Finally, their ship docked in Dairen on the coast of Manchuria. There they were met by the W. W. Adamses and the tall, gaunt, smiling figure of Eloise's father. He had taken a ship across the Gulf of Chihli to meet them.

When they had last seen W. B. Glass a little over two years before, they had not expected to see him again so soon or in this way. It was a moving moment for all of them. Since it was Saturday, they decided to spend the night with the Adamses and stay for Sunday services before catching a Monday morning boat across the gulf to the Shantung Peninsula. The Cauthens were to leave their luggage there while they made a visit to Dr. Glass's home and Eloise's birthplace in Hwanghsien. They would recross the gulf then and proceed to their language school in Peking.

In the services at Dairen the next day, Cauthen heard his first real Chinese singing and preaching. The churches were strong, still feeling the aftereffects of the amazing Shantung revival of the early thirties. With great fervor they sang old tunes to which they had put the words of Scripture verses. Cauthen was intent on the sermon but completely at sea. Hearing the words *woman* and *jelly* quite often, he wondered if they were English transliterations. He found out later that they meant *us* and *here* respectively. Eloise sat through the service bright-eyed and excited. She could hear and understand more than she had ever dreamed possible. Her childhood language had not deserted her.

On Monday they crossed the gulf to what was known as Dragon's Mouth or Lungkow. Dr. Glass had left his car there, and together they drove to Hwanghsien. Eloise Cauthen had left there twelve years before at age seventeen. She had spent four years at Baylor, three years at Southwestern Seminary, and five years as the wife of a pastor. It was quite a homecoming for her.

Hwanghsien lies in a fertile plain between the Gulf of Chihli to the north and mountains to the south that separate it from the rest of the province.

When the Cauthens arrived in Hwanghsien the great fields of tall grain, which had been brought to a peak by the summer rains, were waving in gentle breezes that belied the approaching chills of wintertime. Cauthen had been used to calling the grain highgear; the Chinese called it *kaoliang*. The Chinese farmers would raise wheat on those same fields in the winter. All around their houses, which were scattered all over the plain in small groups, were truck gardens full of onions, cabbages, cucumbers, and okra. Ducks waddled around, vying with the chickens and dogs for vocal honors.

It was all very nostalgic for Eloise. As a child, she had roamed the whole area and had especially cherished picnics into the southern mountains. Even before she left home, however, the countryside had become too unsettled with bandits for such trips. Now it was even more so.

While the Japanese were in control of the area, there was a strong resistance. Chinese guerillas came out of the hills and the mountains at night to harass the Japanese in a variety of ways. The guerillas were farmers in the daytime, but were trained to hide out and fight at night. Called the Eighth Route Army, in Chinese the *Ba Lou,* they constituted a strong organization. At this point, they were just resisters to the Japanese. Later they would fall under Communist persuasion and be a part of the Communist conquest.

This guerilla activity made the Japanese occupation—oppressive at best—an exceedingly fearful thing for the Chinese and frustrating for expatriates such as the American missionaries. Checkpoints were everywhere. Cauthen quickly learned to adopt Glass's patient "it's an opportunity to witness" attitude at the innumerable delays.

Eloise revelled in the experience of being with her father and stepmother and walking ground that was familiar despite obvious changes. With delight she showed Baker the house she had described to him so often. It was called the *Nan Lo* or South House in the small compound of missionary houses in Hwanghsien. Her eyes had a way of sparkling when she was involved in animated conversation, but the emotion and bombardment of memories made them fairly dance. Baker laughed with her and entered into her joy.

The missionaries made much over the two toddling Cauthen children, who took everything in with the "business as usual" attitude that only small children can manage. Some of the Chinese women who had known Eloise as a motherless child and cared for her found even more delight in her children.

Few men were more highly motivated than Baker Cauthen as he entered the language school in Peking. While he was at Hwanghsien the missionaries and the Chinese preachers, knowing that he was Dr. Glass's son-in-law, Eloise's husband, and supposedly well known in his own right, were very gracious about asking him to preach. In fact, he had that opportunity on six different occasions in the week he was there. Though frustrated at the pauses necessary for the interpreter, he preached with great fervor. He longed to preach in the language of the people without restrictions, to let the Spirit flow in the way he had experienced so often since he had begun preaching over a dozen years before.

At the end of one of the services, six adults made professions of faith. The people were visibly moved. Glass realized that his son-in-law's gifts were considerable, even across language and culture barriers. He wondered what the young man could do when he did master the difficult Chinese language.

At a feast that the Hwanghsien Chinese Christians prepared for the missionaries in honor of the Cauthens, Dr. Cauthen sat with the venerable pastor Tsang and talked, with Dr. Glass as interpreter. The old pastor gave the young preacher his whole evening, and Cauthen found himself even more strongly drawn to China.

In their brief stay in Hwanghsien, the Cauthens had an opportunity to transcend two seasons. Late summer fled even while they were there, and the harshness of the winter presaged its potential in a cold wind.

The poverty of the people was a shock. Their crops had been poor, and the people faced a hard winter. Cauthen and Eloise saw a beggar woman picking at garbage. When she started to walk away, she staggered and fell into a flowerbed. The two rushed after her and found that she was weak from lack of food. Cauthen immediately pulled some of the unfamiliar Chinese money from his pocket and pressed it into her withered, crusty hand. To his shock, she got down on her knees and began to bow her head to the ground again and again. Shortly afterward he wrote Charles Maddry, saying, "But for the grace of God, that woman could have been your mother or my mother." Carolyn, a little over two, stood in the Glasses' yard and watched the proceedings. When the Cauthens came back, he reached down and picked up the wide-eyed child. She said, "Daddy, let's pray for the poor people."

After their week in Hwanghsien, they packed their belongings, drove to the gulf, boarded a boat, and crossed overnight to Dairen. There the Adamses saw them off, with all their luggage, on the train that would take them across Japanese-Chinese lines to Peking to begin their study of the Chinese language. Eloise was discovering that she could still speak Chinese to a limited degree and could understand it to a surprisingly broad degree, but she had never learned to read or write it. She was a long way down the road that her husband had to travel; but she, too, had a language task. If Baker was bothered by the fact that his wife was ahead of him, he let no one know. They merely laughed about it.

The Cauthens were to study Chinese at the College of Chinese Studies, founded primarily for expatriates studying in the country. It had a founding board in New York and was run by a man named W. D. Pettus. In its student ranks were missionaries of every persuasion, businessmen, customs officials, and diplomatic personnel from the United States, Britain, and several other countries.

Assigned two connecting bedrooms and a study further down the hall in a hostel where the school boarded its students, the Cauthens ate with the other students in a dining room run on a concession basis by a local Chinese cook. Students with longer tenure told them that newcomers could always be identified by their long faces, which betrayed the digestive problems that inevitably accompanied early encounters with this concession.

Chinese babysitters called *amahs* were employed by the school to keep the children of students. An amah came to the Cauthens' rooms each morning as the mother and father were ready to go to their studies.

Eloise, with a language facility that even advanced students envied, was assigned to an advanced class. Baker, in good humor, began at the lowest rung. "If there had been a lower rung, I would have had to go to that one," he remembers.

As they dug into their routine of study, the nip in the air yielded to the first winter blast. Cauthen had always disliked bitter cold, but found to his surprise that it was because he had never dressed properly. Nor had he ever lived in a house constructed to deal with real cold. He led the family out to purchase woolen underwear and heavy fur-lined coats. With the heated rooms of the language school to retreat to and the proper clothes to wear when going out, he not only could adapt to the cold but was invigorated by it. Later, he was to give that same testimony about the tropics. Knowing him to be often inflexible on issues, his friends were perplexed by his adaptability to circumstances.

Dr. Glass and the veteran missionaries in Shantung had convinced Baker that if he wanted to progress in the language he would have to get out among the people. They urged him to take even his most elementary understanding of the language and make use of it in the marketplace. "Besides, that is a good way to get to know beautiful and intriguing Peking," he reasoned. On weekends, he and his family ventured out in wider and wider circles.

The language school was located near memorial arches in the eastern section of the city. Peking is a walled city, but there is a walled enclosure inside that, called the Forbidden City, which was built by Manchu emperors for their palaces. As winter came, the many lakes there froze, and ice skaters would emerge from everywhere. The "Altar of Heaven" was located south of the city, and even further south were the Ming tombs. But the students were not allowed to go that far.

Peking was built in the days of Kubla Khan. One of the sights is the "Temple of Heaven," a place where the emperor represented the people in religious ceremonies. Custom had the emperor going out the evening before the ceremony to spend the night in a special place. He would then go to the "Temple of Heaven," a great white structure surrounded by carved balistrades, and there pray. Only the emperor was allowed to do this. On their first visit, the Cauthens discovered some very strange sound effects near the place where the emperor would stand. Even the whispers of visitors seemed to be carried mysteriously around the balistrades. Near the "Temple of Heaven" was the "Temple of the New Year." The Cauthens soon learned to identify the forms of Chinese religious expression.

As much as they enjoyed sightseeing—and the Cauthens do even today—they were more committed to trying the language. They journeyed often beyond the city to the villages, where Cauthen tried to "loosen his tongue."

A friend at the Polytechnic Church gave him five dollars before he left Fort Worth and asked him to use it in his work. Shortly after arriving in Peking, he parlayed that five dollars into twelve thousand Chinese tracts about Jesus. He and Eloise went out into the areas beyond the gates of the city and tried to use some of the greetings he had learned. She purposely kept silent, which was quite natural in the Chinese culture, and let him lead the way. It wasn't easy, but she did it. On one such excursion, Baker took a picture scroll of Jesus feeding the five thousand, and, sitting on the steps of a small Chinese temple as children gathered, he tried to tell them the story. It was the first time he had ever tried to tell the Chinese about Jesus in their own language.

Soon it was time for the Christmas break, but there was no chance to go to Hwanghsien to spend it with relatives. Crossing through Japanese lines and making the torturous trip back through Manchuria wasn't practical. In fact, a recent letter had revealed that Dr. Glass and a party had been roughed up a bit by Japanese on a trip to Laichowfu. They decided to accept an invitation to Tsinan to visit with the John Abernathys immediately after Christmas Day. From there they would go on to Kaifeng in Honan Province, where Dr. Buford Nichols and a group of missionaries were building the All-China Seminary—the occasion for Cauthen's initial invitation to the mission field. They left their children in the care of a fellow missionary student named Mary Lucile Saunders.

As they began the trip, the Cauthens chatted with a Chinese policeman, Cauthen eagerly trying out his language. The man queried Mrs. Cauthen about the children and, when she answered him, remarked, "You speak very good Chinese." Then he looked at Baker and smiled. "You should go back and study some more."

They enjoyed telling the story to the Abernathys, and John was impressed that Baker could handle his own disability in such good humor. He congratulated him for it. "Many of the missionary husbands find it quite frustrating when their wives learn the language before they do," he said. "You seem to be handling it quite well. But then Eloise did have quite a head start, didn't she?" "Like thirty years," Eloise laughed.

They stayed with the Abernathys through New Year and a black-eyed-pea-dominated New Year's feast. Then they boarded a train for the trip into Honan Province.

Though they reassured themselves, it was a dangerous trip. An extra locomotive preceded the train by a half-mile to locate any mines that might have been planted along the tracks. The shades were pulled down to discourage indiscriminate firing into the coaches by Chinese guerillas and/or any Communist bands that had not reconciled themselves to working with Chiang Kai-shek's nationalist government against the Japanese.

In Kaifeng, Baker Cauthen saw his first large Chinese church and realized what could be developed.

But it wasn't only what he saw that impressed him. It was also what he heard. He was the closest he had been to the fighting zone and could hear guns firing across the Yellow River. He wondered what role they would play in his future. Then he realized he had committed all of his future to God, and he joined the retreating missionary party and put it out of his mind.

At the beginning of the new year, Baker and Eloise Cauthen sent out their first missionary form letter, featuring a small Chinese print at the top and dated from the College of Chinese Studies in Peking, China. They told of their experiences since leaving the United States and, conscious that they were reaching out to American friends who still questioned why they were there, Cauthen said:

"As I spoke to a group of splendid, intelligent school students, I asked myself, 'Do not such people as these have a right to hear about Jesus?' Certainly they have that right, and we have the responsibility of telling them. I remember that whereas in America there is one preacher for every 670 people, yet in this land, for every ordained preacher there are 131,000 people. Such a contrast needs no comment!"

After telling a bit more about their trip to Honan Province during the Christmas holidays, the Cauthens summarized their letter:

"Since coming to China, four things have forcibly impressed us: First, the poverty of the people which beggars description. Refugee camps, laborers toiling for a pittance, and beggars everywhere are the order of the day. We have actually seen one poor family on the streets trying to sell their baby. Second, the appalling spiritual need. These people do not know about Christ. One man asked us if Jesus is an American. Third, the power of the gospel. Wherever it has been received, it has brought life, hope, and transformation. Fourth, the wide open door for evangelism. To be sure, there are difficulties, but if we have faith enough to keep our eyes on the Christ who walks on the troubled waters, we need have no apprehension of the storms that rage. Thanks be to God for a day of unusual opportunity. Thanks be to him for our privilege of bearing good tidings."

Their language-study year disappeared rapidly. Soon it was spring, and dust storms from off the Gobi Desert came rolling across the ancient city. While the adults choked and sputtered, the children fought debilitating attacks of bronchitis and colds. One day when Eloise returned from class, the amah expressed concern about Carolyn. Eloise rushed to the child to find her limp and obviously suffering from a high fever. She sent the amah to get Baker from the study hall and, with him, took the child to the Rockefeller Medical College in Peking. The firm advice was that the child's tonsils would have to come out. Her body could not handle repeated infections from the diseased organs.

Regulations of the hospital did not allow the mother and father to stay with their child. She was not quite three, but she knew she was being left. It was hard on all of them. The morning after the surgery, however, it was obvious that care for her had been good. Besides, they let her have ice cream. She was already chattering away in Chinese almost as well as English, and she had asked for it. When it came, she had complained that it was cold. The nurse had quickly taken it and warmed it. Then the child wailed. It wasn't ice cream anymore.

Baptist missions allowed missionaries one year of formal study, after which they traditionally went to their station, where they were to continue a second year of study with a resident teacher. As the time drew near for the Cauthens to leave Peking, there was quite a debate in the North China Mission as to where they should go. The

All-China Seminary was still in the planning stages, and there was no real provision for another missionary at this time. Dr. Glass urged in his strong and persuasive voice, "Let them come to Hwanghsien. There's great opportunity to work. There's an extra house. They'll give us evangelistic help, and we can protect their study." If anyone questioned the old patriarch's motives in moving his daughter back to her childhood home, it didn't surface loudly enough to influence anybody's vote. Hwanghsien it would be.

The Cauthens arranged for their Peking teacher, Mr. Pai (pronounced *Bye*), to go with them and continue to teach them. Eloise was making tremendous progress. There was a Chinese flavor to her language that gave the Chinese great delight.

Before moving to Hwanghsien, the Cauthens attended a meeting of the Baptist Young People's Missionary Organization in Shanghai. In the Chinese churches this organization roughly corresponded to a combination of Training Union and Woman's Missionary Union in Southern Baptist churches. The conference was planned to promote Bible study and discussion groups, followed by inspirational periods and evangelistic meetings. The planners especially pressed the cause of frontier missions, urging young people to move out into the frontiers of their own land and preach the gospel there.

Not surprisingly, Cauthen, his reputation growing as a preacher in English and now in halting Chinese, was asked to lead the closing service. One hundred fifty-five young people volunteered at the close of the services. The planners were overjoyed. They had not expected such a harvest. Some were college students; some were already teachers; and some were younger students from the middle schools.

At the end of the conference, Baker and Eloise toured the Central China Mission. Greatly devastated by war, the mission was in Japanese hands. The Cauthens were overwhelmed by the spirit of Chinese Christians there. Adversity seemed to call forth their best. Cauthen wrote:

"On every hand, we hear accounts of new, open doors for the gospel. We were shown one church where before the war only two Sunday School classes could be assembled. Now the same church has more than thirty Sunday School classes. We recently saw on a rainy Monday night more than four hundred people gathered in street chapels to hear of the Master. The turbulent conditions of this land have caused a heart hunger for the gospel which has never before been experienced in China."

In the same letter, Cauthen poured out his conviction that now was a time for reaping. The China Baptist missions had recorded their best year ever from the standpoint of conversions. The convictions that were rising up in the young missionary's heart were definite:

"For more than a hundred years we have sown the gospel seed in this land. Surely this ought to be a time of reaping. Thanks be unto God that when the harvest of the gospel is ripe, it can be reaped in spite of all the wars and disturbances that may rise up to prevent it. While the world is blundering on its suicidal course of greed and hate, it is time for us who love the Lord to press forward the message of the Prince of Peace with every faculty that we can command."

It was an excited family that moved into the Nan Lo house, the two-story home where Eloise Cauthen had been born, in Hwanghsien. Bedrooms were on the second floor. Downstairs were the living room, the dining room, and a study. Cauthen had taken great joy in unpacking his books and setting up his library. Coal stoves heated the thick-walled home; and as the fall chill settled on the place, sunshine coming through the southern windows into his study augmented the heat from the stove and made it a thoroughly delightful place in which to work.

Eloise said one day: "Did you think we would ever get through that year of moving and turbulence? Did you think we would ever get to a moment like this when we could settle in and look forward to doing what God calls us to do?"

Settle in? Cauthen wondered.

CHAPTER TWO

Unsettling the Settled

One of the first tasks facing the young missionaries was to go to Chefoo and get their car out of storage. They had not seen it since it was hoisted from the dock in San Francisco over a year before; but when they claimed it, they found that it had made the long trip without mishap. The children squealed with the delight of recognition, and soon they had it ready to roll up the road to Hwanghsien. One of the Chefoo missionaries and the harbor master strongly requested that they wait until the next day. It was so near dark that they would likely be caught by darkness on the road. Used to a furious driving schedule in Fort Worth, Cauthen decided they could make it.

The road was unlike anything he had ever seen before. Chinese guerillas came out at night and dug deep trenches across the roads to wreck Japanese patrol vehicles. The next day, the Japanese would commandeer the villagers in the area to fill in the ditches. Filled ditches up and down the road between Chefoo and Hwanghsien had settled with the rain, giving the road a washboard quality. They made such painfully slow progress that Cauthen soon realized he was not going to be able to make it before dark. He had no choice but to turn his lights on and continue even more slowly.

They had heard stories of the Chinese guerillas firing indiscriminately at vehicles along the road, knowing that no Chinese would be driving and supposing them to be Japanese. The odds were against any foreigners traveling at night. Most of them were smarter than that. Cauthen began to pray as he gripped the wheel and peered intently ahead.

At last the lights of Hwanghsien appeared. A greatly relieved young missionary and family unloaded at the Nan Lo house. Glass came out to meet them, but he said nothing. It was obvious that

Baker had already said it to himself.

While Cauthen's primary assignment was to study the language, he was given permission to do all the evangelistic work he liked in the outlying areas. The reason was simple. Every such effort increased his language ability and augmented his study. While some missionaries had to be driven out into such work, fearful that their halting language would cause them embarrassment, Cauthen's heart hunger to preach (a hunger he tried to describe to friends in letters as more intense than anything he had ever known in his life) overcame such fears and trepidation.

Eloise was his major companion on evangelistic trips. With tracts and evangelistic posters, and often a Victrola, they trekked to nearby villages. The Victrola was especially good for gathering a crowd. Baker would wind it up, place on it a record such as "My Jesus, I Love Thee" or "Lord, I'm Coming Home," and start the sound. Hearing the music, people would come out of their homes or off the streets, and soon the missionaries had a large crowd.

Baker would signal Eloise to turn off the Victrola. He would unroll a colorful evangelistic picture poster and begin the message by explaining the meaning of the picture. Sometimes the effort was discouraging because of distractions, laughter, and the short attention span of most Chinese peasants. But on one occasion, Baker spied a man giving rapt attention. The thought that somebody was beginning to understand his Chinese was most encouraging to the missionary. After the service, he went to the man and spoke warmly. The man looked at him, turned around, and walked off. Mrs. Cauthen, seeing the problem, followed the man and also spoke to him, hoping that her accent would cross the communications bridge. He ignored her and continued to walk. As the two missionaries stood there puzzled, another Chinese man came up and informed them that the man could neither hear nor speak. Again Baker's sense of humor came to his rescue. They roared with laughter all the way home.

The Cauthens were greatly strengthened by the Christian community in Hwanghsien. It had benefited as much as any center from the North China revival of the early thirties, known as the Shantung Revival. The warm afterglow of that mighty moving of the Spirit was still evident in 1939. The Glasses, Dr. and Mrs. C. L. Culpepper, Dr. and Mrs. Frank Lide, Jane Lide, Florence Lide,

115

Martha Franks, Wilma Weeks, Lucy Wright, and Dr. and Mrs. N. A. Bryan had all been blessed in that revival.

When the new missionaries attended station prayer meetings, warmth of what had happened in these people's lives flowed into theirs. One would read a passage of Scripture. Many would voice prayer concerns. Then, spontaneously, all would get on their knees and spend time in prayer. Cauthen, who, like most American Christians, had been exposed to ceremonial or representative prayer, was caught up in the warmth and fervor of these personal prayers. It kept the missionaries close. It resolved differences. And as Cauthen was to learn, it invoked great power.

The revival effects were even more evident in the churches. Chinese preachers loved expository preaching. People would turn the pages of their Bibles, mark verses, and exclaim to one another over a truth they saw. Humility and love were obvious in their fellowship, and Baker's soul was stirred when he first heard them sing and pray in a worship service.

"It was a strange sound—a noise, but a holy one," he said later. "They would pray out loud—all of them—quietly but fervently. Sounds of prayer would rise all around. The sound of a neighbor praying next to them didn't disturb their praying." Cauthen found a unique advantage in that young Christians learned how to pray from the very beginning.

"But the strongest evidence of the moving of the Spirit in their midst, and in some ways the strangest, was the way they would, without prompting, go from concerted prayer into singing," Cauthen said. "I'm sure it could not have been cultivated. It had to be the result of a great stirring of the Spirit in their midst."

Chinese evangelists were using tent evangelism all over Shantung at that time. They would go into a village, put a tent over a threshing floor, and announce services; and before the tent was struck a new church would be established in the village. Perhaps more than any other evangelistic approach, Cauthen warmed to the tent evangelism concept.

In the front yard of the Nan Lo house, the Cauthens tried out the public address system they had brought. Across the way, seminary students heard the sound of singing coming from the air. They had never before heard such. Several thought the Lord was coming.

116

As Cauthen first began to preach in Chinese, Dr. Glass asked one of the Chinese preachers how it went. He replied, "Ch' a pu li"(not too far off). "But no decisions either," Cauthen remarked.

Despite moments of beauty and encouragement, many who were grim and harsh vied for the upper hand on their daily horizons. They followed the war in Europe on radio, worried that it might somehow come home to them. Expatriates from European countries who were their friends made the war personal. Eloise still had friends in the school she had attended in Chefoo, among them many British. She agonized with them when it looked as if the British Expeditionary Force in the European lowlands might be wiped out. She rejoiced with them when a miraculous rescue was effected at Dunkerque.

It was obvious that Japan, Germany, Italy, and Russia were making common cause; and the perspective from Shantung made that quite ominous. Then tensions from a new source broke over them. A Christian in Hwanghsien was arrested by the Japanese and tortured on charges the Christian community felt sure were false. Later the Christian schools were ordered closed, and posters appeared around the city encouraging the Chinese to have no dealings with missionaries. It was the first real hostility the Cauthens had experienced, though Eloise remembered such incidents from her childhood when battles between Chinese warlords swept back and forth across Shantung.

The missionaries took extra precautions with their children and tried to ignore slights from Chinese with whom they had business dealings.

Baker had a respite in October when he preached his first revival in China. The place was Lungkow, a city of about twenty thousand people, where Dr. Glass had been pastor of a church for many years. Baker preached, and Dr. Glass interpreted in Chinese. Yet twenty-three people made professions of faith. His heart exulted in the fact that the work God had called him to do was effective across the culture and the language barriers of this great land.

When he returned from the Lungkow meeting, Cauthen found that his reputation had been established. The Christians in Hwanghsien invited him to preach for them. They hoped a revival meeting would rally their forces and encourage young believers in the midst of the tremendous anti-Christian feeling around them.

It was as if God chose this particular atmosphere to especially bless the Hwanghsien church. Efforts to disturb the services failed. Although planned as a renewal for the Christians themselves rather than an evangelistic rally, there were ten professions of faith. These were not ordinary professions of faith. Because they were made in a hostile atmosphere, the converts' sincerity was not only not doubted, but their courage was lauded. Baker knew every time he extended an invitation that the people who trusted Christ would be subject to taunts and threats from friends and even relatives.

The North China Mission voted that any missionary should feel free to leave at any time without censure from either the mission or the Foreign Mission Board. Most of the mothers and children left.

That Christmas the missionaries were caught up in their own environment, but not so much that they didn't thrill to the haunting strains of "White Christmas" coming over the shortwave radio.

At the dinner gathering of the missionaries who were left at Hwanghsien during the Christmas season, there was talk about war. What would happen when American and Japanese relations deteriorated? What if Japanese belligerency in the occupation area turned hostile toward Americans?

Early in 1941, relations between the United States and Japan became ominous. The United States State Department urged all nonessential personnel, especially remaining women and children, to evacuate China.

Baker and Eloise talked long into the night and prayed earnestly about what to do. "I don't feel I should go, Baker," Eloise said quietly. "I don't want to place the children in danger. I don't want to worry you unnecessarily, but I just don't feel that the Lord wants me to go."

Baker looked at her intently, his own emotions warring within him. On one hand, he wanted to know that they were safe, that they wouldn't wake up some morning interned and perhaps even separated from each other. At the same time, he wanted desperately to be with her and the children, and he knew he should not leave. Above all there was his confidence in Eloise's dependence on the Lord. Together they decided they would stay and work as long as they could. The decision made, they went ahead with language study and witnessing.

CHAPTER THREE

Evacuation

The next week, Cauthen left with Dr. Glass for a revival in Laichowfu. They had to make the trip by *shantze*, a small covered litter carried on the backs of two mules. It moved at the rate of about three miles an hour. As the two men swayed from side to side in their vehicle, they grew increasingly uncomfortable from the bitter cold. They wondered if they would ever get there.

When they did, they agreed that the effort was all worthwhile. As adversity, tension, and uncertainty swept the land, Christians seemed to be, in direct proportion, strengthened and encouraged by the presence of the Lord. In six days there, Cauthen saw 131 people accept Christ. Young and old responded to the invitation the missionaries extended. Glass continued to marvel at the obvious gifts of his son-in-law. The great fervor, the clarity, the ability to grip a congregation from the very beginning and hold them through until the net was drawn amazed him. He prayed that God would grant Baker many years of harvesting in China.

But he was praying against all outward signs. When they returned to Hwanghsien, Eloise was the only mother among the North China Mission group left except one other who had already decided to evacuate.

The Cauthens tried to keep their lives as normal as possible studying the language in the morning, doing the tasks necessary to keep their household going, and following through on numerous opportunities Baker received to teach and preach. The tensions mounted. New pressures came from the American consul urging Eloise and the children to leave. Ships would be coming to Shanghai in April for that purpose.

One morning, she said to Baker, "The Lord has laid something very special on my heart. If we were to be interned, I could survive.

Perhaps you could survive. But what of the children? I feel that I must move them from danger. But, Baker, I do not feel that I should go back to the United States."

A few days later a letter from Theron Rankin, their Orient secretary, urged them to evacuate from Shantung to an area called Free China, specifically to a station called Kweilin. The two almost wept with gratitude and excitement. This was the answer to their prayers. This was the basis of Eloise's strong feeling. They wrote immediately of their interest and their readiness to proceed. In April a letter came from Richmond and the executive secretary, Maddry. With so much of the mission work being closed down in China, he was obviously grateful that the Cauthens had decided to stay. He said:

"I am certainly happy you are going to Kweilin, and I want you to make a thorough study and investigation of the possibility of this new mission in China. I think we ought to press out from Kweilin into the interior, and I have money in hand and missionary candidates, including a doctor and a nurse, ready to send as soon as you can locate the new mission and perfect your plans. I am greatly thrilled over the idea that you are to lead in the organization of a new mission in Free China. I feel that the Lord has led you in your preparation for this great work. Please know that we are standing by you in every way possible."

Maddry knew that it might be very difficult for Cauthen to get his family into Free China, and he added:

"Let me know just what Eloise and the children will do. If they come home, we will do our best to take care of them, and if they decide to stay in Shanghai or Hong Kong, I'm sure Dr. Rankin will see they are well provided for."

"We'll go to Kweilin," Eloise grinned. "There's no way they'll keep us out." But by late April, it seemed that there was every way that they would be kept out.

First they moved to Shanghai, where consultations continued directly with Rankin and by letter with the Board in Richmond. Everything proceeded as it should, except for one thing. The Hong Kong government would not grant permission for Eloise and the children to pass through to Kweilin. As door after door of inquiry shut, they began to look at each other with the quiet realization that they were going to have to be separated after all.

"But the God who has laid this on our hearts will surely not ask us to be apart long," Eloise said. She steadfastly refused efforts to get her to return to the States while awaiting permission to go to Free China. "No, I want to be closer than that," she said.

Where was closer? Why not the Philippine Islands? The Chinese language school had been moved there. From the very beginning, this sounded like the thing to do. If and when permission came, she could fly from Manila to Hong Kong and then catch one of the night flights over Japanese lines to where Baker would be in Kweilin.

Cauthen held a meeting at the University of Shanghai even while they were preparing for their departure. A long list of interested non-Christian students had been prepared before he came. According to Chinese custom, they came in for personal conferences. Many of them trusted Christ. Cauthen felt more was needed. He finally convinced the university officials that by allowing him to extend an invitation and letting the students make professions of faith before the assembled group in public, great strength would be accomplished in the life of the convert and also in those who witnessed the event. With Cauthen's growing reputation as an effective evangelist, the officials consented. The response was phenomenal.

One of Cauthen's prized possesions was an album that the University of Shanghai students gave him, on which everyone who trusted Christ signed his or her name. He watched many of them baptized on his last Sunday night there.

On April 30 Baker and Eloise, four-year-old Carolyn, and three-year-old Ralph boarded the *Tatuta Maru,* sailing to Manila. As the ship left Shanghai, Baker wondered if he would ever see North China again. Their twenty months there had been filled with incredible spiritual blessing, and during the last few months he had been aware of a deep sense of anointing for his task.

Characteristically, as the coastline faded behind swelling seas, Baker and Eloise turned to thoughts of what was ahead. They had often spoken of the opportunities in the great western stretches of China. Cauthen had a pioneer's longing to carve out a new work, and it seemed as if time and circumstances were affirming his feelings.

On board the *Tatuta Maru,* Cauthen wrote to Charles Maddry in

121

Richmond, explaining further the work he could foresee.

"Eloise and I have often spoken of the vast possibilities in that rapidly changing area. Baptists may think not only in terms of establishing a new mission with intensive local work in the immediate vicinity but of sending out a stream of influence into all the great cities of West China. Millions of people have moved to those areas. These people, in the main, are people of some education and are of the middle class economically. Among those people are many Christians and countless others who are familiar with the Christian message. As they undertake to build in the west a new country, they stand in dire need of spiritual leadership. With our base in Kweilin, which is described by the Chinese as 'The Gateway to the West,' Southern Baptists are in on the ground floor of this vast opportunity. Providentially, there has developed in China a passion among the Chinese Christians for extending the gospel to areas that have not heard about it. A Frontier Missions Movement has come into being, and already a good number of consecrated young people have volunteered their lives and secured their training for this work. Money has been contributed to support their labors. They stand waiting for the 'forward march' to be sounded. It may be in the providence of God that the going of missionaries of Kweilin to plan out steps for the future will be a sounding of the 'forward march . . . .' "

Cauthen identified with this grand notion both conceptually and practically. He had already been useful in inspiring Chinese students to commit themselves to a deeper walk with Jesus Christ. For many of them, that meant volunteering to go wherever God led. Some saw western China as the distant horizons of Christ's call for them. Cauthen's opportunity to join them in the realization of that dream strengthened him as he faced something that was harder than life itself—the thought of leaving Eloise and the children.

When the Cauthens landed in the Philippines, they had only a few suitcases with clothes, some quilts, and Cauthen's most needed books. They also had a loudspeaker which he hoped to take to Kweilin for evangelistic work. Left behind in North China were their car, their piano, their food supply, their furniture, and most of Cauthen's library. Though neither voiced it to the other, both had the feeling they might not see those things again. The much greater pain of facing separation, however, reduced the leaving of

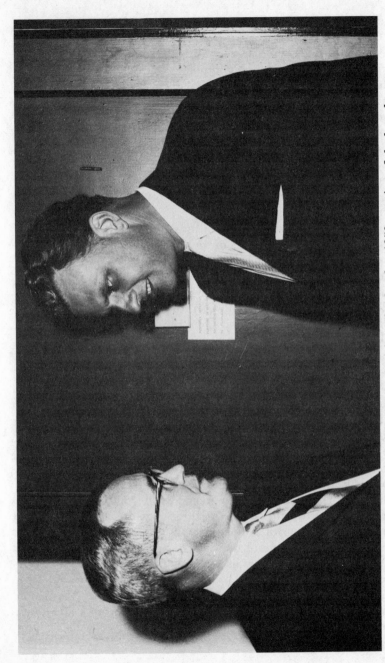

Baker James Cauthen and evangelist Billy Graham visit at the October 1959 meeting of the board.

things to a mere detail.

On board ship, Eloise kept searching the New Testament for any word that would help her accept the impending separation.

When they arrived in the Philippines, several of the missionaries who had been language school students in Peking and had moved to Baguio, north of Manila, were there to meet them. The Hugo Culpeppers, the Rufus Grays, the Bob Dyers, and Fern Harrington, Grace Wilson, and Cleo Morrison were among those students. The Cauthens traveled with them to the beautiful mountain city, where Eloise and the children moved in with the Hugo Culpeppers. They had a few days to get everything squared away and start the pressure to secure permission for Eloise to go into Free China.

The thing that disturbed Baker most was that he found as much insecurity among Americans in the Philippines as among those in China. Dependents were being shipped out daily. As he and Eloise traveled down from Baguio to Manila in preparation for his departure, a vague uneasiness gripped him. At one office where they filled out forms seeking permission for Eloise to go to China, they talked to an old Navy man who said: "Don't give it another thought. All these people leaving doesn't mean a thing. I'll tell you what's really happening. The 'old man' wants to get rid of his wife. He dreamed up this big exodus so he'd have an excuse. Don't worry about it." The Navy man walked off, and Baker and Eloise smiled at each other. It was a good story, but they weren't convinced.

Down on the docks where the ship that would take Baker to Hong Kong was being boarded, they had a good briefing of what he could expect. The Robert Bausum family and a single missionary named Hattie Stallings were in Kweilin. Another free station was a place called Wuchow, where Southern Baptists had a medical mission work. A young doctor named Bill Wallace was working there. Another doctor, Robert Beddoe, was to accompany Baker Cauthen and Charles Culpepper on their trip into the west. Wuchow was to be one of their stops. In fact, Cauthen had been engaged already to preach in a revival in the church there before proceeding to Kweilin.

He and Eloise talked this over in the quiet moments they had in his cabin. Then the ship's whistle blew, indicating that all visitors were to leave.

It was May 18. In two days, they would celebrate their seventh wedding anniversary. They sat on a bunk of his cabin, and he slipped an arm around her as she laid her head on his shoulder. He spoke quietly. "It's not going to be easy, but God will give us the grace."

Together, they knelt and prayed earnestly. Baker prayed for his family, choking up as he did so. Times were so turbulent and situations changing so rapidly that he was almost overcome with fear that he might never see them again. In all of his life, he had never had to lay hold of the promises of God and reach out to the very hands of God more earnestly than he did at this time. Eloise, conscious that her prayer could make Baker's heartbreak even greater, prayed softly. But she believed in a God who could answer prayer. She asked first that God would protect each of them as they were separated and then that God would open the door for her and the children to join him quickly.

When they finished and were composed, they walked hand-in-hand to the deck and the gangplank, where she waited with him until the "all ashore" gong sounded. The heaviness was almost more than they could stand. They made a bit of small talk as they stood there watching the last-minute preparations to launch the ship and the movements of the ship's officer who would sound the "all ashore." Then something changed.

Neither one remembers who noticed first the quiet phenomenon that began to slip over them. Eloise remembers, "Despite the hustle and rush of people preparing to get the ship underway, there came a sudden quietness as if it were all far in the background." She said it was "like a gentle rain." Soon both of them were enveloped by it. Neither one said a thing.

Their anxiety was washed away. Fears disappeared. The ultimate assurance of God's care wrapped them in a warm blanket of awareness of God's presence that neither had ever experienced before.

The totally unique moment was broken by the sound of the "all ashore." They kissed, then smiled at each other; and Eloise went down the ramp to the dock. She turned and looked back at Baker. The assurance was still there in her heart, and he later assured her it was still in his. Both knew that God had done a remarkable thing and had answered their prayers in a way that neither one could have anticipated. While the ship slowly floated away from the dock and then began to move out into Manila Harbor toward a western sun that seemed to race the ship for the horizon, she stood motionless. When the ship was a little more than a speck and the sun a great red ball across the tropical horizon, she was still standing there, watching. "But," she said, "the assurance never left me. Even on the long trip back to Baguio that night, its warmth was as real as the moment it first began to fall over me when I stood at the top of the gangplank holding Baker's hand."

When he could no longer see her on the dock, Baker turned and went back to his quarters. Her last words to him had been, "When you get to Hong Kong, try one more time to get me a permit to come to Kweilin. We'll be ready to leave here at a moment's notice."

He knew that would be the first thing he would do when he got to Hong Kong; but meanwhile, he had something more urgent to do. He went to his cabin and fell on his knees before the presence of the one who was so completely surrounding him. In that memorable moment, he was convinced that God had his family firmly in hand.

CHAPTER FOUR

Inland Bound

In Hong Kong Baker was met by Charles Culpepper, who planned to accompany him to Kweilin after Cauthen finished a round of meetings. Cauthen was shocked to find that it would be four weeks before he could leave Hong Kong, but then he realized that he would have those four weeks to arrange for Eloise and the children to go to Free China with him.

With this thought, Cauthen launched into a grueling round of evangelistic meetings in the Baptist schools and churches of Hong Kong. Still basking in the warmth of God's assurance that had fallen upon him and Eloise, he preached with great power. He remembers it as "a time of unusual blessing in my life." The special power that was increasingly evident in his preaching was never more obvious. Multitudes of students registered decisions in the schools, followed by an equally large number of professions of faith in the churches.

The four weeks passed quickly; but despite repeated trips to the government offices, he did not have Eloise's permit. He had no choice but to proceed inland with hopes that she could soon follow. Culpepper and missionary physician Robert Beddoe, on his way back to join his colleague Bill Wallace in Wuchow, were to make the trip overland to Wuchow with him, as Cauthen was supposed to preach for a week in the church there. They carried a large amount of medical supplies they were going to have to shepherd along the torturous route through Indochina and behind Japanese lines into Free China. Their destination was the Baptist hospital in Wuchow on the West River.

The night before he left Hong Kong, he booked—on faith—a space for Eloise and the children on a Chinese plane that flew once a week over Japanese lines directly into Free China. It was an open ticket. She could use it when and, he had to confess to himself in a moment of doubt, if she was able to get to Hong Kong.

As they took a final meal in the home of a Chinese friend, Dr. Lum Chi Fung, missionary Flora Dodson rushed in with a letter that gave permission for Eloise and the children to come to Hong Kong. Cauthen arose from the table (amidst gasps of gratitude to God) and cabled her immediately.

The party included, besides Cauthen, Culpepper, and Beddoe, a distinguished Chinese physician named Abraham Hsu. Dr. Hsu had been appointed by the Chinese convention as their first medical missionary. He planned to explore for a place to open work in interior China. Culpepper was to work with Hsu before returning to the Japanese-occupied area in Shanghai and then on to Hwanghsien, where he still served as president of the seminary and where he faced an uncertain future because of worsening Japanese-American relationships.

On June 22, 1941, the four men boarded a freighter in Hong Kong bound for the Kwangchow Peninsula on the northern border of Indochina, now known as Vietnam.

Cauthen was elated to be on the way. There was a dance in his eye and a readiness for adventure that had been drained by the exertion of his preaching schedule in Hong Kong on one hand and the anxiety about his family in the Philippines on the other. Now, as the wearied old freighter that was to take them to Kwangchowan plowed its way through the junks in Hong Kong Harbor toward open sea, he exulted in the prospect of reunion with Eloise, Ralph, and Carolyn in Kweilin.

In Baguio, Eloise was even more excited. She quickly made a trip to Manila to arrange for passage to Hong Kong. There her joy turned to horror when she was told that she could not book passage to Hong Kong even with a permit. She did not have United States' permission, and officials didn't think that she would be able to get it to go into war-torn China. Quickly she made her way to the appropriate United States offices. The flash of her eye, her acquaintance with the overall situation, and her determination soon crushed all resistance. One official said, "Lady, you're the craziest woman I've ever met."

"Why?" she asked sweetly.

"There's a war on. Don't you know that?"

She didn't try to explain that she had been living in Japanese-occupied China and had heard the guns of war many times, while he was yet to hear the first shot of real belligerency. She just held her ground, secured her permit, thanked God, returned to the shipping office, and booked her passage, arriving in Hong Kong in early July. To her distress, no one had any word on the progress of the four overland trekkers.

Meanwhile, the trip overland had turned into quite an odyssey. The four men arrived in Kwangchowan and, after considerable haggling, leased four sedan chairs and bearers. Men were also hired to carry baggage and supplies.

The weather waxed hot and sultry. Suits and shirts limp with sweat, they stopped, at Dr. Hsu's urging, and bought black coolie clothing. These clothes—slick, shiny black material on the outside—had a nap on the inside that insulated from both heat and humidity.

Cauthen's new clothing was too big around his waist. He had to lap the waist and roll it to hold it around his slender frame. Ignoring the good-natured jibes of his traveling companions, he hitched up his britches, pulled on his wide-brimmed hat, and climbed into his sedan chair. It seemed they would never get across the border into China, much less to the river where they could catch a steamer to Wuchow.

It was hardly a leisurely trip. In some ways, life around them was going on as it had for centuries, despite changes of dynasty and battles between warlords exchanging territory off and on without rhyme or reason. Not even the establishment of the Republic in 1912 and the nominal unification of China under Generalissimo Chiang Kai-shek in 1928 had changed the pattern. Not even the appearance of Japanese war planes, strafing the roads at random whenever they pleased, had altered it.

Traveling down the roads, they watched Chinese coolies in short pants wade through muddy rice paddies up to their knees, holding ancient wooden plows in place as water buffaloes slowly slogged ahead of them in seeming slow motion.

Little villages appeared from time to time. Tiny markets featured baskets filled with the same kind of foodstuffs that had been sold there for hundreds of years. Cauthen noted that the wheat and millet he had seen in North China was almost completely replaced by the ubiquitous rice in the south.

At places where the road had been bombed, strafed, or rutted by rains, a Chinese crew worked with primitive methods. Four men held the ends of two crossbows to lift giant stones and then let them drop to pound down soil transported to the road from adjacent fields. Periodically, the chairs made back-wrenching detours. The bearers would exchange unpleasantries with the coolies, usually in a dialect that Cauthen could not understand; and then they would move on.

By nightfall, they had found a small inn where they could spend the night. The next morning, sore from the first day's ride and unrefreshed by a less-than-appetizing breakfast of hot tea and rice with some kind of fish pieces in it, they moved out again. That day rain soaked them to the skin, and a continuous round of air-raid alerts interrupted their journey.

Temples, located everywhere in China, had become the nucleus of a unique air-raid system. When planes were spotted, a priest rang his bell in such a way as to signify the direction. The next priest in that direction would ring his, and on and on until the bells had far outdistanced the planes and given the Chinese people a ten- or fifteen-minute warning. The number of bells rung signified how close they were.

The first time Cauthen's party heard the bells, it was obvious the planes were right upon them. Their coolies urged them out, pulled the chairs off the road into the paddies, and then herded them toward bamboo thickets. Hsu led the way. Cauthen brought up the rear, not because he wasn't fast, but because his pants kept falling down. Culpepper would have made it more quickly, he claimed in later days, but for laughing at Cauthen trying to keep his pants up. At any rate, if they were spotted, the planes decided they weren't worth a bomb and flew on, deeper into China.

As the sound of the planes faded, the travelers slogged their way back to the chairs. There, sloughing off as much of the mud as they could, they resumed their positions. Thirty minutes later, they repeated the whole thing.

Cauthen rolled his britches every way he knew how, including tying them in knots. But no matter what he did, each new run still included grabbing them from around his knees and hauling them up under his armpits in order to move.

Not a single one of them lamented leaving that part of the journey behind them when they finally arrived at the river and bargained for passage on a small paddleboat. They rode it for approximately an hour before reaching and haggling a ride on a cable boat.

Cable boats made no better time, but they handled bigger loads. As many as fifty coolies moved along the river bank in front of the boat, pulling it along by giant cables. Exhausted from the problems of moving from one boat to the other, the four men silently listened to the chants of the coolies as they strained into the cables over their shoulders.

The only accommodations available on the boat were cargo boxes on the upper deck, but a camaraderie had developed among the travelers that they began to cherish. Culpepper observed something about his young colleague Cauthen. Beddoe was a talker, and almost anything was a legitimate subject. Cauthen, with a highly refined sense of what constituted appropriate conversation, once or twice became frustrated, slipped from his cargo box, and walked to the back of the boat. Beddoe seemed not to notice, and Cauthen respected the veteran missionary doctor too much to say anything to him.

Finally, they transferred to still a third boat, a steamer with staterooms for them and, bless God, beds. They were too tired to note that it was July the Fourth. The next morning their ship rounded the river into sight of the colorful city of Wuchow, clustered on the side of a hill between the confluence of the West and Fu Rivers.

With the steamer's whistle drowning out any conversation, the four men stood on the deck and waved at the Baptist hospital's doctors and nurses who had gathered to welcome them. Cauthen caught his first glimpse of tall, handsome Bill Wallace standing in their midst and waving shyly. The bachelor physician was already something of a legend.

When they climbed the hill to the hospital, they were shocked at what they saw, despite Bill's warning. The top two floors had been bombed to a shell. They listened, stunned, as Wallace told them of the air raid.

Wallace's report was simple and matter-of-fact. Hsu was able to get more details from the nurses. "He operated right through the air raid," Hsu said to the men. "The nurses say that he made them all go to the shelter, and he stayed in the operating amphitheater, sheltering his patient with his own body. Glass fell over the floor around him and in his hair," Hsu said.

Used to the heroics of his young colleague, Beddoe was more concerned with the destruction of the building. Wallace was more excited about the medicines they had brought in. The four men felt a sense of accomplishment as they saw the young man's excitement.

By the next day, Wallace and Beddoe were back to treating the long lines of people gathered at the clinic, located at the gate below the main hospital. Cauthen was making rounds with the pastor of the Wuchow church, where he was to begin preaching in a revival that night. The week passed fast. Cauthen preached in English with an interpreter, since his Mandarin Chinese was of little use in Cantonese-speaking Kwangsi Province. The results were good, but his mind was on the journey ahead and the possibility that Eloise, Ralph, and Carolyn would be waiting at its end.

Cauthen, Culpepper, and Dr. Hsu finally bade good-bye to Beddoe and Wallace and boarded a steamer heading inland to a place where they could connect with buses going north to Liuchow. The next day, they boarded rickety buses for the next leg of their trip. After sedan chairs, paddleboats, cable boats, and steam boats, the buses sounded good. They were not.

Since gasoline was not available, the Chinese burned charcoal for the engines. This kept them turning over, but gave them little power for the hills that were increasingly in evidence as they moved deeper into the countryside. Periodically, the driver pulled the brake and ordered everybody outside to push. None of the three really minded joining the other sweating passengers in putting their weight into the great hulk of the bus. Culpepper and Hsu had learned to moderate their laughter by the time a rope solved the problem of Cauthen's falling coolie pants.

Cauthen was developing patience in the face of a temper that had been the bane of his existence since he was a child, but he let something get under his skin. Each time they climbed back into the bus, the first thing they saw was a fat Chinese gentleman who refused to budge when the others got out to push. Cauthen told the man, in what Mandarin Chinese he could muster, that he wasn't going to push him any farther. Whether the man understood a word or not, he must have understood the tone of voice. But his look of impassive immobility was the only answer Cauthen received. From Hsu's point of view, that settled the situation.

Smells of dried fish, ripe fruit, and unwashed bodies mingled to dull the appetites of the exhausted travelers. When they finally got to Liuchow and transferred to a train for the final leg of the trip to Kweilin, its seats looked like the height of luxury. Missionary Robert L. Bausum greeted an exhausted but happy trio at the train station in Kweilin.

"Let me take you to my house to change and get cleaned up," Bausum told Cauthen. "You need to go to Kukong to meet your family." Cauthen's face lit up. The traveler's weariness fell away along with the grime and unpleasant memories of his journey. He was in the interior of China. He had made it, and, God willing, his wife and children would soon be with him.

Meanwhile, Culpepper and Hsu quickly made additional transportation arrangements and prepared to press on. Their goal was Chungking in Szechwan Province. Cauthen wished his companions well but, because of his anticipation of his family's arrival, couldn't really put his heart into the parting.

Several nights later, as the flares flickered down the borders of the Kukong runway, Cauthen paced up and down and listened fretfully for sounds of the engines of the Hong Kong flight. Knowing that at times planes had not made it didn't help. Mercifully, he saw the exhaust flashes of the twin engine DC-3 long before he heard the drone of the engines. The plane landed, taxied, and rolled to a stop. As the propellers slowly stopped spinning, the door from the back part of the fuselage swung open. It seemed as though everybody in the world disembarked before a four-year-old girl jumped out ahead of a woman who was helping a three-year-old boy. Baker gathered them into his arms. It was July 31. They had left Shanghai in April. He had left her at the dock in Manila in the middle of May. "Thank you, Lord."

CHAPTER FIVE

The Caves of Kweilin

When the Cauthens arrived in Kweilin, the mission there included Hattie Stallings, the Bausums, and a single man named Oz Quick. The station had once been a big one as a large hospital had been located there along with a church and several missionary homes. A story frequently told is that a fire threatened to jump a storage house to the church. Missionary Alec Herring fell on his knees and prayed God that the fire would not burn the church. His prayer was answered. The wind changed, and the fire destroyed the hospital.

The Cauthens were assigned to a big old house next door to Miss Stallings. Eloise says, "We literally rattled around in it." And it was impossible to warm, as it had neither furnace nor space heaters. Its furnishings consisted of a few chairs and two swaybacked beds in the attic. Some boards were found to firm up the beds. Mattresses were fumigated. With no refrigerator, they had to hang foodstuffs that needed keeping in a screen safe. Nothing could be kept longer than overnight.

Eloise had brought one trunk stuffed with a few linens, some towels, and some clothing for the children and Baker and herself. Baker James had brought a suitcase of clothes overland. That had to be enough. She had squirreled away in their baggage a few cases of extra food, including some S 16 tins of powdered milk. Grateful for each item, she rationed her supplies carefully.

The Sunday after they arrived, they were at the breakfast table in Hattie Stallings' house when the air-raid sirens started wailing. The eggs had just been set before them on the table, but no one had yet had a bite. They were wondering what to do when Miss Stallings jumped up and exclaimed, "Now you all follow me. We don't have much time."

"What shall we bring?" Eloise asked.

"Don't bring anything—just yourselves," the determined lady answered.

Oz Quick came in the door about that time and grabbed Carolyn. Baker James picked up Ralph, and they ran as hard as they could to the edge of the city and then up a sloping and rocky hill.

The caves in the hillside were natural, but more ideal bomb shelters could not have been built. How other people got an earlier warning Cauthen never knew; but when he got there with his family, the caves were full and stuffy. The ceilings were so low they could not stand up. Rough-hewn wooden doors were slammed shut. Then they heard and felt the bomb explosions. The Japanese bombers had seen people fleeing for the caves and had altered their flight to drop explosives in the area.

When the all-clear sounded people hustled out, gasping for fresh air. To their horror, they saw that one of the caves had taken a direct hit. It was only three hundred yards from the cave in which the missionaries had taken refuge, and they beheld the carnage, stunned.

Two church members came up sobbing. One of the deacons had been killed. Cauthen helped Eloise shepherd the children back and then assisted at the clinic in bearing the wounded on stretchers. When they got to the compound, they found that a bomb had hit the area. Homes were damaged but not destroyed. This was to become a way of life in Kweilin.

The new missionaries soon adapted to the environment. Eloise had no stove, but managed to prepare food on a small charcoal pot. She converted a five-gallon gasoline can into an oven, in which she cooked biscuits whenever she could get the ingredients. An old wooden bathtub sufficed as a place to store their rice. There was a room called the bathroom, but it had no flush plumbing. The Cauthens often talked about being able to identify with their pioneering forebears.

They were back in Mandarin-speaking territory and could again use the Chinese language they knew. At the first meeting of the mission group, Bausum, the senior missionary, asked Cauthen, "What do you want to do? We've got Bible School work. We've got orphanage work. We've got evangelistic work. We've got clinic work." Cauthen replied, "Bausum, I'm a preacher. Let me preach."

They agreed that that arrangement suited them both.

Bausum's wife had an accordion and could play it quite well. At night the two families began going to the midcity church, where they organized young people for the task of inviting people in. It was a good time to gather people since the bombers seldom raided Kweilin at night. At dusk, the streets would fill up. Cauthen remarked that it was like East Texas on election night.

Soon Cauthen was preaching every night and making the adjustment to his audiences. Oz Quick pointed out, "In America, people's minds wander. In China, their whole bodies wander." But the missionaries had some encouragement. As Paul said of his experience in Athens, "Some believed."

Because people knew they might well be dead the next day, from either the air raids or disease, they were susceptible to messages of hope and wholeness in Jesus Christ. The missionaries, also knowing that no one of them knew what the next day would hold, were deeply zealous in their task. They learned to put the people into a kind of triage—the off-the-street group in one room, those who became interested into another room, and those who made decisions into still a third room. "It was like a three-ring circus," Cauthen said. Because many Christians were among the refugees, the missionaries discovered other preachers and workers who could strengthen their witness in both preaching and counseling. New life began to flow into the church in Kweilin.

A life-style emerged. During the morning, missionaries studied the language. In the early afternoon Cauthen prepared the message he was going to preach in the evening. While he did this, Eloise took the children into a room they designated school and began teaching them, just as missionaries in the interior of China had taught their children for decades.

At intervals, Eloise looked from the window to the top of a tower in the center of the city. City officials ran a big paper ball to the top of the tower when there was possibility of an air raid. Eloise kept a little cache of food and water in a grab bag so that when there was an alarm, they could pick it up as they went out the door.

On August 1, Cauthen wrote Charles Maddry of the work in Kweilin. He spoke of street preaching and the thousands of people who could be gathered at night. He noted the clinic work where several Chinese doctors ministered near the remains of the old hospital building. He mentioned a Bible school for men and a separate one for women that had been conducted in Kweilin for years and was bursting at the seams as refugees poured in. Then he said:

"However, with all of the wonderful opportunity in this city, we must remember that Kweilin is merely the gateway to western China. It is a strategic center, as is evidenced by the fact that in the last two years a railway has been built through here opening up eight hundred miles of territory which can easily be reached by the gospel. I heard only a few days ago of a university with more than four thousand students where the door stands open wide for the preaching of Christ. It's a significant time in the life of West China. It's a most opportune time for the preaching of the Word. An opportunity for preachers to go from city to city and town to town, winning the lost, enlisting the Christians, and establishing churches is now before us."

Yet everything closed when an air raid came. The whole city was evacuated. Thousands of people poured into the nearby hills. Even the bank loaded its valuables into trucks and moved out to a holding area until the all-clear sounded. Shackled prisoners marched out chain-gang style.

One of the big limestone caves in the mountain to the southwest of the city was called "Old Man Mountain." Two thousand people could crowd into it. Bausum apologized for the long walk. He had an automobile that he had used in the beginning to go to a smaller cave they had almost to themselves, but he ran out of gasoline. He had pushed the car back to the compound, and there it stood.

The Cauthen and Bausum families enjoyed each other. Dorothy Bausum was Carolyn's age. In the caves, Baker pulled the children around him and read *Winnie the Pooh* to them. They used flashlights in the beginning, but when the batteries played out, they resorted to candles and tung oil lamps. Later, oil and tallow were so hard to get that the reading was curtailed. It tended, as Baker said, to "put them to bed with the chickens."

In late November Cauthen's immediate supervisor, M. Theron Rankin, the Foreign Mission Board's area secretary for the Orient, flew into Kweilin on a night flight from Hong Kong to spend several days with the fledgling Free China Mission. He dreamed aloud of the kind of work they could project in the midst of their tremendous opportunity. They considered expanding the medical work, activating the seminary from Canton, which was already refugeeing in the area, capitalizing on the schools that had been relocated there, and mobilizing Christians scattered throughout the area, both north toward the Tibetian Steppes and south toward Liuchow.

It was decided that they should organize two teams—one to move north and one to move south—as the beginning of a radiating work from Kweilin. Cauthen, Bausum, Oz Quick, and Rankin worked out a paper on the subject. As Rankin prepared to return to Hong Kong, he asked Cauthen to polish the paper and send it on to him. Neither man dreamed what lay just ahead for all of them.

On the first of December, Oz Quick became ill with what doctors in the area thought was appendicitis. The most logical action seemed to be to take him to Wuchow and let Bill Wallace operate. The trouble was getting to Wuchow, not to mention the bombing problems there. Finally, it was decided that Oz should play it safe. He returned with Rankin to Hong Kong to have his surgery there. Cauthen, Bausum, and their families saw the two men off the next evening, watching until the plane's exhaust flames could no longer be seen in the darkness of the night.

A few mornings later, December 8, 1941, Bausum knocked on Cauthen's door before breakfast. Cauthen, sleepy-eyed and tousle-haired, opened the door, still belting his bathrobe around him to ward off the morning chill. Cauthen knew that something was wrong. "What is it?" he asked.

"It's war," Bausum said. "The Japanese bombed Pearl Harbor this morning. I heard it over the shortwave radio on the five o'clock news."

"Pearl Harbor!" exlaimed Cauthen. "Was there damage?"

"I couldn't tell," said Bausum. "They said that a lot of ships were sunk and a lot of life was lost, but it wasn't too clear yet."

That afternoon, Chinese newspapers said Americans had retaliated by sending five hundred planes over Tokyo, which turned out to be a bit of unfounded optimism.

The next morning Bausum didn't have to come. Cauthen was at his house, and the news was even worse. Japanese forces were on the offensive all over the Pacific. They landed troops in Hong Kong. They pressed toward Singapore. They landed in the Philippines. Hong Kong fell. The Kweilin missionaries prayed fervently for Rankin and Oz Quick. "And he thought he was playing it safe," Bausum mused.

For the Cauthens, as concerned as they were for their friends in the Philippines, there was even more concern for missionaries already in Japanese hands in Shantung. Eloise, near tears, looked at Baker. "Daddy and Mother!" she said. "And Lois."

Cauthen said, "I feel sure they will be all right. They know the Japanese authorities there now; and while they may be detained, I don't think they will be harmed."

It was nearly spring in 1942 before they received word from Dr. Glass that in fact he was all right though confined to a detention camp in Chefoo. The indefatigable faith of the old missionary shone through his letters.

Though the Cauthens left everything behind when they came out of North China, they had not actually lost them because the mission provided storage and protection. Now, with the war, everyone lost everything. They wrote Baker's parents:

"The war continues to help us eliminate our possessions. We don't know how the car, furniture, and piano are faring in North China. We left our rugs in Baguio, and of course we have no information about them. The bulk of our things, including nearly all my books, the loudspeaker, and many of Eloise's things, are in Hong Kong. I had a bank account in Shanghai, and of course it has 'gone with the wind.' "

They were never to see any of those things again. Yet in the same letter, Cauthen reasoned, "What do a few losses amount to when you have the privilege of being with your loved ones and preaching the message to those who have never heard?"

Being with loved ones and preaching Christ to those who had never before heard made all the hardships of living in Kweilin— running to the caves, being unable to get staples, fighting inflation, living with few conveniences—not only bearable but a unique adventure. When he realized that but for the grace of God his wife and children would have been in Japanese hands in the Philippines, Cauthen could only thank him. He considered the problems as nothing when compared to the excitement of preaching. His was the best of all worlds. He wrote:

"But over against the inconveniences of the war, there stands the glorious opportunity of preaching the gospel that is so abundant here. For months we have continued day by day our evangelistic meetings. We are now preaching twice daily. The people still come eagerly to hear, and their responses are most glorious. Yesterday there were fifteen at our noonday meeting who made profession of faith in the Lord."

The genuine happiness Baker and Eloise enjoyed in the midst of trying circumstances is reflected in a letter that their colleague, Robert Bausum, sent to the Foreign Mission Board's executive secretary shortly after the first of the year:

"We are more grateful than words can tell for the presence with us of the delightful Cauthen family. They are perfectly wonderful, and our five children make a fine and happy lot. I remember Mrs. Cauthen from the time she was returning to China with her parents in 1920 when I was a new missionary. I can still see the little girl of those days in her. Dr. Cauthen is preaching and finding, I believe, all the opportunities he wants to preach. And he is fine at it."

The Kweilin missionaries learned that about two thousand civilian prisoners in Hong Kong's Stanley Prison included several of their colleagues—Flora Dodson, the Cecil Wards, Auris Pender, Dr. Rankin, and Oz Quick, who recovered from his appendicitis but paid a big price for it.

A Chinese refugee brought them a scribbled note, written with a bit of charcoal, from Flora Dodson. She said they were getting two bowls of rice a day with a few beans or a bit of fish or vegetable on it. Their main suffering, she said, was from the cold. Typhoid and dysentery had broken out because their water was not being boiled, and they had no way to do it themselves.

As the rippling effect of the escalated war hit Kweilin, the missionaries there began to feel some problems, too. An aspirin tablet cost a dollar. Gasoline was five dollars a gallon, but it had to be paid for in gold.

The Cauthens received word in late spring that women in Texas had raised and sent to the Foreign Mission Board the princely sum of five thousand to build Baker James Cauthen and his family a home in their new station in Kweilin. But getting the money into China at that time would have reduced it to practically nothing. The board had no choice but to hold on to it.

Baker Cauthen not only preached daily, but also worked diligently with his fellow missionaries to seize the opportunity to train Chinese Christians. In the summer of 1942 he wrote the board, "As we face the future, we are putting our emphasis on two chief lines, evangelism and the training of workers."

He and his fellow workers had already organized evangelistic teams to begin work in the north and in the south. Three other teams were to visit systematically the churches and chapels already existing in areas around Kweilin, encouraging them toward self-support and evangelistic outreach.

News from the war grew worse. From radio broadcasts that summer, they learned that the German Africa corps was threatening Alexandria and Cairo in Egypt and, of course, the vital Suez Canal. The Germans were also driving toward Moscow in Russia.

More painful was word that MacArthur had left the Philippines and that General Wainwright had surrendered his beleaguered forces on the island of Corregidor off the Bataan Peninsula. The Kweilin Mission spent long hours in prayer on behalf of the missionaries caught in the Philippines.

Singapore surrendered on February 15. All the Netherlands Indies surrendered to the Japanese by March 7. Then Burma was lost, and the word came that the Japanese had bombed Australia's northernmost port, Darwin.

The missionaries were skeptical when they heard that American twin-engine bombers under the leadership of a colonel named James Doolittle had actually bombed Tokyo in April of 1942. They had heard some overly optimistic reports before. But, not long after that, word came that one of the Doolittle Raiders had been evacuated through Kweilin. It was true. The event became something of an emotional turning point. Then the shortwave radio revealed that an American naval force turned back the Japanese in the Coral Sea in May and again near Midway in June. Balancing that was word that the Japanese had taken over some of the Aleutian Islands off Alaska. "That's American soil," Bausum said soberly.

The most exciting word yet, however, came to the Kweilin missionaries in a letter from Maddry in July, indicating that information had been received through the State Department that missionaries who had been interned in Hong Kong, along with thirty-one other people from North China, were on a repatriation boat called the *Gripsholm*. "Do you think Daddy and Mother and Lois are with them?" Eloise asked anxiously. "I'm sure they are," Cauthen reassured her.

Late in July, people were awakened by a terrible explosion on the outskirts of Kweilin toward the American Air Base. No warning had been sounded. Everybody was immediately concerned. From their window, the Cauthens saw smoke rising from the direction of the air field. They anxiously scanned the skies but saw no Japanese planes.

When they had first arrived in Kweilin, there had been just a small contingent of American Flying Tigers working out of the Kweilin field. The missionaries had not had a chance to know them well. But right after Pearl Harbor, the Tigers were augumented by and incorporated in an American Air Force contingent. In one sense, this had given them protection from Japanese bombers. In another sense, it made them an even more vital target. Later in the morning of the explosion, an American colonel (who had taken over one of the mission homes for his quarters because of cramped living space on the base) came to the Cauthen house and asked for Baker.

"One of our boys, Lt. Allen, a Louisiana lad, was killed this morning in a crash. We had a patrol up fighting the Japanese north of here. He almost made it back."

"I'm sorry," Cauthen said. "Can we help?"

"It's our first casualty here," the colonel replied. "We want to have a funeral. Would you hold it?"

"Certainly," Cauthen replied. The pastor in him arose immediately to the situation, and by evening eight American soldiers were gathered with the Kweilin missionaries and several Chinese military men in Miss Stallings' house. It was chosen because it had the largest sitting room. Eloise sang two solos. Baker spoke. At the close of the service, the whole group sang "America." Bausum wrote, "It sounded thrilling, but it was a little sad, too." At dusk they buried the young aviator in the foreign cemetery next to the graves of the children of some missionaries named Bailey.

Afterward the Bausums entertained the airmen. Eloise put her ingenious oven to work and brought what she felt sure would be more than enough biscuits. After hearing the exclamation "Homemade biscuits!" she knew there wouldn't be nearly enough.

Dr. Cauthen and Dr. William R. Tolbert in front of the Providence
Baptist Church in Monrovia, Liberia (1960)

CHAPTER SIX

Tested

The fall of 1942 went rapidly. In some ways, it was their most difficult yet. Baker traveled constantly. He worked into Honan Province, back down to Kwangsi as far as Wuchow, and preached often at Liuchow.

In a mountain town far from Kweilin, a knock came on his door late at night. The innkeeper told him a young man was asking for him. Cauthen went down to find one of the young men who had received Christ that summer in his meetings at Kweilin. The young man, who had set up a store in the little town, had never been baptized. Their discussion not only brought on his baptism, but the nucleus for a little church that Baker was unable to begin. A few days later in a still more distant town in the mountains, a young man working in the telegraph office greeted him and indicated that he had also been in the Kweilin meetings and had trusted Christ. That night he introduced Baker to Christian friends he had met since moving to the town, and they too became a small church.

Such moments helped Cauthen survive the anxiety he felt in being away from his family. As he returned from this particular trip, he found that Eloise had had to take the children to the caves nearly every night. After they returned from the caves one night and she had just gotten the children undressed and back in bed, the alarm sounded again, and she had to do it all over again. Baker was constantly amazed at the "good soldier" quality Eloise brought to the most difficult circumstances. He thanked God for his mate's background and her deep call. He shared his feelings with Rankin. "It's their courageous spirit, together with the assurance of the Lord's constant care for them, that enables me to leave them at home while I go about in the evangelistic work."

At Christmas time that year of 1942, the beleaguered little mission's trials increased sharply. With the exchange rate for American dollars unchanged, prices had skyrocketed. Their support now totally inadequate, the missionaries existed by selling some of their things. Baker and Eloise had a problem. Their things were scattered from Hwanghsien to Shanghai to Hong Kong to Baguio and, as they said laughingly, "belong to some Japanese gentleman by now."

To make things worse, Robert Bausum became ill. He and his family were ordered to Wuchow for two months of rest.

Then Eloise found little Ralph, now four years old, burning with fever one morning. A Church Missionary Society doctor, Charlotte Bacon, came to their rescue; but when the fever was gone the little boy couldn't walk. As they gathered around his bed, Dr. Bacon said, "I don't really know what has happened. It could be either polio or tuberculosis of the hip. The problem is that you treat one exactly the opposite from the other. Until I know, I'm afraid to do anything."

"How can we find out?" Eloise asked anxiously.

"We'll just have to pray," the doctor said. And pray they did.

The next afternoon, Sunday, they were holding services in their home for English-speaking people in Kweilin. As Ralph's condition came up for prayer, a young banker said, "I know a Chinese doctor who may be able to help us. His name is Dr. Pan Tse Hwa."

Baker and the banker left immediately to find the doctor. He was hard to find because he was at church. Baker said to the young banker, "I don't mind waiting. Just knowing where he is makes me feel better."

Dr. Pan examined Ralph right after supper that evening and said, "This is polio, and I will show you what to do about it." A disciple of the Sister Kenney method of treatment, the doctor soon had them exercising and massaging Ralph's little legs.

Giving Ralph the attention he needed, in addition to doing the teaching and providing for the family, was a grueling task. But Eloise seemed to be up to it, and God provided special help for her.

During mission meeting one day, Eloise saw a young girl peering through the window. She went out to talk to the girl and found that she was hungry. Eloise fed her and, as the girl ate ravenously, elicited from her the fact that the girl was from a famine area. Relatives sold her into servanthood, but she had run away. She told of beatings, abuse, and degradation, and her body showed the evidence. Neither Eloise nor Baker could bring themselves to send her back. The girl begged them to let her stay and work and earn her keep. Such people were all over Kweilin, but this one was special. They felt that God had sent her to them. Soon the young girl, who was half Chinese and half Filipino and whose Christian name was Mary, was like a member of the household.

This evidence of God's care was needed boost to offset Ralph's illness, heavy travel, constant bombings, rumors of a new Japanese offensive, continued rounds of inflation, and conflict between Chinese Christian factions from different areas. The missionaries struggled prayerfully against this conflict, realizing that their evangelistic opportunity was unparalleled and anything that would dilute the Christian witness tragic.

Baker refused to let himself become discouraged. Long training and self-discipline in looking upward whatever the circumstances, claiming God's victory no matter what was happening around him, and pressing on toward any goal held sway as the months dragged on. Often as he watched little Ralph drag his foot around, his heart would sink as he thought the youngster might have contracted the disease in the caves outside Kweilin. Momentarily, he would chastise himself for doing this to his family. Then he would console himself with some tiny progress in the youngster's condition, turn his heart toward God, and thank him.

Eloise was alternately encouraged and discouraged with correspondence from her father, still confined in North China. Early in 1943, Dr. Glass got a letter out to her:

"Your letter of November 16 arrived here just a few days ago [February 1943]. There was joy in the camp. Mail is so rare that every letter is everybody's letter. We've been passing them around among friends here. Deaver Lawton has not seen them. He is in another camp, and we seldom have any communication. Very, very few letters trickle in from the outside. Sometimes the China Inland Mission hears from their headquarters in Shanghai. We heard that eight thousand 'enemy nationalists' in Shanghai are all to be in internment camps, as we are, by the end of this month. We are not bad off here.

". . . Those in the camp do all the work. This week I am on the sanitation squad. Jessie and Lois are both in the kitchen. They have three groups. So they have to do the cooking every third week. Our camp is well organized, and no one is really overworked. We have to do our own laundry as well, only we have no arrangement for boiling the clothes. We do manage to keep fairly decent."

Eloise looked at Baker with tears in her eyes. "I hope the Lord will forgive me for ever thinking we have a rough time when I realize what Daddy and Mother and Lois and the others are going through." With the children unusually sobered by the letter, and consequently very quiet, the four prayed for their loved ones and colleagues.

Because of Bausum's illness and the need to handle the mission business, Baker did not travel into the country areas during the spring of 1943 as much as he had the previous year; but the stay was fortuitous. With the large concentration of refugee Christian schools in Kweilin, he was much in demand to preach to them. The concept of giving a Christian invitation at the end of a service—that is, inviting people to come forward and make a public profession of their faith—was treated with skepticism in China. "Oriental face," the British missionaries would say knowingly.

But Baker wasn't sure the China heart was, down deep, that much different from the East Texas heart. He preached to the Pooi To-pooi Ching schools for four days and had seventy-three public professions. Most of the converts were baptized a few weeks later. In the Ping Shek school, a three-day meeting yielded more decisions.

As one of the missionaries said, "They don't always understand Baker's Mandarin Chinese, but they always seem to understand what's involved when he begins to draw the net. No one can draw the net like Baker."

Perhaps more than anything else, Baker and Eloise were encouraged by a sense of personal drama. They were convinced that God was dealing with them very directly, leading them, delivering them from tragedy or danger, and manifesting his face to them in situation after situation. Cauthen wrote Rankin in the summer of 1943, "Whatever problems we face, we are encouraged by the memory of his blessing and in desert places are able to 'draw water from the wells of salvation.'"

In the summer of 1943 the Cauthens, exhausted by their schedule, went to a mountain resort area north of Kweilin where a number of missionaries had built retreat homes before the war. Most of the owners were gone now. Their homes, faithfully kept up by servants in the area, were rented out to other missionaries or foreign nationals in the area. The place, in Honan Province, was called Nanyo. Summers in Kweilin were blazing hot and humid, and inflation was spiraling even higher. The missionaries were glad to escape from the city for a while.

Unable to get one of the cabins at Nanyo, the Cauthens stayed in a Chinese inn where accommodations were crude. The only room available was one that had been made from a loft. Despite the relief of the cool weather after the oppressive heat of Kweilin, Baker wasn't sure he had made the right decision. Smoke from the kitchen curling up through cracks in the floor made the room very uncomfortable, but fleas made it even worse.

On the fourth day, they woke up to hear six-year-old Carolyn coughing. Eloise wrapped her robe around her and slipped over to the child, placing a hand on her forehead. "Baker, this child is burning up." Baker got out and knelt by the child's bed. It was obvious she had a high fever.

He dressed and went next door to where a missionary couple who had been there longer were staying. He asked them about the possibility of finding a doctor in the area. They told him a Chinese doctor was supposed to be practicing in a little town at the base of the mountain. Baker made the trip down and talked the doctor into coming back with him. It was after dark when they finally got back to Nanyo and climbed into the little loft. One look at Eloise indicated she was even more worried. The doctor examined the child and said, "Paratyphoid."

"But she's had shots," Eloise protested.

"Good," he replied. "It may modify the disease."

He gave Eloise and Baker instructions for caring for Carolyn, and the rest of the vacation was spent doing just that. Her hair fell out soon after the onset of the disease, and the little bald head increased their distress as they tried to keep her comfortable. Together they sought the Lord, trying not to let visions of their son dragging his polio-weakened leg or their daughter lying sallow-skinned and listless in her bed rob them of their confidence.

As the Israelites of old had laid hold of their deliverance from Egypt again and again to encourage them in times of trouble,

Eloise and Baker laid hold of their deliverance from the Philippines and Japanese concentration camps to the freedom of Western China to encourage them. If ever Baker felt deep pangs of remorse, he would not confess them. If ever he remembered the protestations of his friends at the Polytechnic Church in Fort Worth that he should not take children to such a place, he would not let himself succumb to them.

By the time they got back to Kweilin Carolyn was making rapid improvement, and her hair was growing again. Fellow missionaries, obviously glad to see them, tried not to show their shock at the child's appearance.

Bausum, now recovered from his illness, told of good news over the radio. The Allies had completed their sweep of North Africa and had invaded first Sicily and then Italy. "They've got old Mussolini on the run now," the missionary said.

When he listened to the news broadcasts each morning he made notes for his wife, who was hard of hearing. Those notes became news bulletins for the mission station. "They cleaned all the Japs out of Guadalcanal, and they landed at a place called Tarawa," he said.

"And the Fourteenth Air Force is at least twice as large as it was before you left," Mrs. Bausum added. "You're not going to recognize your congregation out there Sunday afternoon." Bausum had been preaching for Cauthen, who acted as a chaplain for the Protestant boys of the Fourteenth Air Force. The Catholic chaplain had recruited him.

Soon the Cauthens were busier than ever. Baker not only moved back and forth to the new missions that the evangelistic teams had developed, but also expanded his work on the base among the thousands of young American airmen. "They're hungry for the gospel and for encouragement. It's all I can do to remember that what we're here for is to establish New Testament churches among the Chinese," he told his wife.

In the fall they had many occasions for rejoicing. Carolyn was rapidly recovering. "You can't tell the child's been sick!" Mrs. Bausum exclaimed. Ralph continued to respond to the twice-a-day Sister Kenney massage treatments they were giving him. And news came that Eloise's father, her stepmother, and her sister Lois had been repatriated on the *Gripsholm.* They were due in New York before Thanksgiving. Again missionaries' prayers were dominated by rejoicing and praise.

They also sensed strong support from the homeland. Secretary Charles Maddry wrote them that fall:

"The stories of what you're doing in China have created a great impression throughout the South. It's been a wonderful inspiration to our people in the churches. My heart aches often because I fear you and those dear babies do not have enought to eat and wear. We have increased the salary every time it has been recommended by the mission in China, and we stand ready always to do more if necessary, as long as our funds hold out. Please, therefore, let me have a word from you immediately as to your personal needs. I want those babies to have plenty of nourishing food if it can be bought. If you need extra funds or if the Bausums need extra funds for the children, please let me know. You must not hesitate to tell me about your individual and personal needs. Our people will hold the secretary blameable if those dear children were to be undernourished or not properly cared for."

"Bless his heart," Eloise said after Baker read that part of the letter aloud. "He sounds like a grandfather and as if these were his grandchildren."

"Listen to the rest of the letter," Baker said.

"We want you to come home on furlough. I hope that you can come home by next summer at least and earlier if possible. You have a great story to tell, and you will need the rest. I want you to come home and rest up and be ready for the glorious new day that is coming in China when the war is over."

"Home!" Eloise's eyes fairly danced. "Next summer?"

"Next summer," Baker echoed with a broad smile.

By the spring of 1944 Ralph's limp was less pronounced, and no one could tell Carolyn had been ill. Though both Baker and Eloise were thinner than either one of them had ever been before, there were so many things to encourage them that they seemed unusually energetic. And furlough was only a few months away.

That spring a young Chinese lieutenant, Fred Fong, announced his intentions to call on Mary, their young ward. Baker and Eloise immediately took a parental point of view, and a Chinese one at that. As politely as he knew how, Baker asked Lieutenant Fong to secure a letter from his parents that would include a sworn statement that he wasn't already married. It was not at all unusual for a Chinese young man to court and marry a girl and take her home to several other wives. Shortly, she would find herself little more than a servant and often something less.

Lieutenant Fong's intentions were good and his credentials excellent. Baker gave him permission to court the young lady. In a matter of weeks, though she was barely seventeen, she eagerly gave her consent to marry him; and her benefactors gave theirs.

It was a grand occasion. The missionaries made wedding garments, decorated the church, and rehearsed joyously. The children were in the ceremony, which Buford Nichols performed.

Baker's responsibilities among the Protestant airmen increased as the Air Force buildup increased. A Jewish driver came every week in a jeep to take the Cauthens to the air base. One day in April, Sargeant Katz picked them up and commenced his usual "thrilling ride" to the air base. Baker kept an eye peeled to the southwest, where a low cloud seemed to be racing directly toward them. "We'll beat it," Katz predicted confidently in his flat, midwestern accent.

But they didn't. They were soaked to the skin as the rain squall whipped through the open-sided jeep. The sun came out almost immediately, however, and it seemed so warm that they didn't worry about the drenching. But when they were home again after the service it was obvious to Baker that Eloise was chilling. She clasped her arms around her slender body and shook almost uncontrollably after they got into the house. "You've got to go to bed. Let's get you a hot bath, and I'll make you some soup," Baker said.

Early the next morning she was in pain and feverish. "Get me the vitamins," she said. Her younger brother Bryan, now in the Air Force, had come through earlier in the spring and brought them vitamins. Not knowing about such things, she had suggested that they save them until they needed them. He brought her the vitamins and said, "I'm going out to see if I can find a doctor." Soon Dr. Robert Beddoe from Wuchow, who had come over to work in the Kweilin clinic, was by her bed. Dr. Bacon, who had treated Ralph, joined him.

"She has a pleural effusion," they agreed. It was rare, but it sometimes occurred with a severe chill. The doctors were obviously concerned, and that deepened Baker's anxiety. Sharp pain brought

151

them to her side again during the night. The doctors pulled Baker aside after examining her again and said, "Her right lung has collapsed."

"What does that mean?" Baker said. "Can she get along with only one? How long will it be that way?"

"We don't know," they said. An Army doctor from the American air base, Tom Gentry, who had known Eloise when she was at Baylor University, joined the little medical team. He was especially attentive to her needs and obviously worried. "If the other lung collapses, that will be it." He hurried back to the base and returned before morning with more medicine.

Missionary Buford Nichols had come into China over "the hump" a few weeks earlier to work with the Chinese military and, because of the shortage of living space, was sleeping in the Cauthens' downstairs living room on a cot. As the doctors worked with Eloise, he helped Cauthen bundle up the children and take them to the home of one of the other missionary families. When they returned he made Baker a hot drink and urged him to sit down and rest for a few moments. The doctors shuttled back and forth.

Airmen who had come to love them kept coming to the door. These men had often brought them toothpaste, razor blades, and canned goods, asking, "Do you have enough of these things?" Eloise would say, "Well, we are a little short," not wanting to mention that they hadn't seen those things in several years.

Dr. Gentry and Dr. Beddoe sat down with Cauthen late the next evening and discussed the problem. "She is very weak. The poor diet that you people have been on for so long has lowered her resistance." Struggling for a positive word, they added, "But she'll make it unless the other lung goes." Cauthen asked evenly, "What will prevent it?"

Gentry replied, "Well, I know you're a Baptist; but you'll just have to be a good Presbyterian and assume that what will be will be."

During the night an air-raid alert sounded. Baker took comfort in knowing that the children would be taken to the shelters, but decided he had no choice but to be a good Presbyterian about the air raids also.

The morning news was another problem. Suffering servere setbacks in the Pacific, the Japanese seemed determined to wipe out the Americans in West China. After years of static lines, they were driving south through Hunan Province in a fresh new offensive. Word came that Liuchow had fallen.

"You've got to get away," the American consul told the American civilians. "We'll be able to fly you out in a series of evenings, but there's every chance that the Japanese are going to storm right in here. The Chinese army is unable to hold them. This base is all but unprotected."

"But you can't take Eloise now," Gentry told Cauthen. "Moving her would surely kill her."

Days passed. Most Americans were evacuated. Cauthen, looking thin and sallow himself, stayed close to his wife, shuttling back and forth on a few errands and trying to visit with the people who came and asked about his wife. On the seventeenth day, her condition worsened. Beddoe, candid to a fault, said, "I'm afraid that's it, Baker. Her other lung will surely collapse."

He stayed until late in the night, and then left. Baker sat by Eloise and prayed, praising God again for the deliverance that had come when the children were sick, pushing back the doubts and fears that loomed up when he looked at his wife's almost skeletal frame. He tried to keep his hand off his own eye. A serious infection had developed on the lid, and when he had gone for some medicine in his cabinet to fix it he had accidentally doused it with iodine. Dr. Beddoe had looked at it and said, "Well, it could have burned you to death, but it will probably cure your eye."

As dawn came on the eighteenth day, Baker got up, went downstairs, and woke Buford.

"What is it?" Buford said, "Eloise?"

"No change," Baker said. He sat down on the edge of Buford's cot. "Buford, do you believe in covenant prayer?"

"Yes, I do."

Baker opened the Bible that he had been reading. He held it so he could catch the light of morning coming in the downstairs front window. "I've been reading from the book of James."

"Is any sick among you? let him call for the elders of the church; and let them pray over him, anointing him with oil in the name of the Lord: And the prayer of faith shall save the sick, and the Lord shall raise him up; and if he have committed sins, they shall be forgiven him" (5:14-15).

Baker said, "Buford, will you help me anoint Eloise and pray for her? She's going to die unless God intervenes."

Buford was already up, pulling his pants and shirt on. "Do you have some oil?"

"I think there's some in the kitchen," Baker said.

"You go on upstairs. I'll get it," he said.

Baker, Buford, and several other missionaries and trusted Chinese friends were soon gathered, praying fervently. Then Baker dipped his forefinger into the oil and put it on Eloise's hot, sallow brow. Buford dipped his finger into the oil and did the same thing, rubbing gently. The others did likewise. They continued to pray, kneeling for a long time—claiming God's promise.

A commotion downstairs indicated that someone had come in. Buford got up and went down. It was the doctors. Neither Cauthen nor Nichols said anything about their experience.

Later in the day, Baker looked in the door of the bedroom and saw one of the women holding Eloise's head, trying to spoon into her mouth some broth that the doctors had recommended. She did not open her eyes.

The next afternoon, the doctors examined her again. They agreed. "She's turned the corner. She's going to make it."

Tears welled up in Cauthen's eyes. He thanked God quietly but fervently.

The roar of C-47s climbing into the sky above him reminded him that the airlift to remove civilians before the Japanese arrived was continuing. Obviously, Eloise was still in no shape to go; but he would worry about that later. He was going to be busy thanking God for the time being.

CHAPTER SEVEN

Odyssey Home

The third day after Eloise took a turn for the better, Chinese contingents—ragged, demoralized, and obviously the remnants of a defeated army—struggled through the streets of Kweilin. An army jeep drove up to the Cauthen door, and one of the captains said to Baker, "We can get you out tomorrow if your wife can make the trip."

Sharply aware of the deterioration in the military situation, Cauthen desperately wanted to get his wife and children out of Kweilin. And he knew Eloise needed additional medical help. But ringing in his ears was one doctor's comment two days before: "She'll arrive a corpse if you try to take her now."

"I don't know if she's able yet," he said. "The doctor will be here shortly, and I'll ask him if we can move her."

"Let me know," the captain said. "I am holding space for you on tomorrow's flight if you can make it. I can't guarantee how much longer the opportunity will exist." He disliked adding to the missionary's problems, but the situation was growing critical.

By that afternoon, it was obvious that Eloise was stronger. "Get ready to go," the doctor informed Cauthen. "We've got space for you and your family on a plane to Kunming tomorrow morning." Cauthen's face brightened. "We'll be ready," he said fervently, not even asking how Eloise was. The doctor's decision told him all he needed to know.

They had been getting ready to go on furlough before Eloise became sick. What few possessions they had acquired had been sold, and everything else was ready to pack. The two of them had planned the trip fairly systematically, including what the children would wear. Their major problem all along was getting to Kunming. From there, they could catch a CNAC (China National Aviation Corporation) flight to Calcutta. Meanwhile, they would be out of the direct line of Japanese advance.

The next morning when the army ambulance drove up, followed by a jeep loaded with airmen who wanted to help if they could, Chinese Christians packed the yard between the house and the wall. They watched quietly as the airmen went in. The two children came out carrying their luggage (or dragging it). One of the airmen held the door open as the others gingerly followed with a stretcher cradling Eloise. Her pale features and her thinness were accentuated by the bright sunlight. Several of the Chinese Christians caught their breath at the sight of her. Baker held an umbrella over her to shield her from the sun. As they stepped into the courtyard, the Chinese began to sing softly, "God Be with You Till We Meet Again." Cauthen noted that his tears were not the only ones in evidence.

As the airmen placed Eloise in the ambulance and the children in the jeep behind, Cauthen said good-bye to his Chinese friends and climbed into the jeep. He had no way of knowing that he was winding up an era in his life; he did know that despite the problems, it had included some of the best years of his life.

The plane was a typical Air Force evacuation plane with bucket seats on the sides and cargo bins in the middle. Toward the front of the plane, the cargo bin had been arranged for a stretcher, and Eloise was secured there. Two nurses had been assigned to tend her during the trip. Baker and the children were strapped into bucket seats. It was not a long trip, and the DC-3 soon touched down at Kunming Air Force Base. Cauthen breathed a sigh of relief. Such planes were shot down often. Airmen called them "sitting ducks." He was glad this duck was sitting on the gound.

As the rapid Japanese advance continued toward Kweilin, Baker and Eloise realized what might have happened had her sickness come a week later. They thanked God once again for deliverance. At the Air Force hospital, a short, stocky, black-haired nurse with a South Carolina accent was assigned to Eloise. When nurse and patient saw each other, they gasped and fell into each other's arms. She was Betty Gray, who had been a fellow missionary in North China. She had also left the area in 1941. Whereas they went to the Philippines, she returned to the States, joined the Army Nursing Corps, and slowly found her way back to China. The Cauthens could hardly believe the coincidence. With Betty taking care of Eloise at the Air Force hospital, Baker and the children went to a local China Inland Mission hostel. They were there three weeks. Each morning they observed the same ritual. They got up, ate a modest breakfast with their friends, and then caught a cab to the hospital, stopping to buy fresh flowers on the way.

All of them benefited from the better food. Cauthen weighed 120 pounds when they left Kweilin. He had contracted a digestive upset in language school in Peking that had never left him. Though it had not felled him, it was his "thorn in the flesh" during all those years. Once as he posed for a picture with missionaries Rex Ray and Robert Beddoe, a fellow missionary said, "We can entitle this one 'The Three Scarecrows.' "

When their three weeks in Kunming had passed, the doctor met Baker at Eloise's hospital door and said, "She's ready to go. We've booked her on an evacuation plane tomorrow that will take her to Calcutta on a slightly roundabout way. We're going to have to put in for an overnight in Assam at Jorhat. That way, the flight won't be too hard for her. You and your children can catch the CNAC plane to Calcutta and be ready for her when she gets there the next day." Cauthen thanked him profusely and soon completed the arrangements. The next day, they kissed Eloise good-bye as her stretcher was loaded on the plane. She was the only woman and the only civilian patient aboard. Eloise couldn't remember whether she was three racks up or two racks down in the specially constructed plane, but there was another rack a few inches above her nose.

As the Air Force ambulance plane lifted off the Kunming runway with its heavy load and began to climb toward the mountains of Assam, Cauthen and his two children stood by the runway, watching until it disappeared into the blue. When they could no longer see it, they walked back to the cab that would take them around to the CNAC terminal for their own departure. Little Ralph, holding on to one of his father's hands, limped noticeably but kept up gamely. Carolyn, now nearly seven years of age, held on to Cauthen's other hand and perhaps picked up her father's anxiety more readily than her younger brother. As the Japanese assault drew closer to the western airfields of Free China, danger of the daily flights over the hump being intercepted and shot down was increasing.

The hustle and bustle of their own preparations to board the CNAC flight brought merciful remission from that anxiety. Cauthen had carefully prepared the children for the ride, with the aid of Eloise's thinking. They were dressed in layers. Underneath was a sunsuit for the heat they had encountered in China, which they would experience on an even more fearsome scale when they landed in Calcutta. But because of the landing in Assam and because of the cold in the plane, he had them carefully layered so he could add for the cold and strip for the warmth.

The idea seemed to work well except for one thing. He hadn't planned on the two children getting airsick. Shortly after the plane climbed into the sky, he was holding airsick bags in one hand and trying to help the children add sweaters with the other. Three hours later, they landed in Assam at a small place called Ding Chin. There he heard that a plane had been shot down earlier in the week between Kunming and Jorhat. It didn't do anything to alleviate his anxiety.

Again the children's needs took precedence. Their airsickness came in waves on the second leg of the flight until they landed in Calcutta. There the heat was oppressive.

Cauthen stripped the children down to their sunsuits. With children and luggage in tow, he hailed a cab to the American Express Office, where he hoped to line up train reservations and accommodations for a trip into the mountains for a time of additional recuperation. When he described the situation to the American Express officer, he strongly urged Baker not to pursue that course. "That's a hard trip. The accommodations are not good, with the war and all. Besides, that's a hard trip for a well person. Your wife would not make it." Cauthen sighed. What was the next alternative? "I can get you an air-conditioned compartment on a train across India to Bombay. There you would have to take your chances on getting ship passage to the States. Most ships are swinging down south of Australia and then back up the South Pacific to San Francisco because of Japanese submarine activity. The closer we get to whipping the Nips, the meaner they seem to get."

Cauthen booked the air-conditioned compartment, realizing that having it was an act of God since such compartments were almost impossible to secure. The first of several letters given him by the commandant of the air base in Kweilin seemed to make the difference in his acquiring the compartment.

The next day, he and the children were at the air base waiting for the arrival of Eloise's ambulance plane.

There was no way to describe his feelings when, after the last patient was unloaded from the ambulance plane from Jorhat, it was obvious that Eloise had not been on it. Nor could anyone on the plane tell him why. "Did the plane from Kunming get to Jorhat the day before?"

"Oh, yes." No plane had been shot down yesterday. No other plane was due in today from Jorhat.

Perplexed but reassuring himself that it must simply be a matter of the number of people needing to be transferred, he took the children back to the hotel. To his chagrin, his digestive system gave way to one of the particular virulent disturbances prevalent in India. "I guess Chinese bugs and Indian bugs don't mix," he said to himself ruefully.

Both children sensed a problem, but they had been dealing with problems so long that they did not inquire. They kept their anxieties to themselves.

They went through their routine for two more days before they joyously recognized Eloise's frail figure propped up on her elbows on one of the stretchers being unloaded from an ambulance plane from Jorhat.

As soon as he got her situated in the hotel, he went back to the American Express officer. Could he work a miracle again? "Miracles come as you need them, don't they?" the officer grinned. "I've got the compartment again. Be down at the train station this afternoon, and you're all set. Furthermore, I've got your hotel space in Bombay still waiting for you. When you didn't go yesterday, I took a chance and held it for one more day."

"And a ship to the States?" Baker inquired hopefully. "No luck," the agent smiled. "But with your contacts with the Almighty, surely it won't be long." Gratefully, Cauthen thanked him and pursued the mechanics of getting his ailing wife, his children, and what little gear they had from the hotel to the station and onto the train. The air-conditioned compartment was a godsend, as were the supplies of canned goods Baker had been able to buy. It was obvious that the long trip across the back of the subcontinent of India in the heat would have devastated Eloise. Her weakness was still marked,

159

though each day brought new strength.

When his duties with the children subsided and Eloise dozed off into peaceful sleep, Cauthen looked at the countryside passing his window and marveled at God's provisions. He had a sense of being carried along as if angels were working on each problem that came up. The sense of deliverance that began with their departure from North China, which had been dramatically accentuated in his family's deliverance from the Philippines before the outbreak of the war, rose strongly in his consciousness again. In the midst of feelings of well-being, deliverance, and supernatural support, hardships seemed only details of the drama and never problems in themselves.

The passing countryside rapidly changed from rice fields and small villages to hills with an abundance of religiously protected skinny cows wandering amidst skinny people. Men in the area wore the white *dhoti* draped around body and legs to form a loose trouser. Women wore *saris*. Because of his studies in various religions of the world, Cauthen watched for telltale signs of temples, dress, and caste marks. His heart went out to the masses of people stretched across that subcontinent still largely ignorant of hope in Jesus Christ. At times, what he saw as the train crossed the countryside or stopped at frequent small stations moved him to tears— the outcasts and misfits of society, beggars, and children, some obviously suffering from hunger.

Those sights contrasted sharply with evidence of British colonialism with its pomp and tradition, neat gardens, and daily schedules. His abiding prayer was that the people of India might know Christ.

It was a grateful little family that finally settled into a hotel room in Bombay. Eloise, weakened by the trip, welcomed the rest. She offered no protest when Baker insisted on going directly to the harbor to see what transportation opportunities might exist.

At the port commander's office, he brought out the second of his letters from the Fourteenth Air Force commandant. The official was very gracious and said, "We will send you out on the first ship."

But the "first ship" was four weeks later. Wartime security required departure plans to be kept secret. Finally, a military ambulance took Eloise to the ship, where she was admitted to the sick bay. The children were assigned space with some Red Cross ladies, and Baker was assigned a bunk with the servicemen. The submarine menace was real, and everyone wore their life preservers or kept them by their sides.

As the ship pulled out into the Arabian Sea and began its long trip down the coast of the subcontinent, Cauthen waited for the seasickness that he expected the children to have. Instead, they prospered. The sea air was invigorating and the ship's atmosphere challenging.

Their ship was the *General Anderson*. With five-inch and pompom guns located fore and aft and on both lee and windward sides, it looked like a battleship to the kids. Daily the sailors staged gunnery practice to remind themselves and the passengers of potential danger. They also had daily lifeboat drills. It wasn't easy, but Cauthen managed to be assigned to the same boat as the children. Rules are easier to work with than exceptions. But with the mother in the sick bay, the officer of the deck finally made the exception.

Each day, Baker made Eloise a milk shake with powdered milk he had bought in Bombay and took it to her in the sick bay. This unheard-of luxury made a difference. Her health improved rapidly. One memorable day, after they left the safety of Australian waters and began the actual voyage across the Pacific, she was sitting on the bed when he came in with the milk shake. "I'm going to walk," she said. She needed help, but walk she did. The ship's doctor was amazed.

"People with what you've been through don't live, much less recover this fast."

"But there were hundreds of persons on both sides of the ocean praying for me," she said. "And my husband prayed for me." He looked at her curiously.

"Does that really make a difference?"

Well into the trip, Baker began to relax from his anxiety about the children going over the side. With Eloise obviously making progress, he was able to work on his own health. He walked regularly around the ship and noted to his satisfaction that the diarrhea that had plagued him for five years was beginning to let up.

Ever observing, he watched the sailors at their duties. The galley workers carefully weighted all of the garbage before they threw it overboard, to make sure that it would sink. "That's all the Nips need," one sailor told him. "They find a little garbage, and they

161

follow it like a trail until they get to their target. Then Zip! Bam! We're all in lifeboats. And they've got a way of handling that, too," he said knowingly.

Cauthen couldn't appreciate such reassurance. It was almost as bad as the lifeboat drills and the daily hammering of the pom-pom guns during gunnery practice. But Eloise's daily improvement more than made up for that anxiety. And the obvious improvement of the children's health under a regular schedule with good food lifted his hopes tremendously. As he dressed one morning, he realized that even he was gaining weight. "Nobody's going to feel sorry for you by the time you get to the States," Eloise said. "You're beginning to look prosperous again." He smiled. "I imagine I've got a long way to go."

Early one morning, he awoke to a realization that the ship had stopped. They were at anchor. Quickly he dressed the kids, took them to the rail, and pointed out the skyline of Los Angeles. They were home.

Eloise was able to walk ashore. She and the children rested on cots and enjoyed milk and sandwiches served by Red Cross workers as Baker contended with entry formalities. Then a Red Cross worker drove them to the hotel. Once again Baker was in the transportation-seeking business. And again there was a problem. Everybody turned him down with the excuse, "Don't you know there's a war on?" He didn't explain to them just how well he did know there was a war. Using his characteristic method, he sought out the top man and gave the last letter from the Fourteenth Air Force official in Kweilin to the district passenger manager of the Southern Pacific Railroad in Los Angeles. He got his train compartment to Houston, Texas.

A happy little family pressed faces against the train window as the verdant coastline of Los Angeles gave way to the high mountains of the Sierras. The mountains in turn gave way to the deserts that stretched on into Arizona before yielding to the southern Rockies. When they could see nothing but sagebrush, windmills, and telephone poles, Baker announced proudly to the children, "Now we're back in Texas."

He had wired from Los Angeles to Lufkin, to Richmond, and to Fort Worth, where Dr. and Mrs. Glass were living after repatriation. The Glasses journeyed immediately to Houston and notified other friends there.

When their train pulled into the Southern Pacific station in Houston, it was the tall figure of Dr. Glass that they spied first, standing alongside his wife, Jessie. Next to them, Cauthen recognized old friends from Fort Worth days, Doug Hudgins and his lovely wife. Pastor of the First Baptist Church, Houston, Texas, Doug had been telling his congregation stories about his friend Cauthen for a long time.

The travelers could hardly contain the warmth, excitement, and sense of well-being they felt. Eloise was able to walk from the train to the car, where they fixed up the backseat for her to lie down. Following a night in the Hudgins home they bade farewell to the Glasses, and Dr. and Mrs. Hudgins drove them up through the Piney Woods country of East Texas into the familiar environs of Angelina County and finally into the city limits of Lufkin, Texas. It had been just over five years since they left. Baker's mother and father greeted them with tears and smiles, questions and answers, hugs and prayers of praise.

Cauthen preached at the First Baptist Church the next Sunday. This was where he had found a Savior, had heard his call to preach, and had received his ordination for a task that he had no way of knowing at that time would lead him across the world. He realized that this congregation, some of their faces familiar, some unfamiliar, had prayed for him during all the harrowing months since he had last been here. Deeply moved, he preached with a special sense of anointing.

He said: "When we were in Kweilin preaching at the Air Force base one Sunday evening, a tough old sergeant rushed into the service and said, 'I'm sorry. We've got Japs coming in. You're going to have to get to the trenches.' The whole congregation filed out to slit trenches a few hundred yards away. There we all crouched—airmen and missionaries. Eloise and the children were with me. We peered up into the night and realized there were no stars, and we could see no moon. They were up there somewhere, but a blanket of clouds was blocking them from our sight. We could hear the drone of planes. An airman next to us asked, 'Are they Japs?' A veteran on the other side of us replied, 'If they are, there will be a stick of bombs to announce them in just a moment.' Then another one said, 'Those don't sound like Japs. They sound like ours.' As if to punctuate his remarks, lights began springing up from the air base, penetrating the darkened sky all around us. 'They are ours,' another one said excitedly. 'They're putting the lights up to bring our boys in.' "

Cauthen paused and looked at the congregation. "Right now I know how those boys felt," he said. "But around this world, there are people lost in the skies of their own sin and hopelessness. It's up to us to put the lights up and bring them in."

Part III

The Fray

That which is formed in the forge and fired in the furnace inevitably finds its ultimate meaning in the fray. And in the fray, that which came by heavenly design from the forge finds that the furnace was an indispensable prelude to that which follows.

Baker James Cauthen talks with a Thai family in front of the Baptist chapel in Prachinburi, Thailand (1962).

CHAPTER ONE

Destined for Leadership

Baker James Cauthen had not yet reached his thirty-fifth birthday when he emerged with his family from the furnace of his initial missionary term in China. He was deeply conscious of having been in the hands of a God who not only cared and provided for him and his own but who was actively leading him. Shortly after arriving in Lufkin, he wrote Maddry in Richmond:

"The Lord has greatly blessed us in the time that we've been gone. He has repeatedly shown us that his leadership is infinitely better than our planning. The sweetness of his presence has taken the bitterness out of many a cup. We return with hearts filled with gratitude, and we are praying that our again being in this country may have some value for the work of the kingdom."

Maddry's reply revealed how highly he regarded Cauthen and how emotionally involved he had become in the fortunes of the young pastor who had impressed him so much at the time of his appointment. He expressed concern over Ralph and his full recovery from polio as well as over Eloise's full recovery from her near-fatal illness.

But Maddry also revealed the grand plans he had for the young missionary. He sensed that Cauthen had charisma to fire the imagination and elicit the affection of Southern Baptists everywhere. He wrote:

"I want you to take a good long rest and get into shape because we shall want to use you in some of our missionary engagements and deputation work. Many brethren are calling for you for summer assemblies and camp work next summer. We want you to visit the seminaries and colleges. So let me urge you, therefore, that you do not tie yourself up with all the smaller engagements that will besiege you for fulfillment. Our board meets next week, and I'm sure we will take some definite action concerning the larger work we want you to do throughout the South."

Cauthen must have sensed the unique opportunity that was his. He did try to rest, and he tried to be with his family as they reacclimated themselves to their own homeland. A trip to New Orleans Baptist Hospital reassured him that Eloise would recover completely if she did not push herself too hard. The parents were told that Ralph's limp could be further corrected by exercise, and no surgery was recommended. As for Carolyn, she was a bright, excited first grader with no obvious residual effects from her mountaintop scrape with death or from the demands of the odyssey that had been theirs.

Both children let memories of caves and air raids, the hollow-eyed look of their mother fighting death, restricted diets, and all the sights and sounds of the Chinese scene recede into the background. Cauthen observed more than once as he watched the children quickly adjusting back to the States, "Children live blessedly in the present."

And he didn't have time to live too much in the past himself except as he recreated scenes from it in one stirring message after another before congregations large and small.

In the fall he spoke to the Baptist Student Union Convention in Abilene, Texas, and then went on to San Antonio to address the Texas Baptist General Convention. He captivated both groups with his fervent eloquence and the drama of his experiences. Dozens of young men and women, including pastors and their wives, responded to the call to seize the exciting new opportunity that Cauthen promised them the postwar world would bring.

One of the most moving of those early speaking opportunities for Cauthen occurred at Southwestern Seiminary, where the impact of his leaving five years before started a legend. When he stood before the student body and faculty in chapel, his urgent style freely unleashed by obvious acceptance, the result was electric. His successor as missions professor, Frank Means, had gone on to the Foreign Mission Board as promotions secretary, and a young professor from Tennessee named Cal Guy had taken the teaching post.

Guy says, "He held us in the palm of his hand. The authenticity of his message was obvious, and his ability to articulate the demands of the task was unlike anything we had ever heard before. The response was phenomenal."

Despite his demanding schedule, Cauthen watched the turn of world events carefully. During their long odyssey from Kweilin back to the States, a journey that had taken them from May until August, 1944, much had happened to portend the end of the war. The Allied landing in Normandy on D-Day, June 6, 1944, happened when they were crossing the Himalaya Mountains (or the "hump," as it was called). Paris was liberated just about the time they arrived back in Lufkin.

That fall, as Cauthen was preaching to the students in Abilene, MacArthur fulfilled his promise to return to the Philippines. American B-29s were already raiding Japan on a regular basis, and military planners were plotting the invasion of a small island called Iwo Jima and a larger one called Okinawa. Now as 1945 dawned, the American First Army had already pushed through to Germany, and the Battle of the Bulge was being heralded not only as a chapter of heroism on the part of the American forces but as the last hoorah of an exhausted Germany.

In January Cauthen finally sent in a statement of his losses in China, which M. T. Rankin had been requesting of him. Rankin himself was in the process of taking over Charles Maddry's job as executive secretary of the Board. Maddry, who had given himself to leading the Board from the brink of financial disaster through the years of war, was worn out. The big hulk of a man with a great heart stepped aside and let the veteran of Hong Kong's Stanley Prison Camp take over.

When Cauthen submitted the accounting of his losses to Rankin, he said:

"We received a rich personal blessing from the experience of parting with the things we took to China. I'm sure you understand thoroughly what I mean because you had the same experience. Our entire time during these war years in the Orient has been filled with new assurance of the dependability of the promises of God. It is good to believe a promise through faith; it's even better to have proved it through experience."

In replying, Rankin asked Cauthen to come to Richmond to the April Foreign Mission Board meeting to give a personal report of his experiences in West China. While there, Cauthen accepted an invitation from the renowned Dr. Theodore Adams to preach before the historic First Baptist Church in Richmond. Already an admirer of Adams, who was destined to become president of the Baptist World Alliance, Cauthen was humbled and awed by the opportunity. Whether the Richmond congregation was as stirred by the fervent young missionary hero as other congregations is doubtful. He was preaching in the context of a national tragedy.

President Franklin Roosevelt died in Warm Springs, Georgia, that very week; and the country, in shock, tried to sort out its feelings about the loss of the man who had led it so long. Though much uneasiness accompanied Harry Truman's taking over the presidency, the main feeling was one of loss. The American people did not have long to indulge their grief, however, because Allied armies pressed into Berlin proper a few days later. Headlines ballooned with news that Hitler had taken his own life. On the seventh of May, 1945, victory was achieved in Europe.

Events from that point on through the summer were a blur not only for the paripatetic Cauthen, going from church to church and summer assembly to summer assembly while trying to touch base with his family periodically, but for people around the world.

The United Nations charter was signed in San Francisco. Winston Churchill was voted out of office in England. Reports that the Nazis may have killed as many as 6,000,000 Jews were emerging from postwar Europe. Japanese *kamikaze* pilots terrorized American ships in futile last-ditch gestures. With victory in sight, life seemed more precious and death more tragic. News that an eight-square-mile piece of island in the Pacific had cost the lives of 25,849 Marines or that Okinawa had exacted 49,151 American lives was not easy to accept.

Perhaps that explains something. The American public did not react immediately with the kind of shock that it felt subsequently to news that came in August. Something called an atomic bomb had wiped out a Japanese city. A few days later mass annihilation was repeated at another place. The Hiroshima and Nagasaki bombings were now history. Things would never be the same again.

If Baker James Cauthen sensed the change, he didn't try to articulate it. He gave priority to mobilizing Southern Baptists to buy up the opportunities that would be theirs with the cessation of hostilities in the Orient.

He was invited to the Foreign Mission Board again in September to be a member of a Far East Advisory Committee. Rankin was planning an orderly return of missionaries to China and, hopefully, Japan. As the meeting closed and the missionaries, excited by the prospects and awed by the task, began to disperse, Rankin asked Cauthen to wait over for a day to discuss another matter.

As Cauthen settled in a chair before the desk of the Foreign Mission Board's executive secretary the next day, he had no idea what was to be discussed. But his regard for the man made exciting the thought that he would want to consult with him individually. Rankin was a veteran. He had served two terms as a missionary and since 1935 had been secretary for the Orient, a position he had taken at the relatively young age of forty. The thirty-five-year-old Cauthen was not prepared for Rankin's words.

"We want you to be the next secretary of the Orient, Baker." Because his memory is dominated by several things that took place a few days later, Cauthen's memory of the conversation that ensued includes little of the actual exchange. If he was aware of his own youth and his single term of service, as compared to the maturity and the long years of service of many of the missionaries that he would be leading, he did not mention it. His youth had long since become something that he took for granted, and it was not his way to measure himself with others in light of his age. If sharp notions about what ought to be done in the Orient welled up before him with the knowledge that now he could do something about it, he has never mentioned it. One abiding memory is a sense of humility at having been selected by Rankin and, as the secretary assured him, by many of the other missionaries Rankin had consulted.

On October 10 Rankin wired Cauthen in Lufkin, saying, "The Foreign Mission Board unanimously and heartily elected you."

Cauthen replied immediately with a telegram of his own from Houston, where he was preaching a revival:

"If God is leading this decision, he will supply wisdom and strength. It is with a deep sense of my own unworthiness but strong confidence in the sufficiency of his grace that I am ready to undertake this responsibility. Will be anticipating a letter from you."

On the eleventh, Rankin wrote in more detail and included a paragraph that stunned Cauthen:

"While you will be attached to the staff at the headquarters in

Richmond and your permanent headquarters will always be here, you will be expected to spend as much time on the field as you and the executive officers of the board may consider essential to the best interest of our work in the Orient. This matter will always be determined through consultation and as we proceed in the program of work."

Cauthen returned to Lufkin and shared his feelings with Eloise at length. He had said yes to a position that he thought he understood. Rankin had lived in the Orient and worked from a base in Shanghai before the war. Cauthen did not realize that anything had changed. He thought he was accepting a position in which he also would be going back to China, something that he had a deep, overwhelming, unshakeable conviction he must do. Eloise stood with him. "We must go back to China. You must share these feelings with Dr. Rankin."

The subsequent exchange of letters between the two men pictured two consummate diplomats at work in the most sensitive of negotiations.

In a letter dated October 17, Cauthen confessed to Rankin that he had responded to a post in which "I've had before my mind your splendid ministry as secretary of the Orient as a pattern aiding me to form a concept of the task."

He said bluntly that the necessity of living in Richmond rather than on the mission field gave him a "red light." He added:

"When I think of accepting a position which would take me out of the mission field and at the same time would—in my opinion— make me less useful to the Orient than I could be were I actually on the field, I am persuaded that such a step would be at variance with my own convictions."

Cauthen knew the man to whom he was writing. For the next two pages, he raised each counterargument as he anticipated Rankin might raise it; then he answered it. The thrust was that he could not accept the position if it meant staying in Richmond, but he would like to convince them that the position should involve the Orient secretary's living in the Orient and traveling back to the States from time to time. He said the cost would be no problem because the $5,600 salary they offered him in the Orient was presupposing that he would live in Richmond. If he were in the Orient, he could serve on a regular missionary's salary of $1800. The rest could be used for travel.

He pointed out the the family could handle the travel. But even more importantly, if they were in the Orient, Mrs. Cauthen could serve as a missionary. He agreed it would be wise for him to spend some time in Richmond before returning to the Orient. And he left open the door that at some time later he might be willing to locate permanently in Richmond. Finally he said:

"It may be that the board has already thought through this matter of the location of the Secretary for the Orient and has decided definitely that he must be in Richmond for the majority of his time and make only occasional visits to the field. If that decision is of the Lord, I'm sure that he will provide the man to fill the place. And in that case, since I do not feel impressed to leave the mission field, I will be happy to go back to China as a regular missionary."

Rankin's reply not only indicated faster United States mails in those days, but his keenly felt urgency of convincing the young Texas missionary that God had indeed selected him for this position. His letter was dated October 20. It suggested that they get together in El Dorado, Arkansas, on the twenty-sixth since it was not too far from where Cauthen would be preaching in Oklahoma and where he, Rankin, would be speaking. Moreover, he assured Cauthen that he had assumed Cauthen would want to be in China for a period after his introductory time in Richmond. And in other ways he slid with Cauthen to keep the matter open. He did make one strong point, administrator that he was:

"I do think that in accepting this position, it should be clear that you have been elected to a different position from that which I was first elected Secretary of the Orient. At that time, the position carried only field responsibility. Originally, I was not listed as an official of the Foreign Mission Board but rather as an official of the Field Administration. You will be an executive officer of the Foreign Mission Board and will be immediately responsible for the executive administration of the work in the Orient."

The conversation in El Dorado reassured both of them, and Rankin had evidently made further adjustments in his own mind.

The Cauthens made the trip to Richmond in January of 1946. Ice coated the streets when they got there. And once again, they were without winter clothes. For the first few weeks, all four were sick with assorted bronchial ailments. Eloise remembers ruefully, "It was as rough as ever Kweilin was."

Cauthen not only took on the task of Orient administration but busily prepared messages for the Baptist Radio and Television Commission's Baptist Hour. Just before he began taping that series, Rankin took him to the Southern Baptist Convention in Miami, the first at which Rankin would speak as the Foreign Mission Board's executive secretary. Not trusting his own eloquence, he asked Cauthen to speak also. Both men led a charge on Southern Baptists' emotions to solicit funds for relief and rehabilitation. Baptists gave over four million dollars for that purpose that year. It was a kind of thanks offering.

What were Cauthen's thoughts that night as he stood before the great congregation of Southern Baptists in their first postwar convention? The last time he had been before them was in 1939, when he and Eloise stood at the end of a line of fifteen missionaries as Maddry introduced him and then turned prophetically to the Convention and said, "We've caught quite a big fish this time."

Cauthen had honestly felt then that he was walking away from his single-minded ambitions as a young pastor in Angelina County. He had laid aside whatever aspirations he might have had for the kinds of pulpits for which he had trained himself. He had surrendered the opportunities that were multiplying before his increasingly effective eloquence and his growing reputation. He had laid that aside to bury his life in China in response to something far superior to any of the above—the will of God. And in China, he had experienced the hand of God and the reality of God's provision in a way that would undergird his walk the rest of his life.

But now, far from having left the limelight, he was in the middle of it. Far from having abandoned position and status, he was thrust into a place where both were accorded not reluctantly but with honor.

But—if Cauthen knew his heart that night as he prepared to stand before the Convention and lay upon their hearts the challenge of helping to rebuild a broken world in the name of Jesus Christ—nothing had changed. He would soon be taking his family back to China. The Lord had opened wider dimensions for him, but that was the Lord's business. Baker was still in God's hands, and he could trust him implicitly.

CHAPTER TWO

Return to the Orient

Bedecked in lightweight double-breasted summer suits with white shoes and sand-colored straw hats, Baker James Cauthen and M. Theron Rankin boarded a military plane, a Navy Amphibian, on the west coast in the summer of 1946. As they clambered into the vessel that was still equipped for its wartime submarine patrolling assignment, a sailor handed them "Mae West" life jackets and began to give them instructions on ditching the plane if necessary during their flight from the west coast to Pearl Harbor and the Hawaiian Islands.

"I don't know why we do this," he said. "We've never had a survivor yet when one of these things went down."

Rankin looked at Cauthen and grimaced. Cauthen forced a weak smile. "Nothing like a little bit of encouragement with which to start a long voyage," he remarked.

They were on their way back to the Orient. A bizarre request from the China Mission's secretary-treasurer, J. T. Williams, for ten thousand dollars to build a bamboo fence to put around a mission compound had served as the catalyst.

"Ten thousand dollars!" Rankin exclaimed. "You can buy all the bamboo in China for ten thousand dollars."

Cauthen had laughed. "Well, if inflation has continued at the rate it was going when I left Kweilin, that may not be a bad price by now."

"I've got to see for myself," Rankin replied.

Cauthen, quickly grabbing the opportunity, had said, "I'll go with you. Only I'll stay, and Eloise and the kids can come on after me. It will give us a good chance to see the situation together and to get me back on the field where I belong."

Rankin had sensed the area secretary's growing need to be back in China. He had preached himself back several times. Powerful messages on the Baptist Hour radio program and his stirring speech at the Southern Baptist Convention had moved many people, but Rankin knew that more than anything else it revealed Cauthen's own desire to be back in the Orient.

"With conditions changing so fast, I will be able to give the board the kind of firsthand judgment it needs for its decisions," Cauthen argued. "Furthermore, with air travel developing the way it is, I can get back from time to time to maintain the ties with the constituency that will be necessary for advance." Some board members in Richmond resisted because they wanted their secretaries based there. But Cauthen was persuasive; and, in general, they were in awe of the man whose legendary proportions had not suffered from his in-person appearance.

The flight to Pearl Harbor went without incident. After a brief visit with missionaries there, Rankin and Cauthen boarded still another military plane that would fly them to the island of Kwajalein in the Pacific. That the island would become world famous for an explosion of terror called the H-bomb was something that waited to be revealed by time. Right now, it was a speck in the Pacific where they could take a break and take on gasoline.

Shortly after they took off from Pearl Harbor, the pilot turned the ship over to the copilot and came back for a visit with his missionary hitchhikers. Suddenly he held up a hand to silence the conversation. "Listen," he said.

"I don't hear anything," Rankin said.

"Listen."

As if he had answered his own question, the pilot jumped up and ran back to the cockpit. In a minute the plane began a wide arc back toward Pearl Harbor. As Cauthen pressed his face against the window glass, he saw one of the engines windmill to a halt. The airman's skill, however, sharpened during wartime, brought them back safely to Pearl Harbor. Soon the engine was fixed, and they were on their way again. Hours later they had more trouble, but at dawn the pilot brought them down to a little postage stamp of a runway lined with white "gooney birds." The welcoming GIs whistled at the two stiff and weary Americans in white summer suits who climbed out to stretch themselves in the brilliant Pacific sunlight. They had time to do little more than that before the plane was refueled and on its way. Cauthen could hardly believe it when they landed at Shanghai just two days after leaving the American west coast. He predicted that overseas air transportation would revolutionize the mission task.

Cauthen left behind in the United States evidence of the rapid response of his mind to his new responsibilities. He had quickly formulated lines of direction. His convictions about the missionary task are revealed in a Baptist Hour speech in February, 1946, entitled "That the World May Know." His philosophy of missions and missionary strategy is revealed in a report to the board in April of 1946—his first to the full board as area secretary. And his grasp of the broad sweep of opportunity in the Orient is revealed in a hastily developed missions book called *Now Is the Day,* jointly edited by Cauthen, George W. Sadler, Everett Gill, Jr., Nan F. Weeks, and M. Theron Rankin.

The speech on the Baptist Hour, "That the World May Know," was delivered February 3, 1946. In its printed form, it was introduced by Dr. Louie D. Newton, then associate secretary of the Baptist World Alliance. Cauthen said, "The yearning of our Master's heart is that the world may know God." Taking his text from John 17:23, "I in them, and thou in me, that they may be perfected into one; that the world may know that thou didst send me; and lovest them, even as thou lovest me," he spoke vividly of the depth of his missionary convictions.

The logic of that conviction is revealed in statement after statement. For instance:

"To this end, he [Christ] suffered the cruel death of the cross. To this end, he commanded those who love him to go to the ends of the earth telling every mortal of redemption through his blood. To this end, many of his servants have left all to follow their Lord and in some dark corner of the world lay down their lives."

Cauthen's commitment to rally support behind those who had delivered themselves up to task wherever it might lead was already well formed. No one could represent the challenge of their efforts more graphically to the supporting constituency than could this man. The points of his sermon reveal his approach:

Number 1:   The world desperately needs to know God.
Number 2:   As the world turns to Christ in faith, it does know

God.

Number 3:   Inasmuch as the world desperately needs to know
    God and as it turns in faith to Christ does know God, we must
    today face Christ's challenge to do his will that the world may
    know God.

The sermon is developed logically and scripturally and is well
illustrated.

He opened with an experience that he and Eloise had "in a great
Chinese city."

"My wife and I were giving away leaflets and portions of the
Gospels. Presently, we saw a coolie resting on his rickshaw. As I
handed him a tract, I asked, 'Have you ever heard of the gospel of
Jesus?' "

" 'Jesus?' he queried. 'Who is he? Is he an American?' "

Pointing out that the Master was thinking of such in his prayer,
Cauthen used the Scriptures and his experiences in China to drive
his point home. Most illustrations were personal—his own experiences in China. In emphasizing what was to be a persistent recurring message through the years, he said, "Not merely must we pray
and give, but many of us must go." Then he followed it with a line
of repetitive statements typical of his preaching:

"It's not easy to leave loved ones, homeland, and golden opportunities which bid you stay.

"It's not easy to go to the dark places of the earth where you will
be a foreigner to all about you.

"It's not easy to take little ones into regions where they may be
imperiled by war and disease.

"It's not easy to bury your talents under a mass of foreign
customs, language, and limitations so that you actually become like
a grain of wheat falling to the ground to die.

"But if the Lord says, 'Go,' you must go."

It was autobiographical, but that was precisely its power.

In his first major report to the board, delivered on April 9, 1946,
Cauthen revealed his grasp of what had to be done in the Orient.
Always the preacher, he began with a sweep of what had happened
and climaxed with a moving transferance to the present.

"Now the guns of war have been silenced. The long-anticipated
postwar era has come into reality. There is a deep conviction

among all missionaries to the Orient that this new day has brought us to an hour of responsibility and opportunity which must challenge Southern Baptists vitally."

He then cited a number of things to underscore the timeliness of the hour:

"Number 1: In the Orient, there's a high tide of goodwill. Number 2: The sufferings of war have mellowed the hearts of people, making them hungry for a message of life and assurance. Number 3: Confidence in old religions has broken down. Number 4: Among the emerging opportunities for preaching, the radio offers China a new challenge. Number 5: This is a day for stressing the importance of the ministry of preaching in the mission field. We need missionaries of all types in the Orient—doctors, nurses, teachers—but above all, we need missionaries who are preachers."

He pointed out that the suffering in the Orient should be seen as a call to action, that the intellectual awakening developing in the Orient was equally constraining. He emphasized the opportunity for student work and missionary activity among students.

Then he developed his plan of action:

"As we face this new day in the Orient, it is the conviction of all of us, both in the Foreign Mission Board and to the last church in the Southern Baptist Convention, that just as rapidly as it is possible we should return every missionary to the field both in Japan and in China."

He spoke of the need to rehabilitate properties but pointed out:

"This war has taught us in the Orient that our best investments in a mission program are not in buildings and equipment, but are investments in human life. War can sweep away our investments in property in a matter of a few hours, but war with all of its horrors when it comes upon the Christian community is unable to stamp out among those people the light which they have come to know in Christ."

In this simple statement, Cauthen revealed an overriding missionary principle. In a subsequent paragraph, he was more specific: "The objective of mission always is to plant the gospel of Jesus Christ in an area, foster its development to maturity, and then see that work become self-supporting and independent."

He urged a new relationship to the Chinese in which the burden of administration "will be lifted from the shoulders of the missionaries and will be placed on the Chinese themselves."

Cauthen correctly sensed the tide of nationalism and suggested that the board cast its lot with that spirit.

In the closing paragraphs, he identified himself as a missionary:

"Those of us who are missionaries are deeply convinced that whatever may be the immediate costs of travel, they will be justified by keeping Southern Baptists and the Baptists of the Orient so closely united in understanding and brotherhood that our hearts will beat as one in this day of unusual challenge."

Thus Cauthen got in some final licks about his decision to live overseas and commute back and forth as necessary to keep Baptists informed.

The book *Now Is the Day,* published by Broadman Press, was written prior to the open outbreak of war in China between Nationalists and Communists. Cauthen's contributions reveal cautious optimism in the face of uncertain signs:

"It is true that at the time of this writing China is yet divided into two hostile camps, one supporting the national government and the other leaders of Communism. None can minimize the seriousness of this internal situation . . . . Facing the issue of Communism is causing the people to think of the destiny of their whole nation rather than the problems of isolated sections. It may be said, therefore, that the war has done much to stimulate national unity in China" (p. 16).

Prophetically, he wrote:

"The Orient is yet in turmoil; issues are not settled; but it is definite that in the days which lie ahead, this great area of the world will not be content to continue in backwardness, ignorance, poverty, and subservience" (p. 19).

In the book, as in his board report, he urged new efforts to reach university students. Again he urged a partnership with national Christians.

It was almost as if Cauthen were urging his fellow missionaries to lay aside the administrative repsonsibility of churches and institutions that had been theirs. He wanted these to be turned over to the nationals in order that the missionaries might get on with their prime task, which was witnessing to Jesus Christ and preaching.

While the work he was presiding over was limited to Japan and China, Cauthen was deeply aware of the Orient's broad possibilities.

"And what shall we say of the other great lands of the Orient? India, with nearly 400 million people, with all her pathetic burdens and tragedies, is a land wherein we Southern Baptists have not one single missionary" (p. 30).

He undoubtedly remembered his long trek with his ailing wife and small children across the Indian subcontinent two years before. That was the only country he mentioned by way of specific opportunity, though including the others by implication.

What his thoughts lacked in profundity at this stage, they more than made up for in intensity. But they indicate that as he arrived in Shanghai in the summer of 1946 and took up his office as area secretary for the Orient, he knew what he needed to do.

CHAPTER THREE

Disregarding the Clouds

Lucy Smith straightened up from the table on which she was sorting manifests of missionary goods in transit. As she looked around, she decided the Foreign Mission Board's Orient office in Shanghai was beginning to take on some semblance of order again.

After spending the war years at home, she had returned to Shanghai late in 1945 to find the place a shambles. Only the efficient Eurasian Elizabeth Ward made it possible to reassemble things. Elizabeth had worked in the office prior to the war, had been interned by the Japanese during the war, and had walked straight from the internment camp to the office. Not having heard that Dr. Theron Rankin had become the executive secretary of the Foreign Mission Board, she had been expecting him back as the area secretary. Lucy brought her the news that a man named Baker James Cauthen was the new area secretary. Elizabeth remembered the smallish, slender missionary from Shantung who had gone to Free China just before Pearl Harbor. His fiery preaching was even then being talked about. But to her Chinese way of thinking, he seemed awfully young to be area secretary. "Dr. Rankin is quite excited about his becoming area secretary," Lucy said, sensing her concern. "And he and Dr. Rankin will be coming soon."

Now as Lucy looked around the office that she and Elizabeth had reconstructed, she observed that Rankin and Cauthen would have a reasonably orderly place in which to work when they arrived. As she looked out from the eight-story True Light building on Yuen Ming Yuen Road, which also housed the Chinese Baptist Publication Society, it seemed to her that nothing had changed despite the war. But she knew that everything had changed. Listening to the rumblings from North China and the ominous signs that the Communists were daily growing stronger, she wondered if more change was just around the corner.

From the window she saw two rumpled, unshaven men dismount from rickshaws on the street below and start in. She recognized the familiar amble of Theron Rankin at once.

A few minutes later she threw open the office door and said, "Now you two are a sight!" Both men were disheveled. Their spiffy white suits were rumpled and soiled. Despite the August heat, both were wearing overcoats stuffed with things they had been asked to bring in for various missionaries.

"I can't believe this office," Rankin said appreciatively. "It's as if there had been no war." Lucy said, "Well, there has been! But thank Elizabeth Ward for the office."

Rankin turned to Cauthen. "Well, this will be your office. And with Lucy and Elizabeth here, you can't go wrong."

The next day, Baker James Cauthen sat down with Lucy Smith and discussed her role in the office. Lucy had been Rankin's loyal right hand for many years, and there was a little awkwardness. Cauthen sought to break the ice. Lucy quickly put him at ease. She recognized the difference between the two men at once; but, as she said to Cauthen, "I came out as a missionary, and I can do whatever I'm supposed to do." Rankin had confided in her a great deal, but Cauthen already had a reputation for being very private. They would be radically different experiences, she decided. But she could handle that also.

The next day Rankin and Cauthen began to meet with the many missionaries who were coming into Shanghai in preparation for redeployment. Cauthen had written some of them in the spring and counseled with them regarding their return to China.

On the first of September, Lucy Smith arranged transportation for Rankin and Cauthen to travel through Central China to visit abandoned stations and review what needed to be done to rehabilitate mission properties. They planned to go as far south as Canton and then to return to Shanghai and go up north. The trip north was in doubt because of the Communist threat there, but missionaries who had already returned to that area desperately wanted Cauthen and Rankin to come.

Before they left, Cauthen had decided he was going to enjoy working with the efficient and good-humored Lucy Smith and the small, demure, British-accented Elizabeth Ward.

Lucy was a graduate of Oklahoma Baptist University and Southern Baptist Theological Seminary. She had graduated from Southern the same year Cauthen began Southwestern. But since that year was in the middle of the depression and the Foreign Mission Board did not have money to send her to the mission field, she had worked at the Olivet Baptist Church in Oklahoma City until she was appointed in 1936. While at Olivet, she met Eloise Glass. Lucy was in China when she heard that old Dr. Glass's daughter had married a brilliant young preacher named Cauthen.

Cauthen and Rankin's trip went well but was a sobering experience. For one thing, they found the highly regarded missionary Eugene Hill in Canton severely emaciated due to the recurrence of a physical ailment he had incurred during the Japanese occupation. The 220-pound Hill was weighing in at less than 160 pounds when he greeted the shocked pair of administrators. Cauthen took immediate steps to get medical help for Hill, and Rankin noted with satisfaction that the young man could act with dispatch.

By the time Cauthen and Rankin returned to Shanghai, Cauthen thought he knew what needed to be done. This was a part of God's gift to the man. He could take the measure of things quickly. He could ask the penetrating question, isolate the key facts, organize the relevant information, and structure necessary action.

Cauthen shared his three major goals with Rankin even before the executive secretary returned to the United States: "(1) We need to redeploy our missionaries as quickly as possible. (2) We must rehabilitate the properties that relate to our work, whether pastors' homes, church buildings, or schools. (3) We must move out in a massive relief program to people suffering as we have seen in Honan." Rankin knew that the Orient missions were in good hands.

Cauthen began catching up on correspondence that had accumulated. Most of it related either to returning missionaries—where they would serve, where they would live, and so forth—or Chinese requests to resume work that had ceased during the latter years of the war. There was a lot of mission business. He found himself grappling with tasks ranging all the way from import fees to building contracts in an inflationary economy. Much of his time was spent comforting men who, with great anxiety about the separation, were returning to the mission field ahead of their families.

Cauthen drew on his own experiences here. "It always helped me to realize that as much as I cared for them, God cared for them even more. I could trust them in his hands, for he was capable and caring even more than I."

Cauthen realized the sharp pain of separation himself until the S. S. *General Meigs* docked in Shanghai in late September of 1946. Eloise, Ralph, and Carolyn flew into his arms. The little family was back together again on what increasingly seemed to be native soil—China.

Shanghai, incredibly crowded, teemed with five million people in 1946. The place where the Cauthens took up residence on Fu Shing Lu, next door to the China Mission treasurer J. T. Williams, was five miles from the mission's True Light office building. The Cauthens had a car, but it was almost useless in the crowded streets. They took rickshaws wherever they went. Even then, traffic jams of rickshaws, carts, bicycles, and autos were almost overwhelming.

Eloise enrolled Ralph and Carolyn, now respectively eight and nine years old, in the Shanghai American School run by the American community. That helped make the adjustment back to China much easier for the two. They had largely lost their language capability during the two years away. Eloise taught in one of the schools, helped Lucy and Elizabeth prepare for the returning missionaries, entertained them during their time in Shanghai until they could be redeployed, and did whatever else needed to be done. It was a good year.

Particularly exciting for Cauthen was the opening of the All-China Seminary in Shanghai. The dream of such a seminary had brough him to China seven years before. Now it was a reality under the leadership of Dr. Charles Culpepper, with whom Cauthen had been briefly associated in Hwanghsien before their evacuation in 1941.

Late in the fall, Cauthen held a revival meeting at one of the schools in the interior and stood back in surprise when over three hundred students made professions of faith. Missionaries and Chinese pastors alike were overjoyed. The power of this preacher and his ability to reach people of all cultures in the strength of God's Spirit amazed them. For Cauthen, it was evidence of the dramatic new day in China and the desperate need to buy up the opportunity while it existed. Though he tried to ignore a red haze on the northern horizon, in his peripheral vision he could see and hear the rumblings of the Communist threat.

Baker and Eloise spent New Year's Eve, 1946, at the docks greeting the S. S. *Marine Lynx*. It carried a load of returning missionaries to be processed, cared for, and sent out to the stations waiting for them.

The year 1947 seemed to wrap up in a strange and variegated package all that has ever been present in mission work at any time anywhere. But this time it was compressed into a single year. Cauthen and his associates spent hours at docks and in customs offices trying to get through red tape. Government conditions were chaotic because of rampant inflation and civil war pressures in North China from the Communists.

Missionaries who had been evacuated during the war years returned. Stations were reopened, but buildings were in bad condition. Money was needed for a hundred different projects. Cauthen answered an unending stream of correspondence as the returning missionaries assessed the situation and fired back to Shanghai requests for money. Many Chinese workers were on the verge of starvation in some areas, due either to discrimination because of their Christian convictions or to the general status of things where they lived.

Buildings had been stripped of bricks and rocks, leaving only bare walls. Window and door frames were gone. Cauthen patiently dealt with all requests. He had a keen sense of the implications of a problem. He also had a remarkable ability to grasp a workable alternative. He could say no, but he obviously hated saying it. Yet when any matter had long-range implications, he was not afraid to deal with it firmly. But his ingenious mind was always looking for other ways in which to meet the need.

In the spring he broke away from administrative tasks to go to Yangchow for a revival meeting. It became more than that. Hundreds of people made professions of faith in Jesus Christ. Missionaries were inundated with opportunities generated by the response.

Right after that Cauthen returned to Canton, where he visited with Eugene Hill, now recovered from his illness of the year before. The difference in South China, where mission work seemed to have less chaos with which to contend, was sharp. Much encour-

Dr. and Mrs. Cauthen greet guests during the missionary lawn party at
Ridgecrest, North Carolina.

aged, Cauthen returned to Shanghai to find both Eloise and Ralph in the hospital.

They weren't the only ones. Epidemic fevers and influenzas struck many in the mission. With the congregation of large numbers of missionaries in Shanghai being processed before they could move on to the interior, caring for the sick rivaled the paperwork.

One of Cauthen's special concerns was the North China Mission, where he had begun his own missionary labors eight years earlier. Of the eight stations in that area five were closed, either because of Communist control there or because of being too near the fighting to be safe. Three other stations were open, but news coming out of parts of North China was truly scary.

John Abernathy was detained by Communists when he tried to move a relief train sponsored by the American government into a beleaguered city. After his dealings with the Communists, he wrote Cauthen: "The Communists want all or nothing, and they don't intend to get nothing."

The ambiguities were at times overwhelming. In the midst of his effort to settle returning missionaries in 1947, Cauthen had to help evacuate the Lawtons, the Yocums, the Fielders, the Harrises, and Harriet King from Interior China. The only good thing about it was that it allowed him to relocate the Lawtons in Kweilin, where so much of his heart had been planted during the war. They began to rebuild the hospital that was there—a dream Cauthen had long nourished.

Just when the threat of the Communist tide looked as if it would engulf the whole area, it began to recede again. While American negotiators worked feverishly to secure a coalition between Chinese Communists and Nationalists, Cauthen used the lull to make a trip to Japan. There he met Edwin Dozier, already a missionary legend. Dozier, born in Japan, was the son of pioneer missionaries, the C. K. Doziers. He had been the last missionary to leave Japan and the first to return.

Baptist churches in Japan were forced by government pressure during the war into what was called a *kyodan* or United Christian Church. Actually intended to allow the government to control Christian activities, it was administered under the guise of ecumenicity. Baptists, feeling their cherished freedom and their desire to avoid church-state entanglements threatened by the relationship, pulled away. Even as Cauthen arrived to consult with Dozier, sixteen Baptist churches were forming the Japanese Baptist Convention and dreaming of efforts to evangelize Japan. Their dreams were almost laughable when compared to their numbers, but totally realistic when compared to their faith.

For Cauthen it was a good trip. Before, he had seen only two kinds of Japanese—the haughty conquerors and the defeated who were still in China at the close of the war. In Japan he found people determined to put war behind them. They had had too much for too long. Even the devastation wrought at Hiroshima and Nagasaki did not dampen their spirit. He wrote the Foreign Mission Board to prepare a large number of new missionaries to move into Japan as soon as possible.

In September Cauthen and his friend Charles Culpepper left Shanghai on a sentimental but important journey into Northwest China. It was sentimental in that they were going to review the work of a Chinese doctor, Abraham Hsu—the same Dr. Hsu who, in 1941, had traveled with them and Dr. Beddoe into Free China. He had moved on into Northwest China. There, despite tremendous hardships, he and his family, in obedience to what they considered a deep sense of God's leadership, had succeeded in establishing a medical work. Taking an old temple dedicated to an idol known as the King of Death, they had transformed it into a church, a school, and a hospital.

This frontier mission work, as the Chinese called it, highlighted youth meetings and rallies. Cauthen wrote the board, "As Judson's going to Burma stirred American Baptists into action, the going of Dr. Hsu and his fellow workers has stimulated the Baptists of China."

The trip was a hard one for both men and took many days. But when they finally embraced Hsu and saw his work, they decided it was more than worthwhile. Their return journey made the inbound trip look like a piece of cake.

Heavy rains had inundated the countryside; and the Yellow River, known as China's Sorrow, was making a mockery of her banks. When the buses could go no further, Cauthen and Culpepper stood on the banks of the swollen river viewing a landslide that workers convinced them would take at least two weeks to clear. They wondered what they would do.

Cauthen, due to connect on another trip out of Shanghai, was deeply distressed by the situation. He had to reassure himself that Hsu's excitement at seeing them and the opportunity to preach and see eight more people added to the little church was worth more than his travel plans.

As he mulled over the matter, Culpepper walked over to the riverbank. "Cauthen, come here!" he called.

Baker walked over to join the missionary teacher. "Look there!" Culpepper exclaimed, pointing to the river.

There Cauthen watched as *Yang pi fa-tzes*—which were nothing more than rafts made of goatskins blown up with air and attached to bamboo strips—were cruising down the river with piles of melons on top of them. Standing on top of the melons, coolies guided them down the river to the market with long sticks.

Cauthen missed the point. "It's quite a sight, isn't it?"

"Now look there," Culpepper said, pointing to the road where four coolies, holding their empty *Yang pi fa-tzes* on top of their heads, were journeying back upriver after disposing of their melons.

Then Cauthen got the point, but he wasn't sure he was glad. "You'd do that?" he asked Culpepper.

Culpepper smiled. "If you would, I would."

Cauthen grinned. "Let's go."

They gave the coolies five dollars, tied four of the rafts together, and piled their luggage on top. With one coolie to keep the jerry-built operation from foundering, they climbed on.

The two men like to point out now that they made forty miles in four hours without a wrinkle or a spot and climbed on the C-47 flight out of Lanchow's dirt strip right on time for their flight to Shanghai. It was a trip both men remember not only for the uniqueness of the trek but for the remarkable courage and example of Dr. Hsu.

Cauthen returned to Shanghai this time to find his family well, and he thanked God. Other news brought concern. Word had come that a faithful layman from Hwanghsien, with whom Cauthen had talked only a few weeks before in a special meeting in Tsingtao, had been tortured to death by Communists who took over the area around his home. The Red specter once again threw sobering shadows across the excitement of reestablishing the work.

Other news came from Theron Rankin. He and several of the other members of the Foreign Mission Board management had gone to Petersburg, Virginia, for a conference where they prayed and became convinced that they should place before Southern Baptists a brave new Advance Program. Rankin wired Cauthen that he wanted him to come home in April of 1948 to help complete the drafting of the program and to help lace it before Southern Baptists at the 1948 Convention. Rankin wrote:

"The time has come for us to challenge Southern Baptists with the outline of a program of world missions commensurate with the faith that six million Baptists profess and with the potential resources which we unquestionably possess. Such a program, even in minimum outline, will be so vastly larger than anything we have ever seriously contemplated that it will be startling. Even so, the time has come for us to hold that kind of program up before our people."

Cauthen's spirit responded enthusiastically. That was precisely the way he was feeling. During the months he spent advancing on one front while evacuating on the other, he had often quoted the French general Marshall Foch. Foch had reported during World War I, "Our right flank is broken; our left flank is retreating; but we are attacking with the center."

In a letter to a missionary in one of the disturbed areas, Cauthen wrote, "In the midst of these disturbances, we must simply go on working for the Lord. One of the Scriptures that helps me a great deal reads: 'He that regardeth the clouds will not sow, and he that regardeth the winds will not reap.' "

He added, "We could easily see enough in the disturbed conditions of China to cause us to become so discouraged that we feel there's no use to carry on. We must, however, keep our eyes on the Lord Jesus as he walks on water, and we will have strength for the days."

CHAPTER FOUR

The Red Tide

An exhausted Baker James Cauthen boarded a Pan American plane for the long flight back to the United States in the spring of 1948. The early months of the year had not been kind to mission work in China. Inflation shot out of all bounds. One missionary sent two refugee children of a Chinese pastor on a plane to Shanghai, the ticket to be paid by the area office. The ticket came to twelve million Chinese dollars.

Cauthen wrote one of the tersest letters of his career, leaving the missionary no doubt that he had not only exceeded his authority but had placed himself in a difficult position. "What will you say to the rest of the people there who want to escape Communist hands?" Cauthen asked. "And what shall we do with the requests that have been waiting for that money?" he added. Typically, he followed it up with a more gracious letter, which came like a soothing ointment to the missionary, who realized all too well that he had acted with impropriety. Cauthen knew that the tension of the times had authored the man's action. This mixture of firmness and forgiveness in his administrative makeup was growing stronger day by day.

News that five missionaries had been killed in North China in January heightened anxieties. Three were Lutheran missionaries shot by so-called bandits that most people felt were Communist soldiers penetrating Nationalist positions. A single woman with the China Inland Mission had been beaten to death by a marauding Communist band in her home, and another missionary was killed by the explosion of a hand grenade thrown into her apartment by Red guerillas.

Cauthen had relayed to Southern Baptist missionaries advice from the American Consul that interior China missionaries evacuate, then had helped relocate dozens of the missionaries who came out.

He continued to project plans to move into Japan and looked longingly at Okinawa and the island of Taiwan. Here many Chinese Nationalists were already settling as they watched their own government's power to stand off the Communists deteriorate.

On the flight back to the United States, as he alternately slept and jotted down notes for his return, Cauthen allowed his thoughts to turn to what was before him. Rankin's Advance Program was taking shape. Cauthen had suggested possibilities of advance into Singapore, the Philippines, Indonesia, Thailand. If God was closing doors in China, maybe he wanted to open doors somewhere else.

The United States to which Cauthen was flying was busy rehashing the war on one hand and plowing new ground on another. Americans were reading Winston Churchill's *The Gathering Storm* and Dwight D. Eisenhower's *Crusade in Europe*. They were also reading Norman Mailer's *The Naked and the Dead* and Erwin Shaw's *The Young Lions* and pondering the difference between the points of view.

They were going to the movies to see *The Treasure of Sierra Madre* with Humphrey Bogart and *Snake Pit* with Olivia de Havilland. They continued to celebrate the age of heroism with *Battle Ground* and *The Sands of Iwo Jima*.

Americans had bought the so-called Truman Doctrine of the containment of Communism, which they now saw as a pseudoreligion. They were frustrated by their inability to contain it in China—that is, when they thought of China at all. They seemed ready to dump Truman; Dewey was standing in the wings, and everybody said nothing could stop him. New cars were rolling off assembly lines at General Motors, Ford, and Chrysler. Housing developments were going up all over the nation. Cauthen prayed that Rankin would be able to get the attention of Southern Baptists, caught up in this milieu of activity, with the equivalent of a religious Marshall plan. He knew it would not be easy.

Cauthen's stateside sojourn was a whirlwind of activities. First he went to Richmond and worked with Rankin and the Board's other administrative secretaries in completing the draft of the Foreign Mission Board's Program of Advance. Succinctly, the objectives were (1) to strengthen the work in nineteen countries where Southern Baptists were already at work and in six others where they were helping through resources, (2) to open additional strategic centers, (3) to support centers and projects undertaken by "native Baptist conventions," and (4) to increase resources and personnel toward a missionary staff of 1,750 and an operating budget including capital of ten million dollars.

In Memphis in May of 1948, under Rankin's leadership, the Advance Program was laid before Southern Baptists. Part of it included a commitment by Cauthen to the missionaries and nationals in Japan to raise the number of missionaries in that country from its present handful to one hundred by the end of 1950—an almost unheard-of escalation.

The Convention responded not only by promising, through its Executive Committee, 50 percent of its proposed budget for Foreign Missions, but an Advance section to go 100 percent to Foreign Missions. The Board now had a personnel secretary, Samuel Maddox, with whom Cauthen conferred. Maddox and an associate, Edna Frances Dawkins, promised to do everything they could to process and recruit workers for the Orient despite the turmoil going on there.

Cauthen went from Memphis to Fort Worth, where he spoke in chapel at Southwestern Seminary and enjoyed the hospitality of his friends Bill and Genevieve Howse.

The seminarians heard his stories of believers' heroism in the face of Communist atrocities with awe and a fervent desire to be a part of a Christian response. Cauthen's call to advance in the midst of the kind of discouragements going on in North China was compelling and contagious.

He was so "high" after these three stops—Richmond, Memphis, and Fort Worth—that by the time he made the long journey back to the Orient and reached Shanghai, the bottom fell out. For three days he could hardly get out of the bed. He didn't know whether he was sick, depressed, or worn out. But on the fourth day a new crisis in Honan called him back to the office, and the challenge of events did what his own will had not been able to do—restored his energies.

In August he backed Bertha Smith in relocating on the island of Taiwan. And there in her home a small Baptist church was organized at the end of the summer. It was to signify one of the most dramatic evangelistic efforts in the history of the Orient. The little woman—who later told her story in an autobiography, *Go Home and Tell*–drew on her own experiences in the Shantung revival and the spiritual renewal that had been hers there. Then she let God light another fire through her.

Cauthen needed that kind of victory. In November the Communists opened up a new offensive, threatening to take all Manchuria and then move on to Peking. Winston Crawley wrote from the Peking language school on behalf of the missionaries there that after counsel with the American Consul, they felt Cauthen should send a plane for them. Crawley asked whether, if "the Lutheran plane" were available, it could be sent directly to Peking with advance assurance that it could land.

Cauthen replied:

"We advise all our missionaries to return to Shanghai now. Can send Lutheran plane on 8th and 9th. Capacity six thousand pounds per trip including passengers. Planning two trips if necessary. Can group be ready? Are two trips needed? Wire reply. Cauthen."

And so it went, first Peking and then one station after another. Missionaries began to arrive by plane, by bus, by riverboat, by gunboat, and by army and navy conveyances. Cauthen and his colleagues moved the evacuated missionaries south to Canton and Hong Kong. The language students were sent to the Philippines. Wives and children and men who were due furloughs or who were ill were returned to the States.

At times Cauthen felt like a would-be Lone Ranger trying to snatch people out of the jaws of disaster. There was always tension, and there were always questions. "Will we fail? Will we be too late?" Somehow, in the providence of God, they always made it.

In between, he found time to go to Japan. First he went to Hiroshima for the dedication of a church constructed with gifts from the Lottie Moon Christmas Offering as a response to the destruction wrought there by the atomic bomb. Then he went into North Kyushu, where he preached at a number of meetings sponsored by the Japanese Baptist Convention. Despite having to hear through an interpreter, 250 people made professions of faith during those days, to the astonishment of the Japanese. Generally speaking, Cauthen was told, they were reluctant even to extend an invitation because of potential "face loss." Cauthen grinned. "I don't have that problem."

At the close of the preaching mission, Cauthen and Ed Dozier crossed the Japanese Sea to Korea. The trip came about in a most unusual way. The Foreign Mission Board received a letter from a group of Korean Christians who said they didn't know much about Baptists, but what they knew made them think they were Baptists; and they wanted to talk to a Baptist missionary.

Cauthen met the group in Seoul and found out that they were the product of the dedicated work of an American missionary named Malcolm C. Fenwick. Sponsored by a Boston church pastored by A. J. Gordon, he had begun an independent work in Korea at the turn of the century.

Cauthen and Dozier came away awed by their contact. The Christians they visited had survived twenty years of Japanese occupation of Korea at a great cost and with many martyrs. Cauthen said talking to them was like "seeing a people walk into the light, blinking."

Because many of those people spoke Japanese as a result of the long occupation, Dozier attempted to translate as Cauthen spoke. One of the Korean men stood up and told them how much Koreans objected to having to speak in Japanese. Another volunteered the information that he spoke Chinese. The result was that Cauthen asked the dislocated John Abernathys, who had been driven out of Shantung by the Communists, to relocate in Seoul in early 1950 to begin a new work there.

At the end of the year, Cauthen sent a report to the board summing up the philosophy he was basing his actions on during the turmoil in China:

"Southern Baptist can not guarantee that Communism will not overrun China. We can not guarantee that we will be able to reenter areas that we have formerly served till after a long time has passed. We can, however, have a feeling of satisfaction that we are seeking with God's help to seize the opportunities for his kingdom's progress in China today even in the midst of great difficulties. We missionaries remember that God foresaw these problems before he ever brought us to the mission field. The presence of problems is a challenge to our faith and an occasion of rededication to the task to which he has assigned us. We urge the board to remember us in

196

prayer, but do not let unnecessary anxiety fill your hearts as we are confident that the Lord is here to give his guidance every step of the way."

Baker James Cauthen was experiencing in the midst of this a unique spiritual blessing. Dependent every day and in every way upon the Lord as never before, he found the Lord meeting his needs. He testified in a December, 1948, report to the board:

"We have felt in these days of crisis an unusual peace and joy. I personally have been lifted in my spirit in a manner most blessed. We can only account for this by the fact that not merely are we lifting our hearts to God in prayer and placing our simple trust in a living Lord, but you and thousands of our Baptist friends at home are remembering us daily at the throne of grace."

In a report to Rankin, he voiced the same kind of faith in light of the devastating turn of events in China:

"Whatever the future holds, we are grateful for the work which has been accomplished in the past three years. Should the iron curtain drop down over large areas of China, our Baptist brethren in those sections could face an indefinite period of working under most difficult conditions. They are better equipped to carry on that work as a result of the accomplishment of these three years . . . . Having made these efforts as unto God, we commit them in faith to our Lord to bear their full fruit in this land."

From a total of nearly 200 missionaries in China at the beginning of 1948, Cauthen had 106 missionaries and 22 children in China at the end of the year, with 24 missionaries and 18 children in the Philippines. Most of the missionaries were in still-untroubled Central and South China. Only one missionary was left in the interior of China and seven in North China.

In January of 1949, the area office monitored English-speaking news radio broadcasts that told of a big battle above Nanking. Over one million men were ultimately locked in combat in that battle. The result devastated the remaining hopes of missionaries. The Nationalists were all but wiped out, and the Reds began a rapid move into the rest of China that spring.

The most persistent difficulty for most of the missionaries, however, was not the battle but the effort to survive inflation. A currency adopted by the Chinese government in August of 1948 had devalued, according to Cauthen's calculations in a March 1949 report to the board. His figures estimated that it would require 8,850,000 Chinese dollars to buy 1 American dollar at the official rate of exchange.

At that point, Cauthen was encouraged by evidences of Communist toleration for Christian activities in the areas they had taken over. Wise heads who had dealt with the Communists through the years cautioned, however, "Don't let their toleration throw you. It's strictly public relations. When they have everything they want, they will turn the screw."

The evacuation problem was getting personal. Cauthen, Frank Connely, and Lucy Smith talked at length about what would happen if the Communists came as far as Shanghai.

Lucy remembers Cauthen as ever optimistic. "They may not make it. The government might regroup and hold," he would say. When they didn't he would simply smile and say, "We're going to keep hoping for the best." When that didn't come, he would say, "We'll make the best out of what comes."

For Lucy and some of the others who wanted him to be more realistic, this was frustrating. On the other hand, no one could fault his ability to adapt to the situation as rapidly as it changed. Now as he talked with Frank Connely and Lucy, their problem was, "Where should the area office be? If Shanghai is taken by the Communists and we cannot travel in and out, as seems likely, what will we do about the missions in Japan, South China, and the Philippines?"

On the other hand, they did not want to disturb the missionaries congregating in Shanghai, waiting to be redeployed or hoping to work in the burgeoning Baptist work in that city. What to do?

In late March, Cauthen sent Lucy Smith to Hong Kong to find a place for them to live and to open up offices as a new headquarters for the Orient.

By pluck and persistence, she was able to do so. She was also able to get a daily phone hookup with the Shanghai office. Keeping Cauthen posted on things at that end of the line, she inquired when he would be moving the office.

But Cauthen decided to wait it out in Shanghai. In April he saw his friend Charles Culpepper off. Mrs. Culpepper had left earlier in January; and as things deteriorated further, Culpepper decided he might as well return also. He encouraged himself and Cauthen by saying, "Remember, they can't take Christ out of our hearts. They can't take us out of his hand."

But still Cauthen delayed in moving to Hong Kong. For one thing, a peace conference had been called in Peking between the Nationalists and the Communists. For another, the persecution that Christians in Communist-seized territories had endured earlier continued to ease. In his April 1949 report to the board, Cauthen stated the situation in China with guarded optimism but waxed eloquent with confidence when talking about the work in Japan. "We are grateful for the thirty-two missionaries now under appointment for Japan, and we trust we will not fail to persevere in our purpose to place one hundred missionaries in that country at the earliest possible date," he said.

Cauthen called his assistant, Lucy Smith, back to Shanghai in April. In a report to the board that month, he reflected his own determination to try to stay. He said:

"Those of us who remain to work in a land overrun by the Communists are entering a dark valley, but it is lighted by the promises of God. It is absolutely necessary that some of us remain on the field to see what can be done under the new regime. If all missionaries were to withdraw at this point, it would be a tragedy from which we might never recover."

But a lot of people didn't understand his attitude. He added:

"This is not time for defeatism in the missionary enterprise. If we are thrust out in one area, we must enter other open doors. If we can take definite steps toward strengthening our work in Japan and enter new fields as indicated above, the Lord may use our reverses in China to take the gospel to other areas."

Later he had to rethink his own decision. Lucy returned to Hong Kong and called to indicate great unrest among the missionaries in South China. Eugene Hill, who was the stabilizing influence in the South China Mission, was once more very ill. A recurring ulcer was draining the life out of him. According to Lucy, he should be evacuated from Canton to the States as soon as he was strong enough. Many observers felt that the Communists were going to sweep around Shanghai, move into the Canton area of South China, and let the Nationalists cope with the problems in Shanghai before the Communists had to take them on. Because of this, many missionaries were in turmoil. Lucy told Cauthen on one of their daily calls, "You really need to come."

Cauthen agreed. But should he leave his family? What if he couldn't get back in to them? How would he feel? He finally decided, with no one's counsel but his wife's, that he would take them with him. She packed some suitcases, and late in the evening they boarded a ship on which he had secured passage to Hong Kong. In the middle of the night, he went back to the office in a rickshaw to get some papers he had forgotten. Even then, he had the uneasy feeling he might not be back.

The ship sailed before dawn. As Eloise and Baker looked at the familiar Shanghai skyline, they wondered if they would ever see it again. And would they ever see their household goods and personal belongings? They wouldn't.

Cauthen flew his family to Baguio in the Philippines and then returned to Hong Kong.

In Hong Kong, Cauthen was swept immediately into a round of counseling to help the South China missionaries make their decisions. Many misunderstood his counsel to stay and wait as long as possible. If that was his thought, why wasn't he in Shanghai? Cauthen fully intended to return to Shanghai. Only, when he returned to Hong Kong after visiting Kweilin and Canton and finished the work in the office, there was no way to get back to Shanghai. Over the telephone he arranged for his food supplies—which all missionaries laid in for the anticipated transition between the Nationalists and Communists—to be given to needy missionaries in the area. Other missionaries were counseled to move out whenever they were ready. Each missionary was urged to make his own decision.

Cauthen agonized over his inability to get back to Shanghai, but thanked God that he had been led to bring out his family when he did.

Another major challenge involved meeting in the Canton area with Chinese Christians who were worried about extra harshness that might come their way if missionaries were still there. They finally decided that if the missionaries wanted to stay, the Chinese would support them. This at least cleared the way for those who felt they should try to work under a Communist government to do so with Chinese Christian support.

Finally, Cauthen decided that he could get away to Baguio in the Philippines to settle the new missionaries there and see his family. Then came word that Shanghai was under final Communist assault. The agony he felt is expressed in his report to the board in June of 1949:

"As I left Canton, I experienced one of the sharpest struggles I've ever known. The reports from Shanghai were so definite that there was no question concerning the crisis having arisen. I was torn between whether to rush back to Shanghai or go to Baguio to help our new missionaries as I had promised and leave the matter of getting back to Shanghai in the hands of the Lord. I got no peace on the question until the following morning. But then came a clear impression that it was my duty to go on to Baguio and leave everything to him we serve. We called Shanghai that evening on the telephone and found that all of our people were safe and well, and they felt it was right for me to be away. Dr. Connely had written such helpful letters telling how the people understood my absence that my heart was gratefully comforted. I need not tell the board how utterly miserable it would make me feel if anyone should think that I would leave the missionaries in Shanghai in time of trial. I suppose that would come as near killing me as anything I could imagine."

When Cauthen returned from Baguio, he brought Eloise and the children to Hong Kong with him. He was able to move missionaries into Bangkok, opening up another new work. Greene Strother had flown there following his evacuation from Nanking; and now Mr. and Mrs. Ed Galloway, who had been with Bill Wallace in Wuchow, were sent to Bangkok.

After these matters were completed, Cauthen again tried to secure transportation to Shanghai. Finally he arranged to book passage to Taiwan and from there into Shanghai. He got his ticket, but within hours he got the news that Shanghai had fallen and that the ticket was no good.

Lucy contacted Connely on the phone just a few hours before the phone center fell. Connely assured her they were in good shape.

The Foreign Mission Board had twenty-nine missionaries still in Shanghai and eleven others still in Central China when the Communist takeover in that area was complete. Cauthen, anticipating criticism, wrote the board twelve facts to explain the situation:

1. These missionaries have remained in China by their own decision, in keeping with the clearly stated policy of the Foreign Mission Board to support fully each missionary's decision to go or stay as made through his best judgment and impressions of the Lord's leadership.

2. These decisions have been arrived at through a period of more than six months of careful study and earnest prayer.

3. These decisions were tested by the availability of adequate transportation up to within a few days of the fall of Shanghai, including a good part of the time the city was under siege.

4. Every possible preparation has been made for the physical and financial needs of the missionaries.

5. Many other missionaries of various boards are remaining to work under the Communist regime. Northern Presbyterians have fifty or more, including several families with children. Methodists, Episcopalians, Catholics, and many others are adequately represented. The China Inland Mission with seven hundred people on the field has not undertaken to evacuate their staff.

6. The United States government has not advised business and missionary interests to abandon their activities in China.

7. The United States government is leaving its consular staffs in Shanghai and other cities to deal with the new regime.

8. There are fifteen hundred Americans in Shanghai alone, and it is possible that with the eyes of the world focused upon the world's fourth largest city and its adjacent area, there will be considerable safety in numbers.

9. In the light of developments in Communist-held areas of China and other lands, it is to be supposed that even if the Communists may not permit other people to enter China, they will likely permit people to leave if they consider it necessary to do so.

10. Newspaper men and dealers in oil, tobacco, and other lines of commerce have stayed. The missionary has stayed not to gain, but to give.

11. Heroic examples such as those of Carey, Judson, Livingstone, and Paton inspire those who have stayed. The

experience of our missionaries under Japanese occupation and internment strengthens our hearts. The missionary labors of Paul furnish a mighty encouragement.

12. The unbreakable promise of the Lord Jesus to be with his servants to the end of the age is our unfailing source of strength.

Fortunately, Cauthen was able to maintain daily contact with Frank Connely and the Shanghai group by telephone for a number of weeks. In June he made three trips—one to Kweilin, another to Bangkok, and a third to Taiwan. He gave most of his attention to getting the work in Bangkok underway, but also secured help for the burgeoning work growing up around Bertha Smith in Taiwan.

Communist threats left him a little uncertain about how much weight to let down on the work in Taiwan. Who was to say the Communists would not sweep right on across the straits and take that island also? They had already declared it to be a part of China, they understood China to be theirs.

In his December report of 1949, Cauthen confirmed that all of the Southern Baptist mission stations in China, with the exception of those in Macao and Hong Kong, and of course the island of Taiwan, were in Communist hands. He wrote, "On Thanksgiving Day word came that Kweilin had been occupied, and today the fall of Wuchow is confirmed."

Wuchow had the hearts of the China missionaries because of the winsome personality of Bill Wallace. The bachelor doctor had survived Japanese occupation of the city by pulling the hospital out on boats and keeping it functioning either on barges on the rivers or in strange cities. When the Japanese war was over, he had returned the same entourage to the hospital compound and reclaimed it.

Wallace had almost died in the summer of 1948 from a seige of paratyphoid, a fact Cauthen recorded in a report to the board when he asked for their prayers on behalf of the slender doctor.

As the missionaries in Wuchow made their decisions, Bill Wallace urged those with families to leave. The Galloways went on to Bangkok. Beddoe and his wife had already retired and returned to the States. Finally, Wallace and two missionary women—a nurse, Everley Hayes, and an evangelistic worker, Jessie Green—decided to stay. Wallace explained in urging Ed Galloway to go and defending his decision to stay, "I'm just one piece of man . . . ."

That summer, Cauthen had gone to Wuchow. He and Wallace had talked long and hard, but Bill was convinced he was doing the right thing. Everley and Jessie could not be dissuaded either. Proud of them and knowing that somebody was going to have to try to stay, Cauthen was grateful. He promised them his prayers as he boarded the amphibious plane for the flight back to Canton. As the plane cleared the water and banked over the city, Cauthen saw the white-clad staffers waving from the hospital roof. He breathed a prayer of gratitude for people like them.

Cauthen's major relief from the intensity of those months during the hectic events of 1949 came as he preached in Macao and Hong Kong. In Macao, an unusual movement saw 160 people accept Christ. At the close of the year, Cauthen wrote:

"The heart of China is open to the gospel of Jesus. May God grant that the trials of the present day will cause the people of this land to thirst more for the waters of salvation, and may we—at whatever it may cost—do our duty before God by giving them strength."

CHAPTER FIVE

A New Diaspora

As secretary for the Orient for the Baptist Foreign Mission Board, Baker James Cauthen was presiding over a missionary enterprise in rapid transition in the spring of 1950. Mission work in Japan was progressing well, and the possibility for one hundred missionaries there was strongly increased by a tremendous response to personnel needs being voiced throughout the United States by the Foreign Mission Board. In Taiwan, the work was growing rapidly in the revival and miracle atmosphere surrounding its beginnings. Most of the missionaries in the Philippines were still in the language school there. The work in Bangkok was definitely of toehold dimensions. China was closed.

But Cauthen believed that none of this would thwart the purposes of God. Somehow, God would do something bigger than any victories yet achieved. Cauthen wanted to know what that was.

Could God be creating a new diaspora? Could the doors be closing in China and missionaries expelled in order to plant a gospel witness in areas that Baptists had not yet the courage to dream about?

He began a journey in January to answer that question. His itinerary took him from Hong Kong to the Philippines to Borneo, then to Indonesia. His goal was to contact overseas Chinese in those places. They constituted a larger dispersion than that of the Jews during the New Testament period when Paul began his missionary journeys. And Southern Baptists had a lot of displaced Chinese-speaking missionaries. God opened doors for him in remarkable ways. He was told in Hong Kong that it would be impossible to get a visa into Indonesia from the Dutch Embassy. When he got there, he found that the receptionist was a young Chinese woman who had met him in church the week before. He got his visa.

Cauthen arrived on the island of Java after stops in the Philippines and Borneo, at a port city called Surabaya. Landing in a pouring rain, he checked into a hotel, redressed, and then went to the nearest Chinese restaurant. He inquired of the owner, in Chinese, if he could be directed to a church. Directions were freely given. Climbing back into the rickshaw, Cauthen found that it was raining again. He made his way, with dampened clothes but not dampened spirits, to a small Christian church. The pastor listened to his inquiries but said he really needed to go to the other end of the island to Djakarta. Cauthen copied some names from him, secured a letter of reference, arranged transportation, and the next morning flew to Djakarta. The people he contacted there thought there would be a good opportunity to relocate missionaries in Indonesia.

Thanking God and continuing to travel under a strong sense of God's leadership, he flew on to Ceylon. But his target was India, so he did not stay over in Ceylon. He often wondered, in light of the fact that so many doors closed in India during those days, if he made a mistake. His efforts for establishing missionaries in India seemed promising, but applications that were filed for entrance were not successful.

Stopovers in Singapore and the Malaysian Peninsula quickly paid dividends. But efforts to stop in Saigon in French Indochina were thwarted.

When he returned to Hong Kong he had been gone a month, but mission work for a quarter of a century was laid out in his mind and heart.

After his January odyssey, Baker Cauthen packed up his family and boarded an American ship for a transpacific voyage home. With brief stops in Japan and Honolulu, the little family found their time aboard ship restful. That rest was desperately needed. The hustle and bustle in Hong Kong was as demanding as it had been in Shanghai, and they had never really caught their breath after the move from Shanghai.

Cauthen had agreed, at the Foreign Mission Board's insistence, to spend six months in Richmond in 1950—a concession to the board's earlier yielding to the location of the Orient office in China.

Time passed rapidly. He spent the first part of March lecturing at Southern Baptist Theological Seminary in Louisville. He spent the period from the March meeting of the board till its April meeting in Richmond consulting with secretaries and board members and handling a backlog of correspondence. Mail was coming in now from not only Communist China and the Hong Kong-Macao island of freedom, but also from rapidly developing mission work in Japan and beachheads in Korea, Taiwan, Thailand (old Siam), and the Philippines.

He took a quick trip to the southwestern United States in late April to hold a week's revival meeting at First Baptist Church, Oklahoma City, with his old friend Herschel Hobbs. Then he went to Texas, first to speak at Southwestern Seminary and visit with Bill and Genevieve Howse, and then to speak at Baylor and renew acquaintance with faculty and friends there. He spoke at churches in Dallas, Alexandria, and Austin, Texas, before going back to Richmond. Quick trips to Maryland and Chicago brought him back just in time to confront a new crisis.

He heard it first on the radio. North Korean troops had invaded South Korea. Crossing the thirty-eighth parallel in force, the Communist North was intent on subduing the free South. The United Nations organization was called into action. It seemed highly probable that a new international conflict was in the winds. Was this a third world war? Was it another all-out Pacific war?

Cauthen's first concern was the Abernathys. Seoul was overrun almost immediately, and it was several hours before he heard that the Abernathys had been evacuated. Though they had had to leave everything, they were safe in Japan. "Thank God for that," Cauthen told Eloise. "Now let's pray for the Christians who've got to deal with a new kind of test of their faith."

The next crisis came from the Philippine Islands. Winston Crawley wrote that Chinese teachers working with the missionaries there were thinking about leaving. Should the missionaries leave? "No," Cauthen said. "If you even talk about it, that may cause the Chinese to go ahead and leave and escalate the problem." His modus operandi in these matters was always to proceed slowly. Its wisdom was confirmed again and again. He erred with it at times, but it served him so well that it always seemed to be his first choice of action (or nonaction).

Another crisis emerged out of Shanghai, where the Communist climate that initially had been so tolerant toward Christians changed radically. Almost immediately, most missionary families who had tried to stay on in Shanghai applied for exit visas. Cauthen urged them to reconsider but promised that he would support whatever decision they made. By the end of August, only thirty-one missionaries were left in Communist China. Cauthen reported to the board that only five of these were men. More importantly, perhaps history should note that twenty-six of them were women.

By September 14, as Cauthen prepared to return with his family to Hong Kong, only twenty-one missionaries were left in Communist territory. He projected that by the end of October the number would be down to fifteen due to inability to renew expired passports.

On the encouraging side, Dr. N. A. Bryan and Dr. Greene Strother, both veteran China missionaries, were in Indonesia exploring possibilities there. Also, three missionary families were seeking to settle in India. Too, despite the fact that Japan was right on the edge of the new war, the missionary force there had climbed to sixty-seven. The one hundred goal by the end of 1950 looked increasingly reachable. Such an escalation of missionary work in a single year had never before been experienced by Southern Baptists. Cauthen's six months at home, with the fervency of his call to go out into all the world, helped escalate the response of Baptist people.

Whether he was reassuring himself or the board, his feelings about these crises surfaced in his report:

"The entire Orient is unstable. We are faced with the necessity of projecting our Christian witness in the midst of instability with all the consequent losses and readjustments which become necessary or having no witness at all. If we walk by sight, we would simply abandon our work in the Orient and wait for better days. If we walk by faith, we continue looking at a Savior who is adequate for every emergency and go on serving him. We are not discouraged because final victory belongs to the Lord we serve."

Soon after returning to Hong Kong, Cauthen measured the situation. All missionaries still in China were under new pressures. He made sure that they had funds and that they knew the board would support whatever decision they made. Bill Wallace and Everley Hayes were reported under a special umbrella of hostility. Jessie

Baker James Cauthen holding his second grandchild, Steven Ralph Cauthen (1967)

Green had to leave. "I don't know how long they can stay," she said of Wallace and Hayes.

After settling his family, Cauthen left for a preaching crusade in Japan. Rankin joined Cauthen there, along with Duke McCall and W. A. Criswell, Cauthen's old friend from Baylor days. The results exceeded the new Baptist missionaries' wildest dreams. Over eight thousand people expressed interest in becoming Christians. The crusade gave the struggling churches in Japan new confidence in spite of their almost infinitesimally small numbers when compared to the nation's dense population. At the end of the year, there were thirty-two Baptist churches in Japan.

But the good news from Japan didn't offset the tragedy in Korea and the increasing danger to missionaries and Christians as the anti-American spirit grew sharply in China. In cautiously couched words, Cauthen wrote Ruth Pettigrew in Hunan Province in late December:

"With this growing propaganda, our Chinese friends may find they will get along better if missionaries are not in their midst. This development may come differently in various areas, and people in each location will have to study it themselves.

"I've expressed to others that the time has come for the missionaries to leave China unless they have a positive sense of the Lord's command to remain. This is to say a person should remain in China not simply because he is willing to do so but rather because he is aware of Christ's clear command to stay on."

The next day, word came from Canton that Bill Wallace, the beloved missionary doctor, had been arrested as an American spy in Wuchow. The word of Bill Wallace's imprisonment came from a Catholic Maryknoll missionary who revealed that several of their missionaries had also been imprisoned. Cauthen knew that the Maryknollers were especially appreciative of Wallace, who often treated them and cared for them in times of illness. Also, when Cauthen, Culpepper, Beddoe, and Hsu went through Wuchow in 1941, they had been the recipients of Maryknoller hospitality.

Missionaries in the office at Hong Kong gathered to pray. In hopes that the difficulty would resolve itself quickly, and also to avoid causing problems for other missionaries, they decided not to make too much of the news. Cauthen sat down to write to the rest of the missionaries. In a letter dated December 28, 1950, he said:

"This letter is occasioned by the report that Dr. Wallace was taken into custody on December 19 . . . . I am writing this letter so that you might join in prayer for Dr. Wallace . . . . There is no way of estimating the amount of good which has been accomplished by your remaining in China up to this point. The gradual withdrawing of missionaries has enabled the work to adjust itself splendidly. It does not follow, however, that the presence of the missionary in these days ahead can produce those same contributions. The growing anti-American spirit may make the liabilities both to the missionary personally and to the work outweigh the contribution he could make. It's for this reason one should stay only on the basis of a deep assurance of God's command to do so."

Word came shortly after February 10 that on that date Bill Wallace had died in prison. The Communists said he hanged himself in a cell. Details from Everley Hayes and the Chinese who claimed his body confirmed what the missionaries in their hearts already knew. He had not taken his life. He had been murdered.

As missionaries gathered in the Hong Kong office with Cauthen, Jaxie Short said, "It's very strange. I was praying for him late last night when suddenly I had the feeling I didn't have to pray for him anymore . . . that everything was all right. I didn't understand it then. Now I do."

Many of the missionaries felt that God had uniquely prepared Bill Wallace to lay down his life in this way. Despite their sorrow at his loss, they tried to resist the anger they felt toward the Communists.

Cauthen steeled his own thoughts from any tendency to second-guess decisions that had been made. The work had to go on. The way was still forward.

Frank Connely finally got out of Shanghai. Cauthen, Lucy Smith, and others who had worked with him closely and loved him deeply welcomed him with gratitude to God for his safety. But the report that he brought was disturbing. He told of Baptists being buried alive for their Christian witness, of more than forty leaders who had suffered martyrdom. "We could not afford to stay," he said. "We were endangering the Chinese leaders by our presence." He reported sadly that 75 percent of the churches with which he was in contact had been closed.

Cauthen continued to provide for missionaries who were able to come out of China, but his thoughts were preoccupied with redeployment. "God has not closed this door without having something special in mind," he confided to Lucy Smith. John Abernathy had been able to get back into Korea and, along with Dr. N. A. Bryan and old China hand Rex Ray, was carrying on a strong relief program as well as gathering the Christians who had fled into the perimeter around Pusan.

That summer, Cauthen went back to the United States to brief a group of missionaries who would begin the work in Southeast Asia. They met at Ridgecrest. Stockwell Sears, Charles Cowherd, and W. B. Johnson were to go to Djakarta, Indonesia. Buford Nichols and another group were to go into India. Still others were to go into Singapore. "We must press on," Cauthen said. "Too many people have laid down their lives in Christ's name for us to neglect the opportunities before us."

The Southern Baptist Convention met in San Francisco in 1951, but Cauthen was not able to get there. Eugene Hill, who had been able to come out of Communist-held Canton, attended the Convention and presented a beautiful posthumous tribute to the martyred Wallace.

Cauthen faced another decision. As Rankin pointed out to him, since his work was expanding all over Asia, he needed to be available to all areas. Moreover, he needed to interpret to the supporting constituency the challenge of the new areas and the need for advance. Now was the time, Rankin held, to bring the area office back to Richmond.

Cauthen, after the six-month period, knew in his heart that Rankin was right. When he returned to Hong Kong, he consented. In his letter to Rankin, he made a condition. "Let me spend a year in Japan helping undergird the work there and see if we can't get the Korean work started," he said. It was agreed that Cauthen and his family would move to Tokyo in the summer of 1951 and return to the States to take up residence in Richmond in the summer of 1952.

In his reports to the board Cauthen tried to avoid preoccupation with what was happening in China, but his feeling inevitably crept in. After Wallace's death in 1951, he reported:

"A nationwide Communist purge has produced a reign of terror.

People are imprisoned daily, and several times each week mass executions are reported. Accusation meetings and mock trials with propaganda to fire crowds wildly clamoring for the blood of victims precede public executions. People are living in terrible fear. Nobody knows when an old friend will seek to curry favor with the authorities by denouncing his associates as spies and reactionaries. Cities are filled with an endless round of rallies, parades, and demonstrations designed to fan the flames of hatred against America and build up support for the war in Korea."

Cauthen was distressed in midyear to learn that his friend Henry Lin was under arrest and possibly dead. It was difficult to get the facts because letters came out coded and obscure to protect both the writers and the receivers. Dr. Lin had been president of Shanghai University while Dr. Cauthen had his offices in Shanghai, and the two had become good friends. Prior to the evacuation, Cauthen had gone out to the Shanghai University campus to visit with missionaries there concerning their plans. Dr. Lin had requested an audience. In the conference he had poured out his heart. Should he move to Taiwan? He had property there. Relatives were already there. His well-known anti-Communist views would surely bring retribution if he stayed. Cauthen counseled with him, trying his best simply to hold up the possibilities, the alternatives, and the assurance that God would lead him if he would seek his guidance. It was a troubled man who left Cauthen later in the day. But the next day, as the conferences continued, Lin came back. "My mind is clear now," he said. "I must stay here."

As word came of his arrest and possible death, Cauthen prayed again for the Christians who had been won as a part of the great missionary witness through the years and must now suffer for their faith. "God, help them and make their witness fruitful," he prayed.

Continuing to feel God's hand in all that was happening, he added in the same report:

"In the meantime, we thank God for open doors in other lands where millions of people are waiting for the gospel. The Chinese populations in many of these areas give us splendid opportunity to project work which serves as a spearhead for a general ministry to the people as a whole. God will lead in redeployment of forces so that the tragedies of China will become the occasion of advance in other lands."

At the end of the year Buford Nichols, W. B. Johnson, Stockwell Sears, and Charles Cowherd landed in Djakarta to open mission work there, fulfilling a dream that had begun two years earlier. Eugene Hill relocated in Singapore to help open work in Malaya (later called Malaysia), and the work in Taiwan had been strengthened by other former China missionaries who joined Bertha Smith. The Philippines and Thailand enlarged their missions with former China missionaries as well as with new appointees, many of them the result of Cauthen's impassioned preaching during trips home in the postwar years.

By December 1951 the last China missionary of Southern Baptists, Pearl Johnson, was out of Communist China.

In early 1952 Cauthen faced a new series of crises. W. B. Johnson wired him from Djakarta that the missionaries there were unable to get permission to stay. Cauthen booked the first flight he could get and flew to Djakarta. After running into roadblocks on lower government levels, Cauthen, Johnson, and the others prayerfully considered God's leadership and decided to go directly to the top authorities. A man named Abednego consented to see him. Admitting that their application had not been approved, Abednego asked, "The Baptists? Who are the Baptists?"

"I felt it was a tremendous opportunity to share our particular witness with him," Cauthen wrote Rankin. "I shared with him our commitment to religious freedom, to separation of church and state, to the autonomy of individual congregations and Baptist respect for others." Abednego was impressed and granted permission. He confided to Cauthen, "I'm on the United Nations commission for religious freedom." Baker Cauthen replied, "Sir, I hope you will be able to give Indonesia that kind of opportunity." When Abednego later asked Cauthen how many missionaries he would bring, Cauthen swallowed hard, prayed silently, and guessed boldly. "Twenty-five." Abednego was puzzled. "Why so many?"

Other efforts did not go so well. Baptist missionaries were denied the right to stay in India despite a variety of approaches.

Mission work did progress in Thailand and, under the leadership of Eugene Hill, flourished in Singapore and Malaysia. This was in spite of Malaysia's own Communist threat, which prevented the missionaries from traveling in the countryside.

Back in Japan, Cauthen bade farewell to the associates who had worked with him. Lucy Smith had already make up her mind that she wasn't going to Richmond. She continued working in Japan for several years and then returned to Hong Kong.

In September 1952 the Cauthens returned to the United States, visited briefly in Texas, and then set up housekeeping in Richmond, Virginia. They bought a small house on Cutshaw, just two blocks off of Monument Avenue and about fifteen blocks from the Foreign Mission Board's headquarters. Carolyn, fifteen, and Ralph, fourteen, enrolled at Richmond's Thomas Jefferson High School, and the whole family joined the First Baptist Church. Baker Cauthen had ended another era in his life. At this point he did not dream that a still larger task lay just around the corner.

CHAPTER SIX

The Mantle of Leadership

Baker James Cauthen's life in Richmond maintained the same hectic pace it had in the Orient. It included incessant rounds of correspondence, consultations over crises, intermittent trips to preach, denominational meetings, periodic overseas trips, and a constant effort to interpret to church members both the mission challenge and their responsibility.

Within weeks after Cauthen arrived in Richmond, Theron Rankin declared that the Foreign Mission Board was in a new crisis. Under Rankin's leadership and the promise of the Advance Program, the board had heavy commitments of missionaries in Japan and heavy costs in the relocation of missionaries throughout the Orient. Record new appointments brought the board to the point where it absolutely depended on the Advance funds that had come in so beautifully in 1950 and 1951. By midyear 1952 the promise was not there. The possibility of being overextended loomed large. Rankin slowed down appointments and sent his colleagues around the Convention territory to inform people how important the Cooperative Program Advance funds were and how necessary the Lottie Moon Christmas Offering would be at this time.

Cauthen, perhaps the most sought-after speaker among the Foreign Mission Board staff or missionaries, had to fight for time to stay with his correspondence and administrative tasks. He said later that he learned two very important lessons: First, when you take a cause to the heart of the churches, they will respond to it; second, when you slow down missionary appointments, it takes a long time to get them started again. Later he was to cut back every place else, but never again in terms of the appointment of missionaries. "Southern Baptist money will follow the lives of their youth," he was to tell the staff again and again.

He went into the year 1953, however, with encouragement. Reports from Southern Baptist churches indicated that the Lottie Moon Offering would reach new highs. Mission work in the Orient was taking on a semblance of stability it had not had in two decades and a promise it had never before had. Korea was a phenomenon. John Abernathy wrote an article entitled "Found: Ten Thousand Baptists." By the end of 1952 he was listing 130 churches in the Korean Baptist Convention.

Missionaries in Taiwan found a Baptist constituency in refugees from the mainland but also discovered that adversity had brought about a deep spiritual revival. The work in Siam (to be known as Thailand) was taking hold slowly against Buddhist resistance, and the same could be said for Singapore and Malaysia. Work in the Philippines was beginning to expand beyond the Chinese; and the first missionaries directly appointed to the Philippines, the Ed Gordons, were sent out. In Japan the mission had not yet expanded to include one hundred missionaries, but the number was close to their goal. Missionaries were projecting a plan to place a missionary in every prefecture throughout the country.

Work in Hong Kong was under the leadership of the Hong Kong Baptist Association, whose ranks were swelled by refugees. It prospered despite problems and intermittent fears that Communists would move in and take over the area.

In Richmond, the Cauthens quickly adjusted to their new way of life. But then, if there was any one thing they had learned over the years, it was how to adjust to a new way of life. Their house on Cutshaw Avenue was small but comfortable. Eloise, having lost everything she owned in 1941 in Hwanghsien and having lost it again in 1949 in Shanghai, had again assembled the basic things of a household.

Ralph and Carolyn were making high marks at Thomas Jefferson High School and getting involved in youth activities at First Baptist Church. Eloise began teaching a class at the church and speaking and teaching mission studies in and around Richmond. "Once a missionary, always a missionary," she laughed.

Encouraging offerings in late 1952 and reports coming in 1953 gave everybody new hope about continuation of the Advance Program. Cauthen, however, believed that the board had lost valuable ground in mission volunteers when word went out that the board would have to cut back appointments. In an almost personal crusade, he redoubled his efforts to "call out the called." At a missions day in Louisville Seminary in February of 1953, he made an impassioned plea on behalf of the open doors in Southeast Asia.

In his February report to the board he indicated that by the end of 1953, all able-bodied China missionaries would be redeployed. He called the board to prayer again for India, where efforts to enter continued to be dominated by frustration.

In the April board meeting Cauthen recognized a belated but much hoped-for goal, the appointment of one hundred missionaries in Japan. He underlined efforts to set up student centers alongside the great universities, where the Communists were vying for young Japanese minds. He pointed out a new effort in theological education to train young Japanese pastors. "After all, 100 missionaries in a country of 83,000,000 . . ."

Cauthen enjoyed fellowship with the staff. Members would often walk from the board's headquarters on 2037 Monument Avenue the few blocks over to Broad Street where the William Byrd Hotel was located. The Byrd coffee shop provided their favorite atmosphere for occasional coffee breaks and lunches together. Some of the more imaginative work of the board emerged in these informal sessions. Rankin especially seemed to enjoy this time with his colleagues.

In his May report to the board, Cauthen said, "There is mounting evidence that God is bringing out of the tragedy of China advance in the Kingdom."

Cauthen was especially busy in April and May taping sermons with the Radio and Television Commission in Atlanta for the July, August, and September broadcasts of the Baptist Hour. That he was asked to take this prestigious assignment again was evidence of the high regard Baptists everywhere had for his pulpit ability. "As an advocative-type preacher," one reported, "he is without peer."

At the Southern Baptist Convention, May 6-10, 1953, in Houston, Texas, major responsibilities for board personnel fell on the Thursday evening Foreign Mission presentation. Many at the Convention thought it was the high point of the meeting. Rankin, elated at their reception, expressed his satisfaction to his colleagues. Driving back to Richmond, he told his wife, "I believe it (the Advance) has caught on. I am satisfied. For the first time, I feel that I can lay down my work with complete satisfaction about the Advance Program."

This did not mean that Rankin felt his goals had been reached. In his April report he said, "It is becoming evident that we have advanced only to the door, where we are seeing the world in a new way . . . . Plans and achievements which we have thought of as being large now appear to be small."

Plans had been laid for Rankin to go to South America in June with Dr. Everett Gill, the secretary for that area. He shared his anticipation over the trip with his colleagues—Gill of Latin America, Cauthen of the Orient, the veteran George Sadler of Africa, Europe, and the Middle East, and Frank Means, the secretary for education and promotion. Samuel Maddox, the personnel secretary, had resigned to return to the pastorate; but Rankin was excited about a young Richmond pastor, Elmer West, who had been elected to the post at the April board meeting. He believed West could help the board accelerate the number of appointments and also make sure the right kind of people were appointed.

There is no way to describe the shock his colleagues felt when he shared with them the report of a routine medical examination, undergone in preparation for his trip. He had leukemia. Although he didn't know exactly what to expect, he had the sense of finality that the disease brought at that time. He thought he might write a book that he tentatively entitled *The World and I*. But in the days that followed, his colleagues watched helplessly as he grew rapidly weaker. Within three weeks, he found it difficult to maintain his schedule. One day in the office he confided to Cauthen, "I feel like all my way, every experience has been the opening of a door into something God had for me. That's the way I feel about this experience."

Rankin was a model for Cauthen. The idea of losing him was almost unthinkable. Cauthen had planned a vacation trip, taking Eloise and the children with him to Glorieta Baptist Assembly, then north to the Colorado Rockies and on to Yellowstone Park. Should he go? "By all means," Rankin said. "This thing hasn't gotten me yet."

The Cauthens left, praying daily for him. Cauthen spoke at Glorieta; then the family journeyed north through Colorado into Wyoming and Yellowstone Park. Before they left they had driven by the Rankin house, and Valeria and Theron had walked to the car with them. Rankin stood between the two large hollies in front of his home in Richmond and waved brightly as the Cauthens drove off.

"Wait a minute, sir. We have a message for you." Baker looked at Eloise, surprised. He had no way of knowing that the ranger at the gate of Yellowstone Park would know who he was, much less have a message for him. The ranger smiled. "We've been on the lookout for your car."

The message was simple. It told him that Rankin was dead. A phone call to Richmond from a park booth revealed that Rankin had spoken briefly at the June meeting of the board, charging the candidates and bringing an abbreviated report. But within days he was too weak to go to his office. On the twenty-seventh of June he passed away.

At the funeral service at First Baptist Church, Rankin's longtime friend J. B. Witherspoon said:

"So well known and beloved a man needs no other monument than the life he lived, no other praise than the work he accomplished, no other portraiture than the character and spirit and purpose that showed in all his ministry. He had one ambition and that not for himself, and he pursued it with all his heart; it was to serve Christ in his world purpose."

The Cauthens, shocked and sobered by the swiftness of the event, found a quiet spot on the side of one of the national park's scenic roads. There they gathered as a family and held their own quiet memorial service for the man who had been their immediate supervisor since their appointment as missionaries fourteen years before, first as their area secretary and then as their executive secretary. Eloise was aware, as others would later be, that Rankin's purposeful life-style and his world view of the missionary task and Baptist responsibility had greatly influenced her husband.

Did their thoughts turn to Rankin's successor? Surely. Just as surely as did the thoughts of foreign and home missionaries, Baptist leaders, and Baptist laymen around the country. Who would succeed him? The elder statesman on the administrative team was George Sadler, and the board had designated him acting executive secretary so they would not be without the ability to act during the interim. Cauthen also learned that the board would meet in special session in July and that he (Cauthen) was needed for that meeting.

Another possibility for the executive secretary's position was Frank Means, who had joined the Polytechnic Church while Baker was its pastor and had been ordained under Baker's leadership at that church. After succeeding Cauthen as professor of missions at Southwestern for several years, Means had responded to Rankin's request to come to the board and pick up the educational and promotional tasks. His administrative skills and imaginative leadership had won a lot of admiration.

Everett Gill was the secretary for Latin America. No one questioned his dedication or effectiveness, but he did not seem to be under serious consideration as Rankin's successor.

And, of course, there were professors and pastors and denominational leaders elsewhere in the Convention who had great missionary hearts and known administrative skills. But the Cauthens must have known, despite an inherent and cultivated humility in such things, that they were foremost in the minds of many, many people.

"No one can elicit response from Baptists like Baker," one said. "He is without peer in causing Baptists to lift their eyes upon the world as a field white unto harvest," another said.

But the Foreign Mission Board was strongly Virginia-influenced. Baker was a Texan, new to Richmond, trained at Southwestern, and utterly foreign in many ways to the Virginia Baptist scene and the Virginia mind-set. But Virginians, too, responded to dedication. They had been moved through the years by stories of the commitment and sacrifice and faithfulness of the Cauthens during the Japanese war and later during the Communist threat in China. They, too, had been moved by his enterprising administration in perceiving the closed doors in China as an opportunity to pry open East and Southeast Asia for Christ and for Baptist missions with, from a historical point of view, lightninglike quickness.

But the Cauthens themselves were in love with the Orient. Their commitment to China was deep. "We'll go back someday," they both told themselves. "Missionaries will return to China. We'll find believers faithful and the church stronger," they would say to each another after periods of fervent prayer for their Chinese brethren. Even now, living in Richmond, they looked forward to the time when they would move back to the field even for a short period.

They saw themselves as missionaries, and the executive secretary's position would preclude such closeness with the Orient.

The Cauthens made it back to Richmond in time for the called meeting of the board on July 9. Of the forty-seven board members, forty-four were in attendance. Long discussions were interrupted with seasons of prayer. Policies were clarified, and personalities were considered. Whether because a consensus could not be reached or because of an earnest desire for additional time to seek God's leadership—neither minutes nor memories reveal—a motion was made and adopted that the selection of an executive secretary be deferred until the annual meeting in October. A motion to have Sadler, the acting executive secretary, designated interim executive secretary until that meeting was adopted unanimously.

Cauthen and the other administrative secretaries returned to their desks. Often approached by men indicating their commitment to see him elected, Cauthen hardly knew how to respond. During the next few months he busied himself with the work of the Orient, which was as demanding as ever, and tried his best to put the election out of his mind. Letters and calls made it difficult.

At one point after Eloise and Baker had prayed fervently about the matter, they felt that perhaps they should notify Howard Jenkins, the Richmond layman who served as president of the Foreign Mission Board, that they would like Baker's name withdrawn from consideration. "But how can we do that if we do not know it is God's will?" Eloise asked. She was only voicing Baker's feelings. They must not run from what God would have them do. Again they prayed. Then they agreed. "We will leave the matter in God's hands."

Foreign Missions Week at Ridgecrest came. Baker, despite heavy responsibilities related to the expanding work in the Orient and people's speculations regarding Rankin's successor, packed up his family and went to Ridgecrest for the week. He had been assigned to teach a group of teenagers, a job some in his place might have dismissed as beneath him.

One of those teenagers was a boy named Sam Cannata. Sam later volunteered for missions, made his way through medical school, and was appointed a missionary doctor to Rhodesia. Still later he pioneered Baptist work in Ethiopia, where he was called upon to suffer in Christ's name in a number of ways—not the least of which was being arrested and held without charges for many days.

Just before he suffered these things, he wrote concerning Cauthen:

"Dr. Cauthen had the assignment of teaching a group of teenagers. I'll never forget his faithfulness to that group. And many days during that week, I marveled to see him taking extra time with those young people, counseling them, praying with them about God's will in their lives, etc. At the time I felt, and today I still feel, that this was a true sign of greatness. With the burdens of his work and all that was at stake, he could have easily excused himself."

In October the board reconvened in its annual meeting. After routine business and reports were complete, Howard Jenkins called the meeting into executive session for the purpose of considering the election of an executive secretary.

Cauthen was quickly nominated, and the nomination was followed by strong words of praise. Jimmy Morgan, a board member from Fort Worth, Texas, a longtime friend of Cauthen, led in the praise. Two men vocally supported George Sadler, the interim executive secretary and longtime secretary for Africa, Europe, and the Middle East. They were Reuben Alley, editor of the *Religious Herald,* the Virginia Baptist paper, and Dr. Ralph McDanel of the University of Richmond, a history professor and man of much influence. Alley's voice was to surface again and again regarding Cauthen's leadership during the years of his active ministry as the venerable and highly respected editor of the *Herald.* Those in attendance believed his opposition was not so much to Cauthen as to the Texas influence.

Cauthen was elected. Sensing the minorities' feeling, a member of the board, rather than moving to make the election unanimous, moved that "the board pledge the newly elected executive secretary our wholehearted and unanimous support." There was no opposition, and the board adjourned.

While these deliberations were going on Cauthen was in his office, as were the other administrative secretaries. Dr. J. W. Storer, the Southern Baptist Convention president at the time, and Dr. John Buchannan, a board member from Alabama, placed the results of the meeting before Cauthen. After they had stated the board's decision, a quiet calm came upon him. He'd left the matter in the hands of the Lord, and this was the result. It was the call of duty. No matter how inadequate he might feel, God would equip him with whatever he needed for the task.

He asked, "Should I meet with the Administrative Committee first?" "No," Buchannan said. "You just tell the board when we reconvene this afternoon."

Cauthen was forty-three years old.

A quiet, expectant group heard his acceptance speech. Cauthen spoke simply, directly, and quietly. The strong, demanding rhetoric that characterized his preaching was absent. The simple clarity that characterized all of his expressions was clearly in evidence. He said:

> "Mr. President, Members of the Board, and Friends:
>
> "Fourteen years ago my wife and I came to Richmond for appointment as missionaries to China. That step was taken after much prayer and heart-searching because we had thought our work was to be at Southwestern Seminary and in the leadership of a growing church in which God had given us a happy ministry. There had come, however, a strong conviction of God's leadership to go to the mission field.
>
> "Throughout the days of war in the Pacific we were reassured many times that God had led us in the step we had taken.
>
> "When Dr. Rankin was elected executive secretary of the Foreign Mission Board in 1945, I was asked to become secretary for the Orient with headquarters in Richmond. We had a very strong conviction at that time that the Lord wanted us to return to the Orient. Dr. Rankin requested us to meet him in Arkansas to discuss the matter, and he fully understood our impressions. He stated that he saw no reason why the responsibility could not be carried out both in keeping with our own impressions and the planning at the board.
>
> "We laid hand to the task on the basis of giving to it whatever might be required for its accomplishment. This meant that we would spend as much time in the Orient and as much time in Richmond as would be needed.
>
> "Through the years of crisis in the Orient we have had many occasions for being grateful for this arrangement, as we have faced responsibilities of relief, rehabilitation, Communist

emergency, expansion of the work in Japan, entering new fields, and redeployment of the China missionary staff.

"About a year ago there came into the hearts of the secretaries in Richmond a strong conviction that the time had come for the secretary for the Orient to be in the Richmond office, due to the need for a larger amount of information available in Richmond concerning the new areas into which we were entering. Although we longed to remain in the Orient, it seemed to us at that time that it was the right step to take to come to Richmond in keeping with the request made.

"None of us had any idea that Dr. Rankin would be so soon called to be with the Lord. Even yet we can hardly realize that he will not be back in his office.

"Following the emergency meeting of the Board in July, Dr. Sadler told me that there was some suggestion of my name as executive secretary. We immediately began to pray that we might know God's guidance in our own hearts in case this eventuality had to be faced.

"In praying we sought to know whether we should request the board not to consider our names at all, but throughout the entire experience there came repeatedly convictions in our hearts that we should leave the matter in the hands of God.

"After earnest prayer throughout the whole Southern Baptist Convention and on mission fields around the world and after careful deliberation on the part of those of you who make up this board, there has come a sense of direction toward the action taken today. Inasmuch as we have sought to leave our own hearts completely in the hands of God for his direction, we can feel nothing else except a solemn call of duty at this time.

"If it were a matter of considering whether we are worthy or capable of such a responsibility, we would not in the least consider it, but there is an assurance that if God is directing he will give his enabling grace.

"There are many assets in the work of foreign missions at this time. The board has some reserve funds in hand. The missionary staff is larger than ever before. The greatest asset, however, is the unity within the board and the staff. This must be preserved at all times.

"It is much encouragement to think of working with honored men of God such as Dr. Sadler, Dr. Gill, Dr. Means, Mr. West, Mr. Deane, Mr. Scofield, and others who make up the staff of this board. The comradeship that we all enjoy and the team spirit that prevails must always remain an outstanding feature of the life of this board.

"My coming into the responsibility of executive secretary immediately affects the work of the Orient. I should like to request the board to ask Dr. Sadler to continue as interim executive secretary until the end of the year and permit me to make a rapid trip immediately to the Orient to confer with the missions in that area concerning arrangements for their work.

"All of us recognize the remarkable administrative abilities that God has given to Dr. Frank K. Means. I regard him personally most highly. It was my privilege to serve at one time as his pastor, professor of missions, and also to preach his ordination sermon.

"One of the first matters we shall ask the executive committee to consider is that of studying ways to further relate Dr. Means to the general administration of this board.

"Although Dr. Rankin is no longer with us physically, his presence in our midst will be very powerfully felt. He will enter vitally with me into the responsibilities I will face day by day, and his great life and noble ideals will stand as a constant inspiration to us all.

"I cast myself upon your prayers. I know that I will find from this board the same undergirding, comradeship, and prayerful support you have always extended during the eight years I have served as secretary for the Orient and as a missionary to China. We are laborers together with God, and he is able to do far more than we can ask or think."

CHAPTER SEVEN

Another Man's Dream

Cauthen's election was widely acclaimed by Southern Baptists as the news was spread through both the Baptist press and secular newspapers. In fact, they were prepared for it. Cauthen was already something of a legend because of his exploits in wartime China and constant exposure to Southern Baptists through preaching engagements and Baptist Hour assignments. According to Cal Guy, professor of missions at Southwestern Baptist Theological Seminary, "Baptists would have been shocked at any other choice."

Clifton J. Allen of the Sunday School Board wrote Cauthen:

"Surely God has been preparing you for this critical place of leadership. Your background of study, your personal experience on the mission fields, your burden of the world's lost millions, and your personal capacities all combine to make it possible for you to lead Southern Baptists in an advance which, please God, will never stop."

A professor from Baylor days, Frank E. Burkhalter, wrote:

"Ever since I first came to know you during your student days at Baylor, I held you and your family in the highest esteem, and I shall pray earnestly every morning that God will use you in leading Southern Baptists to far larger accomplishments in foreign missions than have ever been achieved before."

Cauthen had also endeared himself to the lay persons in Southern Baptist life. An engineer, Henry S. Boling, who worked with the Southern Baptist Radio and Television Commission, wrote him:

"It's with a great deal of pleasure and no surprise that I read of your election to the secretaryship of the Foreign Mission Board. During your thirteen weeks on our Baptist Hour this year, I heard every program an average of five to seven times each and was thrilled every time."

W. O. Vaught, who served on the Foreign Mission Board with Cauthen twice and closed out his second term of service as president of the board, remembers, "In all of my years as a Southern Baptist, Dr. Cauthen's election was more universally accepted and felt to be the will of God than any other I can remember."

Again and again, Cauthen replied to congratulatory notes with a single phrase: "We lay hand to this task with a profound conviction of God's mandate and assurance of his enabling grace." He had built his whole ministry on those two pillars—God's mandate and God's grace. The mandate kept him from ever questioning why he was where he was or why God was calling him to face whatever it was he had to face. God's enabling grace was a constant assurance that in anything God brought him to, God would equip him to do what there was to do.

The Foreign Mission Board's press release of October 14, 1953, stated the situation Cauthen inherited:

"As executive secretary of the Southern Baptist world mission enterprise, Dr. Cauthen will direct the work of 57 employees in the home office in Richmond and 910 foreign missionaries in 32 countries. The Board's budget for 1954, adopted at the October meeting, totals approximately $6,461,465.00."

In Frank Means Cauthen had a friend he hoped would be his right hand in the years ahead. As editor of the *Commission,* Means wrote in the postelection editorial:

"The board's choice has met with hearty approval in all parts of the Southern Baptist Convention. If sentiments expressed are an indication, the people in the churches have already accepted Dr. Cauthen's leadership and are eager for an advance program in overseas missions to move forward at an accelerated rate."

Means reviewed Cauthen's experience as a missionary and as an area secretary, then said, "Under Dr. Cauthen's leadership, we may confidently expect continued advance into unoccupied areas, conscious that virtually every venture of that sort is, to use his phrase, 'a calculated risk.' Beachheads will thus be established upon which larger undertakings can be based."

But Cauthen's opportunity to answer the hundreds of congratulatory letters was brief. He had already planned a trip to the Orient. Now the trip assumed new dimensions. He would need to take soundings for the election for his own replacement as area secretary and also say good-bye to those he had served in that capacity. Sadler was to serve as interim secretary until January 1 to allow Cauthen to wind up his work in the Orient.

Cauthen already had his eye on his replacement. He was J. Winston Crawley, the young language student who had been spokesman for his fellow students when it become necessary to evacuate from Peking and relocate in the Philippines. He was also one of the key men in getting mission work started in the Philippines when China closed behind him. He was young; yet Cauthen had been young. He was a first-term missionary; yet Cauthen had had only a single term as a missionary. But Cauthen kept his counsel until he could read the thoughts of other missionaries in personal conference during this trip.

After he left, a letter that he had prepared was circulated to all of the missionaries. In the letter Cauthen revealed a bit of his heart. "From the time I was eight years old, there has been in my heart a conviction of God's call to duty," he said. "In pastoral responsibilities, seminary teaching, missionary experience, and as secretary for the Orient, there has been assurance of his command." Again he referred to God's mandate and God's enabling grace. He affirmed that he saw himself not as a director or as a boss "but rather as a pastor whose privilege it would be to serve God's flock." He affirmed the unity of the board's staff, and he referred again to Rankin and his example. "Although he's not here in the flesh, he is felt most definitely in our midst; and his ideals enter into all our considerations."

Cauthen declared that while he would not surrender his love for the Orient, he was going to find opportunity for discovering an equal love for Latin America, Africa, Europe, and the Middle East. Baker Cauthen was to be a man for all nations.

His deep sense of comradeship with his wife emerged. "Mrs. Cauthen joins me in greetings to each of you and in anticipation of sharing with you this task for our Master's glory."

The weeks and months fell away under the onslaught of responsibilities, unexpected turns of events, and travels in every direction. There were too many to recall, but they called upon the energies of the youth, experience, and spiritual resources he brought to the task.

Returning from the Orient, Cauthen quickly planned a trip to Latin America. He had no way of knowing the true significance of that trip at the time he planned it. Presenting in the spring his final report to the board on his work in the Orient, he recommended the election of James Winston Crawley, the young Philippines missionary, as his successor to the Orient. Then before another board meeting could roll around, Everett Gill died following a brief illness—the board's second major loss in ten months.

"Although Dr. Gill had not been well for several months," Cauthen told the board, "none of us had any idea at the April meeting of the board that he might not be with us today." He pointed out that it would be difficult to measure the magnitude of the loss. Gill had fulfilled a unique role both in administration and in personality at the Foreign Mission Board.

Porter Routh, secretary-treasurer of the Southern Baptist Convention's Executive Committee, remembers that it was Everett Gill who, following Cauthen's election, quipped, "We can all get back to our work now. All of us have been so busy writing our acceptance speeches that we couldn't answer our mail." The comment broke the ice, as Routh remembers, and helped unite the little family of administrators around their new leader.

Therefore, when Cauthen actually left for his Latin American trip, he had the same problem as when he went to the Orient a few months earlier: to take soundings on a new area secretary.

By October he had the man—Frank Means. He had planned to pull Frank into an administrative role as a special associate. "I felt I especially needed Frank's help because of his sharp grasp of financial matters," he said. "But then I decided that wasn't a job I could put off on somebody else. It was something I was going to have to learn myself."

Executive committee members of the Foreign Mission Board through the years can testify that Cauthen has learned his lessons well. A steel-trap mind has ingested fianancial realities with both a broad view and a grasp of detail that have left seasoned businessmen in awe. Many have remarked to preacher colleagues, "We couldn't find enough to pay that man if he were in business."

Seeing the area secretaries as key associates in his task, Cauthen decided that having Means in the position of a Latin American secretary would not only take care of that position but still make

Dr. Baker James Cauthen congratulates newly appointed foreign missionaries.

him available for administrative help.

In November the board sent Elmer West to the Orient to review personnel needs. In sending him, Cauthen said he felt sure it was going to mark a new era in personnel recruitment. West and his associates were to feel both the backing of their new executive secretary and the heat of his hopes for rising appointments.

Cauthen was quickly known as a "men and money" man. Every message, from no matter what quarter it began, soon centered on the need for young men and women throughout Southern Baptist life to surrender themselves to the missionary task and for Southern Baptists to back those lives with sacrificial giving. The 1,750 missionaries that Rankin had hoped to attain in the Advance Program constituted a goal to which Cauthen was single-mindedly committed. All of his preaching began to zero in on that point. He quickly announced an interim goal of 1,000 missionaries by 1955.

A Southern Baptist committee on world evangelism in December of 1954 reported Baker James Cauthen as saying, "The basic requirement for an expanded mission undertaking is a much larger missionary staff." Cauthen pointed out that if increase kept going at its present rate, it would take from fifteen to eighteen years to reach a mission staff of 1,750. He called for a rapid escalation of that effort, and the committee responded by urging that all phases of Southern Baptist life gear in behind.

Meanwhile, Cauthen and his family came under the white hot light of publicity as they never had before. Articles in *Home Life* magazine pictured sixteen-year-old Carolyn and fifteen-year-old Ralph around their new home in Richmond, Eloise in the garden, and Baker reclining in a chair with a good book and listening to classical music. Their homelife was dissected and shared with Baptist readers in the typical way that such articles were written in those days.

Cauthen not only preached day in and day out in every kind of situation, but also wrote many articles. When he took the time, he had a surprising flair for it.

Writing in a Sunday School Board publication called the *Teacher,* in an article entitled "Missions in the Heart of God," Cauthen began:

"I write these lines aboard a transpacific airliner whose four powerful engines take us swiftly through the skies. The calm, blue waters of the ocean reflect the gleaming sunlight, while fields of snow-white clouds add beauty to the heavens.

"But in the Orient, to which I go, are teeming millions of fellow mortals who know little of beauty in their lives. These soaring wings ere long will bear me to Japan, where heavy hearts are hidden behind friendly smiles. War and stinging defeat have kept the nation confused and groping for her way."

Though always erudite, Cauthen was not always as spontaneous or as aesthetic. The sheer press of events pushed him more and more to simple and clear declarative statements. Seldom, therefore, did readers discover in his writing his extremely sensitive side. That was reserved for the hearer. His preaching grew richer in such dimensions and his emotional involvement even more authentic.

By mid-1955 Cauthen had led the Convention and its various agencies to gear up for a special world missions emphasis in 1957. It was to be highlighted by a special stewardship emphasis week October 29—November 5, 1956, to be designated World Missions Week. That was to commence a series of special emphases leading up to the year 1964, the Baptist Jubilee anniversary of the organization of the Baptist Convention in America. Adoniram Judson's missionary journey to Burma had occurred 150 years before.

Cauthen felt that the new emphasis would make it possible to reach the minimum objective of 1,750 missionaries that Rankin's Advance Program called for by the Jubilee anniversary. He began to address every decision and relate every priority to that goal. Later that year he brought in another one of "his men." Eugene Hill, his good friend from Canton, China, was still fighting health battles that began under the Japanese occupation. He was brought in to succeed Frank Means as secretary of education and promotion.

Excitement was beginning to be generated throughout Southern Baptist life about the world missions task. Advance of its world missions program was, according to some, the singular accomplishment of Baker James Cauthen, who seemed to be everywhere at once. But Cauthen was charged with an administrative task, also. The board demanded that he bring in an associate. Rogers Smith, who had been elected earlier to be an associate in the department of education and promotion, was asked to become Cauthen's associate in 1958.

Cauthen got a scare when Crawley, in the Orient in 1955, developed a malignancy; but quick and effective surgery restored him to good health. Cauthen admired Crawley's "business as usual" spirit. When he discovered he was ill, Crawley refused to come to the States for medical attention, but used doctors available in Japan.

Elmer West was authorized in 1955 to add another associate in personnel in the person of Bill Cody. His responsibility was to set up a division for mission volunteers who were not yet ready for candidacy so that they could be cultivated toward that point. In 1957 West added still another associate, James E. Stertz, and in 1959, Luke B. Smith. In 1960 a fourth associate, Jesse C. Fletcher, was added to work in the western part of the United States. Edna Frances Dawkins, another associate, had been there when West came on the scene.

All of this was in line with Cauthen's unswerving commitment to building the missionary force to the 1,750 mark by the Jubilee Advance in 1964.

Increasingly, board members began to hear a familiar sound. It was the testimonies of newly appointed missionaries saying that they had heard God's call to the missionary task while listening to Baker James Cauthen. These had heard him preach at the convention, at Ridgecrest, at their church during their Lottie Moon emphasis, at an evangelism conference, at an associational meeting, at a special youth rally, at a chapel period at a Baptist college, or on a missions day at a Southern Baptist seminary. One board member listening to such testimonies remarked to a staff member sitting beside him, "I believe God is using him to call out 1,750 missionaries by himself."

Cauthen would have denied such thinking. Thinking of himself as part of a team, he saw the administrative staff as a family. He tried not to think of those who were his men and those who were Rankin's men. But when Sadler retired in 1957 and Cornell Goerner was brought in as the new secretary for Africa, Europe, and the Middle East, many noted that Cauthen now had his own men on the front lines in all area work.

But not everything turned up roses. As advance escalated, criticism emerged. Cauthen's constant pressure for escalating mission-

234

ary appointments was viewed by some as an unwillingness to come to grips with the need for quality people. Cauthen moved to head off such criticism by affirming wherever he could a careful screening process. He followed personnel department recommendations to begin an orientation conference as early as 1955, saying, "If we can prevent even one appointee from becoming frustrated and resigning, we will have achieved something worth more than all of the conference costs." At that point Cauthen also indicated one of his ongoing concerns—missionaries who resign. Resignation, unless bad health precluded further service, was almost beyond his understanding.

Others said that his approach to mission volunteers and also to missionaries on the field unloaded a great deal of guilt on them and prevented free action in terms of their own dynamic sense of God's leadership. In personal conferences, however, people always found him generous and understanding.

"When you get him in personal conference, the pastor's heart is evident," one missionary said. "No matter how tough he's been in letters or in decisions mediated through the area secretaries, when you get in personal conference with him, he's as gentle as a spring rain," said another.

Cauthen did not go to Africa until 1957. That was in part for the same reason he had gone to both the Orient and Latin America—a new area secretary. And in part it was a recognition that Africa was going to be a most difficult area to relate to. Africa had been George Sadler's territory, and many Africa missionaries had wanted him to succeed Rankin. Members of the Nigerian mission especially had been frustrated by some of Cauthen's decisions, which they interpreted as limiting their traditional autonomy. But as usual, in face-to-face encounter, he was well received. He came back recommending Goerner's election and new moves into developing countries in southern and eastern Africa.

Cauthen felt, correctly, that the Foreign Mission Board's free church tradition especially equipped it to ride the new tide of nationalism in Africa. He backed Goerner strongly in a policy of expansion into such countries as Northern (now Zambia and Malawi) and Southern Rhodesia, Kenya, and Tanganyika (now Tanzania) and into such West African countries as Guinea and Ghana.

In 1958 Cauthen reflected on the first ten years of Southern Baptists' Advance Program. There had been 625 missionaries at the beginning. In the April 1958 report, he reported 1,203 missionaries under appointment. The Board's income, $4,700,000 in 1948, had climbed to almost $14,000,000. Whereas missionaries worked in twenty-eight countries ten years before, they were now established in thirty-eight countries. The headquarters staff had grown from thirty-seven persons to eighty-two, and a new headquarters building further west on Monument Avenue was nearing completion.

Cauthen continued to press for an increased rate of missionary appointments, holding up a 1964 goal of 1,800 missionaries instead of the 1,750 that had been a part of the Rankin Advance Program. This seemed to be an effort not to restate the Rankin program, but to reflect his own schedule for increasing the number of missionary appointments each year.

Cauthen recognized a missionary commitment throughout Southern Baptist life, and he strove to utilize it wherever it was found. But he also recognized the importance of keeping the foreign mission task in the hands of the Foreign Mission Board rather than parceling it out to other Southern Baptist agencies that also felt a missions commitment. His staff members marveled at the way he could stand up and carry the day in interagency debates. Then they would despair when he would turn around and, aware that he had won the battle, "give away most of the spoils."

The aggressive Radio and Television Commission was in the forefront of efforts to be utilized in the overseas tasks. Cauthen responded with a series of new moves to keep the board's leadership in media efforts overseas. In his 1958 report he said, "Another aspect of missions advance lies in our using to a greater degree facilities for a large-scale communication of the gospel. This calls for much greater use of audiovisual materials, radio, television, newspaper publicity, and the work of publication agencies." But then he took the lead in trying to involve the Radio and Television Commission in supportive relationships.

Cauthen had a keen understanding of the Convention support necessary for the missions endeavor. Because of it, he gave himself unendingly to the task of preaching in churches large and small. He always accepted an invitation on the basis of first come, first served rather than on the basis of the largest or most influential church. Pastors soon sensed that Cauthen would do this and responded with unqualified loyalty. As some of these men assumed higher responsibilities in Southern Baptist Convention life, they didn't forget.

The editor of the Georgia Baptist *Christian Index,* John Jeter Hurt, once said, "Cauthen can have anything he wants anytime. Southern Baptists are not going to let him down."

In January of 1959 Cauthen led his staff into the new headquarters building on Monument Avenue and led his family out to a beautiful new home in Chesterfield County south of the James River. The yard gave him an opportunity to walk and work and get his mind off of the increasing tensions of his task. His doctor had noticed a slight tendency to high blood pressure and urged him to get some exercise and watch his diet. At the latter point, he had already cultivated some very spartan habits—a residue of his China experience—and needed little urging. He quickly controlled a fifty-year-old man's tendency to gain weight by reducing his intake and adding exercise.

Cauthen made another trip to Africa in 1960, along with Cornell Goerner, to explore opportunities for opening new mission work. The Congo was in terrible turmoil at that time, and Cauthen used the opportunity upon returning to the United States to address the racial question again. He had made strong statements on behalf of racial justice as early as 1958, and many people resistant to blacks' demands for equal rights were reluctant to schedule missionaries for fear of what they might say on the subject. Some men gave Cauthen his due for leading out in this area. But his extreme graciousness with all people, even those with whom he radically differed, caused others to downplay his role in civil rights. If it could be analyzed speech by speech, Cauthen and his fellow missionaries probably used the missionary wedge to open more doors in the deep South than were ever opened by other, more pontifical efforts.

In the summer of 1960 Cauthen performed a tender and traditional task. He gave his daughter, Carolyn, in marriage—during a fierce rainstorm in Richmond, Virginia—to a young theological student named Bill Mathews.

Carolyn had attended Mars Hill College in North Carolina, then

Baylor University. Ralph was at Mars Hill himself. This marked a change in the life-style of the Cauthens. Eloise went on the road with Baker. Their salvations from the tensions of office were an automobile and books. As they drove she would read at length to him; or when she was driving, he would read to her. Traveling from engagement to engagement, meeting to meeting, often driving late into the night to make connections, they yet found the time together refreshing. Many times, of course, the connections were too tight to allow this luxury. But whenever they could, they bought up the opportunity. And the two of them, always close, drew even closer.

Eloise's companionship was especially propitious for Cauthen, who, though he felt close to many people, was never one to nurture extremely close friends. "He keeps his own counsel," even those closest to him would say. "There's something about the man that you can't really level with," others complained. "He sits back in that chair and looks at you, and there's no way you're going to give him really bad news."

Moreover, they knew his persuasiveness could be overwhelming. Some of the biggest and most blustery leaders in Southern Baptist life wilted before the narrowed gaze and measured words of the Foreign Mission Board's executive secretary. His own staff was sharply aware of his persuasiveness. More than one staff member went into his office with the declared purpose of "telling it like it is," only to come out sheepishly confessing that it wasn't "like that" after all.

As the time neared for the Baptist Jubilee Advance meeting of the Convention in Atlantic City, it became obvious that Cauthen was not only going to be able to announce to Baptists of the world that Rankin's 1948 advance goals had been reached, but that new vistas beyond were visible.

As he looked back over the years, however, there were some scars. Because conflict was so painful to Cauthen, he does not recall these particular events except in terms of their healed dimensions and long-range implications.

The New Life Movement is an example. A missionary from Japan, Dub Jackson, sent a film that he had produced to promote a special evangelistic campaign in Japan in 1962. He wanted to show it at the Southern Baptist Convention in Miami in 1960. Staff members advised that it would not be appropriate; but Cauthen, recognizing the deep interest of many Convention leaders, decided to let the film be shown. The matter subsequently developed into a full-fledged, primarily Texas-supported evangelistic effort in Japan that was highly successsful but equally controversial.

Despite reactions even within his staff, Cauthen spoke warmly of the campaign, preached in it, and remembers it as a major contribution to new evangelistic thrusts throughout the world. Because of it he recommended that a consultant on evangelism be added to the staff, pointing out that the Foreign Mission Board would be initiating such efforts in the future.

But neither conflict nor controversy robbed Cauthen of a deep awareness that the close of 1963, Rankin's dream was a reality. The 1,750 missionaries he had prayed for were in excess of 1,800 missionaries in fifty-three countries. The $10,000,000 he had prayed for had given way to a budget of $22,133,031.96 for 1964. How did he celebrate it? "The reaching of this objective is not a summons to relax but a summons to gird up afresh for the battle. A glance at the map of the world with its vast areas where we have no witness brings a sense of rebuke to our hearts."

He had completed that which he set out to do in the memory of the one who had inspired him and preceded him, M. Theron Rankin. He was now casting down a gauntlet for the projection of his own dream.

CHAPTER EIGHT

Dreaming a New Dream

An aura of undeniable success in what he had accomplished accompanied the Foreign Mission Board's celebration of Baker James Cauthen's tenth anniversary as executive secretary at the close of 1963. From Cauthen's point of view, what he had accomplished was the completion of Theron Rankin's goal. An executive of the Woman's Missionary Union was later to say, "Before Cauthen, very few people knew about Rankin. In constantly stating Rankin's dream, Cauthen made him famous."

Cauthen would have denied that, and so would Rankin's followers. Many of them felt that Rankin's perception of principles and grasp of both the technology and the methodology of missions were superior to Cauthen's. But the same group felt that God raised up Cauthen with the particular gifts that were needed at precisely that time to galvanize Southern Baptists toward cooperation and commitment to the missionary task. "Rankin could never move an audience as Cauthen can," one former staff member said. "But in a small group, he was absolutely scintillating."

Interestingly, such comparisons were never brought to Cauthen's attention. Editors didn't write about them, and individuals didn't talk to him about them. Cauthen has never voiced any but gracious words about Rankin or acknowledged anything other than a personal debt to his executive secretary's inspirational leadership. Now that debt was paid, and he was free to dream his own dreams.

Staff members, who had found Cauthen resolutely resistant to any ideas that would drain off energies directed toward expanding the missionary force and establishing new beachheads around the world, were suddenly surprised to find him open to new ideas, probing and even provoking them to explore the frontiers of their own thinking for a "new program of advance." At the end of his first ten years, the shape of the Foreign Mission Board's staff was approximately as Cauthen had received it. The personnel department had been enlarged. A consultant for medical matters had been added. And, as mentioned earlier, a consultant on evangelism had also been added.

Tension that had grown between Cauthen and his personnel department over the escalation of missionary appointments came to a head in 1963, when all but two of the department members left for other positions. The secretary of that department, Elmer West, took a pastorate in northern Virginia, but not before Cauthen tried to persuade him to take a new area secretaryship that would constitute the first major enlargement of that section of missionary administration. West, who often differed with Cauthen although he had profound respect for the latter's "single-minded dedication to the cause of missions," declined.

Jesse C. Fletcher, a Texan and a Southwestern Seminary graduate, was named secretary of the personnel department and quickly rebuilt it. The Virginia editor, Reuben Alley, suggested in an editorial that West's leaving was the result of administrative resistance to higher standards for appointees. Alley was probably among those disturbed when the statesmanlike Virginia layman L. Howard Jenkins, retiring after thirty years as president of the board, had been replaced by a Jacksonville, Florida, pastor named Homer Lindsey. The latter favored a strong conservative and evangelistic outlook on the part of the board. Some of them reminded colleagues of their fears at the time Cauthen was elected.

Despite these voices, the pace quickened at the board. New work was opened in another dozen countries within a very brief period of time, and the missionary force soon bounded over two thousand and into the top position among missionary agencies in the United States.

Cauthen enthusiastically accepted Fletcher's plan for another short-term program. A missionary associate program for older men and women with especially needed experience was instituted in late 1962 to work in English-language opportunities overseas. It was Cauthen's openness to a whole new advance thrust that, Fletcher felt, caused him to buy the short-term program for young college graduates between the ages of twenty-one and twenty-seven. The program was named the missionary journeyman program and was placed under the leadership of the associate personnel secretary, Louis Cobbs. Following on the heels of the popular national Peace Corps from the Kennedy era, it quickly caught the imagination and support of Southern Baptists.

At the Baptist Jubilee Advance Celebration in Atlantic City in June of 1964, Cauthen pointed to new horizons with a shocking call for five thousand missionaries at the earliest possible date, expansion into new geographical areas, development of new programs of work, and commitment of more than $65,000,000 a year to underwrite the task.

Many people felt that it was a visionary call to higher ground. Others thought Cauthen was still voicing the men and money theme when he needed to explore new methods and new relationships with nationals. Some ecumenical groups of missionaries were caught up in what was called "six continent missions." This view de-emphasized sending boards and highlighted special relationships between sharing and receiving bodies of believers. Advocates of it were especially critical of Cauthen.

Cauthen thought his new program of advance more imaginative than that. He emphasized working with university students, expanding radio and television work, more mature partnerships with national constituencies, a broader spectrum of leadership training programs, new commitment to agricultural missions and self-help programs, and a new approach to medical missions that would take into consideration the improved medical care being provided in nations where Southern Baptists were working.

Critics, including Southwestern Seminary missions professor Cal Guy, thought there was too much emphasis on institutions and too little on self-supporting churches and national leadership. Southeastern Seminary professor Luther Copeland read the problem from the other direction. Baptists were trying to go it alone when a more ecumenical approach was desperately needed.

It wasn't an easy period in which to get Southern Baptists' attention. Incidents that altered everyone's way of perceiving things stalked Cauthen's years of leadership. The beat generation was followed by the hippies, the free-speech movement, and the youth craze. The hard facts of the Communist world became evident in Hungary. Then the United States civil rights movement heated up to preoccupy everybody with Little Rock in 1957, sit-ins in 1960, freedom riders in 1961, James Meredith at Old Miss in 1962, and Wallace at the schoolhouse door in Alabama in 1963.

In 1957 came Sputnik, and in 1961 Alan Shepard became the first Amercian to probe space. In 1962 Glenn orbited the earth.

The Kennedy era began in 1960, and the Bay of Pigs incident and the Kennedy-Khrushchev debates occurred the very next year. Something was happening in Vietnam that few people understood. In 1962 they were too occupied with the Cuban missile crisis to worry and took little note of the Diem brothers' assassination in Saigon in 1963.

One reason so many people failed to be preoccupied with Vietnam was an event that happened in Dallas in November of 1963. The charismatic young president, John F. Kennedy, was downed by an assassin's bullet. The bloom came off many roses everywhere.

Foreign missions felt the repercussions of that and subsequent events more than most people realize, but Cauthen realized that and periodically tried to speak to it. In the Tonkin Gulf incident he saw not Russia's influence but Chinese Communism. That concerned him less, however, than the civil rights murders in Mississippi, which shocked the nonwhite world where most of Southern Baptists' mission enterprises were carried on. Cauthen made an impassioned speech to Baptists gathered at Ridgecrest, North Carolina, that summer, urging them not to let the missionaries pay all the costs for racial wrongs in the United States. Even before the Mississippi murders, he had said:

"The majority of the work we do across the world is amid nonwhite people. It would be hard to overstate the shock that these people experience when stories of racial disturbances in our land find major space in their newspapers. It's particularly sad when any story goes out of people of any race being refused admittance into a house of worship."

Pointing out that the Foreign Mission Board might even find it necessary to bring missionaries out of troubled areas because of racial tensions in the United States, he added, "We need to pray for the guidance of the living God that we may be able to show clearly that Christian love includes all people regardless of race, of nationality, or of circumstance."

Baker Cauthen was, at this point, one of the acknowledged statesmen in Baptist life around the world as well as in Southern

Baptist life. But Southern Baptists were beginning to honor him in new ways. Southwestern Seminary named him one of its distinguished alumni in 1964, along with his good friend W. L. Howse.

That summer Baker and Eloise Cauthen journeyed back to the Orient together. Among other things, Cauthen wanted to measure the impact of the continuing evangelistic crusades from visiting American preachers and laymen in the Orient. Some missionaries felt that they spent more time getting ready to entertain "weekend missionaries" than they did doing their own missionary work. Others felt that the impetus was needed. They saw that national Christians, who were infinitesimal minorities, drew great strength when they met the Americans. These often were men and women of stature, education, and means who came from abroad to share their faith in a simple manner.

Cauthen refused to be polarized on the matter. Instead, he called for due process. "Let the missions call for such crusades," he said. "Then we are in the right position to respond." He urged that such matters be channeled through the board's consultant on evangelism and church development, Joseph Underwood. The latter had been brought to the Foreign Mission Board to try to head off the fragmentation of such efforts throughout the convention. Cauthen greatly feared the fragmentation of Southern Baptist world missions. He saw some of the zealous but uncoordinated efforts as a threat to the cooperative concentration through the board that had brought rapid growth.

In the mid-sixties a Brazilian pastor who had grown up in the Southern Baptist work in Brazil, Rubens Lopez, came to the United States. He used the Southern Baptist Convention's Foreign Missions Night to call for a crusade of the Americas. Cauthen responded warmly to the call and made a tremendous investment of Foreign Mission Board personnel and planning. The program was a series of simultaneous revivals working up and down both the northern and southern hemispheres. Many people thought they were less than successful. Others felt that they welded in a positive way the ties between Baptists in the various countries involved.

In 1965 Cauthen received an honorary doctorate from Hardin-Simmons University and delivered the baccalaureate sermon there. He tried to speak to the missionary task in its twentieth-century context. United States ground troops had been committed to Vietnam earlier in the year, and it was to be the year of the Selma march in Alabama and the Watts riots in Los Angeles. In a Ridgecrest speech that summer, Cauthen said, "Our century is one which can be described in terms of overflowing benevolence and extreme cruelty." Contrasting foreign aid and concentration camps, he called it a century of longings for peace yet one filled with horrors of war. There were scientific breakthroughs, expansion of knowledge and new freedoms, and yet frustration and ignorance as to how to handle those very fruits.

In that same year of 1965, Cauthen responded to increasing pressure. Southern Baptists on state convention levels, pastors, seminaries, colleges, and lay people wanted to have more of a say in foreign missions. He convened the first Foreign Mission Board Consultation on World Missions with 281 participants in Miami Beach just prior to the Baptist World Alliance in the summer of 1965. Cauthen explained that the consultation was designed to help the Foreign Mission Board implement its new program of advance, which called for an overseas missions staff of 5,000 as soon as possible.

The consultation group debated the role of institutions and social ministries. It looked at the use of radio and television and other mass media, large-scale evangelistic campaigns, the involvement in missions of Southern Baptists traveling and working overseas. Other considerations were short-term programs of missionary service, the need for more definitive orientation of new missionaries, and the overall strategy of missions.

The personnel department had convinced Cauthen and its area leadership of the need to underwrite a fourteen-week orientation program for new missionaries beginning the next fall. Two orientation cycles would be run each year—one in the fall and one in the spring. Training programs for missionary journeymen were to be held each summer. The first group of missionary journeymen was sent out in the summer of 1965. Cauthen undergirded it as strongly as he dared, realizing that many missionaries believed that any short-term program would undermine emphasis on career missions.

In an editorial in the *Commission* in 1966, Cauthen recognized a tender moment in his own life. His beloved mother passed away, five years after the death of his father. He wrote of her:

"Her love for missions was profound. It was not easy for her to see us go to China as missionaries with two babies in 1939 when war already was spread across the land and the terrible destruction of World War II was about to break. It was hard for her to endure the times when wartime conditions made communication slow and difficult."

He said, "During her illness, her faith was like a brilliant light, and her eagerness to enter heaven's door was evident. In talking with me one day about the message of life, she said, 'Tell the people that it's all true.' " Then he added poignantly, "Now she is on the golden shore, and heaven seems so very near."

In 1966 such things as Black Power and the rhetoric that went with it were heating up civil rights discussions. Radical theologians were heating up theological discussions with the cry that "God is dead." Cauthen tried to speak to such issues periodically, usually taking as a forum a staff chapel period, a convention meeting, or the Ridgecrest or Glorieta service he made traditionally his own on Sunday mornings.

Cauthen's experience in the Orient, both as a missionary and as an administrator during turbulent times, uniquely equipped him to deal with some of the things he faced during the sixties. He now was at the helm of the rapidly growing mission enterprise. Crises in Nigeria, Israel, Vietnam, Indonesia, and Chile, to mention but a few, gave him ample opportunity for statesmanlike calls to stand steady and not lose sight of the big picture. When natural disasters around the world called for response, he suggested a measured response. He knew full well that the next week's headlines could move attention in other directions and that gearing up beyond ability to sustain a program was a classic mistake in a volatile situation.

In June 1967 a new Arab-Israeli war broke out just as Cauthen and the secretary for Europe and the Middle East, J. D. Hughey, were preparing for a trip to that area. It was necessary to evacuate missionaries from Jordon, Lebanon, and Gaza. Missionaries in Israel were able to stand. Cauthen left on July 2 to join Hughey, who had gone ahead to Beirut. They toured the whole area, set in motion several relief projects, and then went on to Yemen, where a new hospital project was commencing. It would be Southern Baptists' closest venture to Mecca, Cauthen liked to point out. While evangelistic opportunities would be limited, the Christian witness through the hospital would be unmistakable. But Cauthen's view was not totally accepted.

Mission strategists like Cal Guy felt that such a tremendous investment of money and personnel into a resistant area was unwise. Guy told his students, many of whom were added to the Foreign Mission Board's missionary force, that advance ought to be made in directions of response. He advocated token forces in resistant areas until the situation ripened and favored heavy commitments of men and money in areas obviously responsive to the Holy Spirit.

In 1968 Cauthen decided to reorganize his growing Richmond staff. Under the long-standing high priority of increased missionary appointments, the personnel department had grown significantly with regional personnel representatives, an orientation director, and even a small data processing center. After a series of studies, the data processing center gave way to a full-scale computer operation. The same study yielded a management report from a consulting firm indicating that the board ought to be organized in two divisions—one an Overseas Division and the other a Homeside Division. Cauthen's original idea was to name Winston Crawley director of the Overseas Division with the area secretaries and consultants under him and to move Frank Means into the Homeside Division with the business office, the treasury, the personnel department, and the department of missionary education and promotion under him. Means declined, preferring to stay with Latin America. Cauthen urged that the Foreign Mission Board proceed with organization of the Overseas Division, and he recommended Crawley for that role. Rogers Smith, his administrative associate, was cast in a supportive rather than an administrative role. Crawley's role, on the other hand, became strongly administrative. He became Cauthen's direct link to the area work and to the fields, though some of the area secretaries continued to seek out and get direct contact with Cauthen.

In late 1968 Cauthen approached the board with a decision to restructure the staff into three divisions. Besides the Overseas Division, he suggested a Missions Support Division and a Management Services Division. The board bought the concept. Then Cauthen revealed that he had asked Jesse C. Fletcher to head the new Missions Support Division. Fletcher had been Cauthen's personnel secretary since 1963. Eugene Hill, secretary of education and promotion, was the senior officer in point of service and in missionary experience, but he himself had suggested to Cauthen that because of his (Hill's) proximity to retirement, Fletcher should take the new division.

The board approved, but some members expressed the feeling that Cauthen had inadvertently bypassed customary procedure in the process. Cauthen's ability to deal verbally with objection and argument and at the same time pour oil on troubled waters soon put down the flame. Fletcher joined Crawley in a division chief's role. They were soon joined by Sidney Reber, who had served as a missionary associate in Singapore, as the mission's business manager. A former Internal Revenue Service executive, Reber took over the Management Services Division, which was composed of the old business office and treasurer's department.

These three men, along with Rogers Smith and Cauthen, became the chief planning body, though Cauthen constantly included the area secretaries and department heads on major deliberations to maintain as broad an input as possible. He felt warmly toward all his staff and had great confidence in their ability to function as a team.

He adroitly negotiated the tensions between the new divisions as they struggled to define their particular responsibilities in reference to the others. Fletcher and Crawley particularly wrestled with the problem because individual members of their divisions constantly suggested that the other division was going to overwhelm some of their prerogatives. Crawley, with a keen mind and a strong historical perspective, patiently worked through these problems with the younger administrator, both feeling the full support and understanding of Cauthen.

As the new structure moved into the last year of the decade, Cauthen called upon them to plan creatively toward the decade of the seventies. At that point they were only responding to the spirit of the times. Apollo II had landed on the moon, and there was much talk about futurism. Some were predicting famine in the world by 1975, but predictions were so numerous that even the more dramatic got lost in the sheer number.

Crawley and Cauthen became the architects for a "strategy of the seventies" as the new decade dawned, with Cauthen its lead interpreter.

The decade of the seventies also heralded the 125th anniversary of the Southern Baptist Convention and the Foreign Mission Board. Under the editorship of area secretary J. D. Hughey, Cauthen collaborated with Fletcher, Hill, Crawley, Goerner, Hughey, and Means to prepare a new Foreign Mission Board history entitled *Advance: a History of Southern Baptist Foreign Missions.*

With a Lottie Moon offering that topped fifteen million dollars for the first time and a budget in excess of thirty million dollars, with missionary appointments running over 200 annually and with over 2,500 missionaries in seventy-one countries, Cauthen had every right to feel a deep sense of satisfaction. If he did, he masked it under a continuing concern for what was yet to be done.

In an April 14, 1970, report he said to the board:

"How far will this enterprise grow? This question we will leave in the hands of God. We know that our task is to communicate the blessed message of redemption to all mankind. We believe that we honor our Lord as the churches share what the people lay upon the altar of their giving that the world may know about Jesus. We commit ourselves to the objectives which are before us, having glimpsed them in faith and confidence in God's power and leadership. We in no way feel that the present objectives represent the maximum of what God may expect from the people called Baptists. We will leave these expectations to our Lord to be revealed to us in prayer and faith as we experience more of his guidance and as we seek to be stewards of his remarkable blessings."

That summer the Cauthens journeyed first to Hong Kong, and then on to Japan for the 1970 meeting of the Baptist World Alliance. Cauthen spoke to over eight thousand people there just twenty-five years after the end of World War II and only twenty-four years after he and Missionary Ed Dozier traveled up and down that war-stricken country to plan Southern Baptists' reentry.

In 1971 Baker James Cauthen was named an outstanding alumnus of Baylor University. Few things gratified him more. But the newsmaker of the year emerged from the nation's capital, where it was announced that Richard Nixon would visit Red China. The news produced ambivalent feelings in Cauthen and other leaders at the Foreign Mission Board. On one hand, the thought that a window might be opened in China, where so many Baptist Christians had struggled so long in a relatively underground situation, was exciting. On the other hand, the possibility that the United States would in any way develop a rapprochement with a government so hostile to the Christian faith was disturbing.

The Foreign Mission Board voted to request from the president a meeting with Dr. Cauthen, so that hopes and needs regarding Chinese Christians could be voiced in advance of his trip.

Billy Graham, with well-known rapport with President Nixon, was urged to intercede. Graham did, and word came back from Henry Kissinger's office that the White House was open to such an interchange. When the interchange came, it boiled down to Cauthen, Crawley, Fletcher, Parks, and Hill in consultation with an aide of Dr. Kissinger. What long-range, or for that matter short-range, impact the consultation had is known only to God. Cauthen's prime concern, and he expressed it in a most articulate way, was that the faithful allies on Taiwan not be sold down the river as a price for rapprochement with China. Further, if any information could be secured on the Christian churches surviving in China or any help be opened up to them, Baptists were deeply interested.

The world watched Nixon's visit with great interest, but no immediate response came regarding Christians in China. The expulsion of Taiwan from the United Nations confirmed some of Cauthen's other fears.

Too many other things were happening, however, for anyone to become preoccupied with this turn of events. The most serious was a devaluation of the dollar by President Nixon, which dramatically reduced the buying power of Southern Baptist dollars overseas. It amounted to a sudden 10 percent tax on mission dollars as currencies began to float against the dollar.

Cauthen grabbed it first of all as a challenge for the Lottie Moon Christmas Offering in the fall of 1971, then went before the Southern Baptist Convention Executive Committee in the spring of 1972 to ask for the best possible Cooperative Program allocation. Other Baptist leaders, desperately needing additional funds themselves, groaned at the prospect but found it hard to argue with Cauthen's persuasiveness and the genuineness of the issue. "He always gets what he wants," one agency head marveled.

"And he always will," John Jeter Hurt, then editor of the Texas

E. H. Westmoreland, board member, Texas, speaks at a dinner in Richmond honoring Dr. and Mrs. Cauthen on the occasion of his twentieth anniversary as executive secretary of the Foreign Mission Board.

Baptist Standard, added.

In fact, he didn't. Cauthen's efforts were often disparaged by the leaders of the Southern Baptist Convention Executive Committee. As other agency leaders and their associates came in with charts and graphs and recent arguments, Cauthen came in with an impassioned plea. "He always preaches to us," some complained.

But those close to Cauthen knew he felt a deep sense of commitment to the other agencies and their needs. He steadfastly refused to press for more than 50 percent of the Southern Baptist Convention's Cooperative Program funds for foreign missions. But he made no apologies for that figure. He pointed out that when the Baptist dollar was invested in the local church, the association, the state convention, and the Home Mission Board, most of it was invested in the homeland. Even with 50 percent of the Southern Baptist Convention budget and an equivalent Lottie Moon Christmas Offering, Baptists were giving only 4 percent of their collection-plate dollar to world missions. "We don't mean to make an apology about that," he said to staff members again and again as they prepared their presentations.

Cauthen's pastoral approach to his task assumed even larger proportions than his administrative stance as he neared the end of his second decade as executive secretary. When Paul and Nancy Potter, missionaries in the Dominican Republic, were found hacked to death in their bedroom, Cauthen's concern was boundless. For months he kept in contact with the mission, with relatives, and with the surviving children to ascertain their needs and to offer any care.

This was true in other crises. Few people who've witnessed the firmness of Cauthen when dealing with a moral lapse on the part of missionaries will forget it. But those people are equally amazed at the pastoral concern that followed administrative decision making. The grossest sins could not keep the missionary involved from Cauthen's pastoral care. But neither could that spare the missionary his administrative resoluteness.

In 1973 the University of Richmond honored him with a Doctor of Divinity degree. The citation pointed out that under his leadership the overseas missionary staff had increased from 900 to 2,510 serving in seventy-seven countries.

Even more gratifying ceremonies came as the board celebrated

Cauthen's twentieth anniversary. The board presented the Cauthens with an automobile, created a special endowment fund for foreign missions bearing their name, named the board's chapel in Cauthen's honor, commissioned portraits of the two, and authorized a biography. The Cauthens' son and his family and their daughter were a part of the ceremonies, which were marked by celebration, nostalgia, and affection.

Douglas Hudgins, president of the board and executive secretary of Mississippi Baptists, presided over the meeting. He said of Cauthen, "He is Mr. Foreign Missions to Southern Baptists."

But the task wasn't over. The battle wasn't finished. A new challenge lay just around the corner.

CHAPTER NINE

Preacher, Husband, Father

To the casual observer of the Cauthens and events that have swept them through the main currents of history, there is a danger of losing sight of the man himself—and even more so of the woman who walks by his side.

On his twentieth anniversary as executive secretary of the Foreign Mission Board, Baker James Cauthen was a bit more than one year shy of his sixty-fifth birthday. He was winsomely gray and more slender than slight, as he had been in younger years. He was good-humored with an easy way of conversation about him, still capable of great intensity toward any problem or challenge— particularly preaching—and still energetic. The years since have not detracted.

Cauthen's health had always been good, but then he had always watched it carefully. As a younger man he would get eight hours of sleep by marking them off from the time he went to bed, whenever that might be. He just didn't get up until he'd had eight hours. He still prefers that, but likes to read in bed and sometimes reads deep into his allotted time.

In 1976 he underwent the first surgery of his life aside from a tonsillectomy. A polyp was removed from his colon. And as the surgeon said, "since we were in there," he lost his appendix also.

A few years earlier Franklin Fowler, the board's medical adviser, discovered a slightly elevated blood pressure during one of Cauthen's annual physicals and prescribed a more restricted diet and walking or jogging. Cauthen has been faithful at both.

Eloise says she is constantly amazed at his ability to decide that something ought to be done and then to do it. He grew up watching his eating habits and never did overeat. Although he loved coffee, he was convinced after he came back to the United States

254

that it was disturbing his digestion, so he gave it up. He drank tea in China and substituted that for coffee when he decided the latter was counterproductive. More recently, he decided that sugar was a problem and gave that up. He's never smoked or used alcohol; nor has it ever been a temptation. But he is remarkably free from intolerance toward people who have struggled with these or any other habits questionable either in relationship to health or witness.

As a youngster he did not participate in sports, but he got all the exercise he ever needed from doing his after-school jobs. At Baylor and at Southwestern Seminary, when his studies caused him to become too tense, he would take a break and go for a walk. At the seminary he would walk west from the campus across the railroad tracks, then proceed south on McCart until he intersected a country road. God gave him some deep insights on those walks, he said. He found places to walk in every place he's ever lived, including the neighborhood where he now lives south of the James River in Richmond.

Golf and tennis? A few not-so-rewarding attempts. Yard work? It was a no-no until they bought their present house and the children were gone. Then, as Eloise says, "It was like a conversion." He suddenly found it a solution for office tensions and a source of great satisfaction. Azaleas and rhododendrons began to blossom around the yard. The grass took on a healthy green as he limed, fertilized, and seeded it annually. The leaves were raked down the hill into a ditch or occasionally stored for mulch.

Because he traveled so much, family life was cherished even more for its scarcity. Family fun was a block of time both kids remember, especially from their China days. Family fun could be created out of almost any free moment that God gave them. Ralph Cauthen remembers discovering a small hole in the floor of one of the limestone caves where they used to take refuge in air raids. He also recalls the excitement he felt when his daddy pointed out a fish swimming in the water at the bottom of that hole. Both he and Carolyn remember sitting on their father's lap as he read *Winnie the Pooh* to them during those times. They may have heard the explosions that indicated potential destruction from Japanese bombers, but they can barely remember it.

They remember family picnics in West China, outings in Shanghai, and rowboats and beach walks in Hong Kong. They remember trips to the mountains in Tokyo. They remember long, pleasant evenings spent listening to classical music or lying on the floor with their father, perusing the *Encyclopedia Britannica*.

"If ever a family enjoyed the encyclopedia, it was our family," Carolyn remembers. "And my own intellectual curiosity and deep love for astronomy, geology, and archaeology come directly as an inheritance from my father and his avid interests."

Missionary magazines from time to time carried family portraits of the Cauthens, including pictures of the children and Eloise in various domestic dimensions. Ralph laughs and says, "That was all true, but it didn't tell the whole story."

On the other hand, both children suffered to some extent from that work their father had been called to do. Ralph remembers nine different places for nine different grades. Both wince as they remember the "superfundamentalist" youngsters who matriculated at Thomas Jefferson High School in Richmond carrying their Bibles with their books and their sincere conviction that they were in the midst of a corrupt society.

"I was a bit of a loner, and it's not really surprising," said Ralph. "Nor did I feel close to the Chinese because we lived in 'little Americas' in my more formative years. My best friend in Shanghai was a German who also spoke English."

In Tokyo both the children first got involved in peer groups of teenagers. The groups were, for the most part, children of evangelical missionaries and more zealous than their parents in their dedication to "separate living."

The result was that when Carolyn went to Mars Hill and then to Baylor, and Ralph followed suit to Mars Hill but then went on to Furman, both were faced with identity crises.

"In part, it was the problem of living in the home of a famous man and in his shadow," Ralph says.

"Our parents are such strong people, though loving and sensitive, that I guess I had to find myself away from them," Carolyn says. Carolyn had thoughts of becoming a missionary for a time and felt some pressure to do so. "But Dad kept telling me it was something the Lord would have to show me," she remembers. "He did not put any pressure on me." Others felt that Cauthen preached to the kids when he laid down strong calls for commitment to young people in places like Ridgecrest and Glorieta. Carolyn in retrospect does not feel that way; nor does Ralph.

Carolyn went to Southeastern Seminary for a year before marrying Bill Mathews. The two decided almost immediately that Southern Baptist training was too restrictive, and they moved to Duke University. There the brilliant young Mathews decided he wanted to concentrate on philosophy and prepare himself for college teaching. Carolyn kept step with him all the way, working as a librarian in many of the institutions with which he was then connected either as a student or as a teacher.

Bill subsequently began a photography business in Michigan. Carolyn continues to work as a librarian in the University of Michigan at Dearborn. Her insatiable quest for knowledge, which she attributes to her father's influence, finds expression as she coordinates the library's purchasing program. Bill and Carolyn both feel that their religious pilgrimage has diverged from that of their parents.

"It's not one of our major topics of discussion on family get-togethers," Carolyn laughs. "But they're never pushy, always understanding," she adds.

Ralph, licensed to preach by the First Baptist Church of Richmond during his college days, soon decided that wasn't what God wanted him to do or who he was as a person. He made a run at seminary training with a year at Southern Baptist Theological Seminary in Louisville, then responded to the Kennedy charisma and the Peace Corps drama by becoming one of the first volunteers and accepting an assignment in the Philippines.

"It was ideal for me," Ralph remembers. "It was not only cross-cultural—something I was very much at home with—but it was a place where I could serve on a one-to-one basis and find my own identity."

When Ralph returned to the States he married Jane Campbell and entered graduate school to become a social worker. He now coordinates social work activities in High Point, North Carolina. He and Jane live with their two boys in nearby Greensboro. The boys, John and Steve, are frequent visitors to their grandparents' home in Richmond, where their presence brings much delight.

Ralph and Jane joined a Methodist church in the North Carolina community where they live. Like Carolyn, Ralph feels that there was a period during which he moved away from his parents to seek his own identity, but now finds a warm relationship with them.

An example comes from the summer before Cauthen's twentieth anniversary as executive secretary, at the close of one of the magnificent Ridgecrest services. Some three thousand people had been deeply moved by his preaching and by the many who responded to the invitation. Baker Cauthen called on his son, Ralph, to bring the benediction. Ralph did so in a sincere, gentle, and articulate way that pleased his father. This observer felt that it was a milestone moment between father and son. Ralph confirms this. "It was a good experience for me."

Both Ralph and Carolyn underscore one of the major contributions that their family has made to them. Baker and Eloise Cauthen have always been close and openly affectionate. They touch each other often. In front of the children, they embraced freely and naturally. "I remember that so well," Carolyn said. "It still warms me, and it's undoubtedly a part of who I am."

Others have noticed this, too. In fact, many people who feel that Baker James Cauthen keeps his own counsel and is an essentially private person suspect there are two to whom he tells everything. One is Eloise Glass Cauthen. The other is a Father God.

"I've never pressed him to talk," Eloise says. "Yet he always takes time to share significant events with me." But Eloise can be as close with his thoughts as he is. "That's a closed corporation if I ever saw one," a former staff person said.

God has allowed the two of them to reach their mature years with a personal attractiveness, a grace, and a sensitivity that leaves new acquaintances charmed and older acquaintances ever grateful for their faithfulness and friendship.

When the board's staff people have illness or difficulty in their families, both Cauthens respond pastorally but are careful not to push themselves upon people. There is an Oriental shyness about both in this sense.

Their life-style since the children left has been built completely around his demanding schedule. Whenever possible they drive to engagements, and Eloise goes with him not only to share the driving but to share their lives.

Classical music is a vital part of their homelife today and their leisure. The Foreign Mission Board gave them a beautiful stereo set on his tenth anniversary, and their collection of classical music has been designed to fit almost every mood. "I turn it up for the newspaper," he laughs, "but it's soft when I study."

The collection includes Wagner, Beethoven, Mozart, and Cauthen's favorite performer, Heifetz. Eloise prefers piano concertos and is partial to Rachmaninoff and Rubinstein.

On the twentieth anniversary the staff gave the Cauthens *Encyclopedia Britannica III,* and Cauthen has been working his way through it with great gusto. He laces his sermons with illustrations from it, and casual conversations reveal not only the range of his interest but the grasp of his understanding. Cauthen says, "The universe has just exploded for me as I study anthropology, archaeology, geology, and space. All of it is shouting praises of the Creator."

The Cauthens like to entertain friends; and if he has a vice, it's dominoes and a Texas game called 42. "He doesn't make many mistakes," his longtime associate, Rogers Smith, says. "And he wins well and loses well."

But ultimately, Baker James Cauthen's life-style can only be understood in terms of his preaching. Since he's preaching all the time, preparation for preaching dominates any time not committed to his administrative tasks.

Frank Means calls him a preaching administrator. "Rankin was a business administrator, but Cauthen is a preaching administrator," Means says. "But Cauthen has a deep interest in financial affairs and the ability to amass the relevant data of a matter in a way that's almost awesome. He's very insecure when he doesn't have enough information. I've seen him halt a matter being presented to the board by saying icily, 'We have more staff work to do.' What he really means is that some staff person hasn't kept him informed, and new information has developed in the discussion. And if it's information he hasn't heard before, that's not the place he wants to hear it. But you don't really know the man till you see him as a preacher," Means adds.

Cauthen himself says, "I see myself as a Chinese coolie carrying a heavy load on a pole. If I put office work on one end and preaching on the other, they can balance each other."

When he leaves the office, he leaves his work on his desk or in his briefcase. If he's on his way to preach, that's all he thinks about. Unlike most preacher-administrators, Cauthen seldom preaches the same sermon twice. "I have to preach fresh," he says. Neither does he try to prepare from scratch for each assignment. He keeps a notebook on texts and ideas and is constantly making notes in it out of his own extensive devotional life. The notebook is always at hand. During tense periods at the board, when problems become worrisome, or when he is carrying great burdens for individuals and is up in the middle of the night in deep prayer, he opens the Scriptures. Often he perceives things that he knows could be shared profitably from the pulpit. He jots down notes and sometimes even outlines.

Then as he prepares for a preaching trip, he often begins by flipping through his notebook or his heavily marked Bible. "Invariably, just the right text and possibly some thoughts on the matter will be there waiting for me—as if God had already anticipated the assignment and had begun getting me ready for it," Cauthen says.

On the plane or sitting in the airport or in the car with Eloise driving, Baker thinks through what he wants to say and makes notes. He speaks from an outline on almost any kind of paper. He outlines fully, even extensively, and keeps the outline with him in the pulpit. He says, "In earlier years, I didn't keep the outline with me; but now I find that I need it." There's a twinkle in his eye as he says so. His notes are written in a small, difficult-to-read script that moves uphill from left to right. When chided about his penmanship, he always grins and says, "When I retire, I'm going to refresh my typing."

Preparations of thoughts and notes are not, however, the major preparation that Cauthen makes for preaching. "He gets off by himself and talks with God about it," Eloise says. "Sometimes I'll leave the room to give him a chance to be alone. More often, he leaves the room. If it's at Ridgecreast or Glorieta, he has special trails all worked out; and he'll make his way up one of those trails to a promontory where he can think it through and talk to God about it."

Observers feel that Cauthen comes as inspired to the pulpit as any preacher in Southern Baptist life. As he preaches, he is a dynamo of action. He leans into the pulpit with his left hand on one side and his right hand on the other, his left foot forward. He lets his voice carry most of the emphasis, but every now and then he backs away and a stabbing right finger adds emphasis. He does not shout, but his voice gets louder and louder, rising on crescendos. Then it settles again to begin a new round of rising. At times he and the audience can get caught up in an interaction that's absolutely magnetic. Those who can back off from what he's saying long enough to observe him are alarmed. "The man's going to have a stroke," a fellow staff member once said, watching him rise to the challenge of speaking to the Southern Baptist Convention.

"Oh, Southern Baptists!" Cauthen voices that phrase with all the fervor that he has felt in his Master's voice when the latter yearned over Jerusalem. And again and again, Southern Baptists have responded to that cry. "Yonder lies the challenge," he will say. "Yonder on the horizons stands our Master bidding us to follow him," he will add. Yet somehow, Cauthen has resisted clichés in a way that is almost miraculous in light of the number of times he preaches in a given week.

Cauthen's skill as an administrator revolves around his personal presence. His psychic strength, as some would refer to it, can be almost overwhelming. Men who hold prominent positions back off before the strength of his rhetoric and the power of his gaze. This has made a problem for him that he's never fully recognized, according to some critics. The problem is that people tend to tell him what he wants to hear instead of leveling with him. On the other hand, he vows he doesn't want yes men around. He says he wants men who will tell it like it is and differ with him if they have a differing point of view. When I was on Cauthen's staff, I struck that kind of bargain with him. Cauthen felt that if he could trust where a man was going to come out, the man could disagree with him at any length; and the matter would be all right.

Many are not aware of this dimension in Cauthen. A challenge made by a state leader was brought back to his attention. Cauthen replied, "Well, when the time comes to be forthright, I believe that you should be clear. Let there be no lack of clarity. State your position in love. Find the right thing to do and do it." He narrows his eyes even as he gives this advice. "Somebody has to be willing to be responsible, has to be willing to stand as a lightning rod. A leader can not evade responsibility," Cauthen states firmly.

One of the great weaknesses Cauthen has felt in his own personality has rarely been seen by others—a temper. Because of this, Cauthen says he doesn't trust himself to respond either verbally or in writing if a matter arouses his feelings. "I wait on any letter that causes me to feel that way. The other person may need the time also," he says, grinning. Cauthen has a deep sense of need to wait on God in such matters. Quoting the Scripture verse "He shall choose our inheritance for us," Cauthen says, "No problem takes the Lord by surprise. And I'm aware that he often chooses to bless me through a problem. I found out a long time ago that I used up too much precious energy reacting to a matter when what I needed to do was to seek God's leadership."

Eloise says that Cauthen wakes up in the night when he has a problem, takes his Bible, and goes off to pray. Asked about it, he said, "Yes, some of my best prayer experiences come in the night as I wrestle with a problem. I try to let each problem be a call to thanksgiving; then I try to let the Scripture passage flow through my mind that seems related to the problem. Sometimes the problem satisfies itself. Sometimes the solution emerges in prayer. Sometimes it comes as I work with the individuals involved."

Six Scripture passages have been particularly helpful to Cauthen in problem solving. "God has given me, over a period of time, a set of Scripture references that are anchor points for me," he says. "I often repeat them back to God as a part of my prayer life with him."

> "Be strong and of a good courage . . . for the Lord thy God is with thee" (Josh. 1:9).

> "He shall choose our inheritance for us" (Ps. 47:4).

> "Cast thy burden upon the Lord, and he shall sustain thee" (Ps. 55:22).

> "If thou wouldest believe, thou shouldest see the glory of God" (John 11:40).

> "Have faith in God" (Mark 11:22).

> "And the man believed the word that Jesus had spoken unto him, and he went his way" (John 4:50).

He says softly, "I cannot put into words what these Scripture verses have meant to me in the long hours of many nights."

If there's a point at which Cauthen's preaching and his administration as a missionary statesman have come together, it's at the point of the missionary volunteer. Unlike some preachers, Cauthen is not a record keeper. Oh, he may be able to point out that there were ten thousand people present at a place where he spoke and that several hundred made decisions, but he doesn't keep records. Nor would there be any way for an interested person to secure such totals. For one thing, they would run into the tens of thousands. Hundreds have come at Falls Creek Assembly in Oklahoma as he served as camp pastor, hundreds more each summer at Ridgecrest and Glorieta, and hundreds more in state Baptist conventions, Baptist Student Union conventions, and evangelistic conferences. Scores have come in services in both large and small churches from the east coast to the west coast. Thousands have come in the Orient and in Africa and in Latin America to invitations he has extended.

Some have criticized him, saying that he moves so many people to make a personal response under the emotional strength of his message that he leaves behind him the problem of those who subsequently do not feel that they've been called. "He leaves a great guilt burden," one says.

Not surprisingly, Cauthen himself does not share that opinion. "When people respond to the best notion that God plants in their lives, they're never losers. They're always ahead. God may not continue to lead them in that path; but if they respond to the leadership that they have at that time, then it will be easier for them the next time God leads them."

Many of his invitations include this phrase: "Unless God closes the door or redirects your path, you will follow him to the mission field and serve there in his strength." Many people feel that the invitation needs to be more positive, that going overseas is not a matter of default but a matter of deep direction. Cauthen would agree, but the influence of Keith Falconer on him from his earliest days has not lessened. In his Bible he keeps on a small typed half-sheet of paper Falconer's words: "While vast continents are shrouded in almost utter darkness and hundreds of millions suffer the horrors of heathenism and Islam, the burden of proof lies upon you to show that the circumstances in which God has placed you were meant by him to keep you out of the mission field."

CHAPTER TEN

The Final Challenge

January 1974 opened a critical and perhaps final phase in Baker James Cauthen's administration as executive secretary of the Southern Baptist Convention's Foreign Mission Board. Whether the challenge emerged because of the spirit of the times, in the providence of God as a catalyst toward new growth, or as a power play within Southern Baptist life at a time when many felt that Cauthen, the "untouchable" who could not be "challenged," was because of age vulnerable, is at best speculation.

Prior to his sixty-fifth birthday, Cauthen asked the board to undertake a review of its retirement policy. The board fixed sixty-five as the normal retirement age for its executives with an annual review to continue up to age seventy.

Was Cauthen going to announce his retirement? Many asked. Cauthen doesn't talk about retirement, though there has been a lot of speculation as to who in his staff or who in Southern Baptist life might succeed him.

"When Cauthen leaves the board, the other agencies will swoop in to try to get a larger share of the pie," one Baptist editor predicts.

But Cauthen, under the strong urging of the board, was still on the scene in January of 1974 when a report of a Southern Baptist Executive Committee subcommittee called the Committe of Fifteen made Southern Baptist newspapers with what amounted to a series of challenges about the administration of each agency. The Foreign Mission Board was not spared; and though some people feel that Cauthen overreacted, everything within him was galvanized to answer. In some ways, all that he had done seemed to be up for judgment in what the Committee of Fifteen was suggesting. Some feel his decision to accept the board's option to continue past age sixty-five was made at this point.

The Executive Committee of the Southern Baptist Convention felt in the early seventies that it was time to take another look at the way the agencies had responded to a Southern Baptist Convention study made by a group called the Branch Committee in 1958 and 1959. A subcommittee was appointed to make this study, but later had their mandate expanded to study anything related to the agencies.

In January of 1974 the Committee of Fifteen released what amounted to a critique and a call for a "Southern Baptist Convention Executive Committee study of home and foreign mission strategy."

When Cauthen and fellow staff members began to read over the recommendations of the Committee of Fifteen, they collectively felt misrepresented in the implications of the critique and alarmed at its possible repercussions among the supporting constituency and its potential for the future.

Among the concerns expressed were the board's missionary education and promotion programs, its support of the Cooperative Program, its retirement program, "the problem of decline of potential candidates," the need to include objectives other than numbers of missionaries and number of fields, the possibility that the force was too thinly scattered, the committee's finding that "missionaries are resigning in number faster than in former years," a gap between overall administrative insight and local application of administrative policy, and the home office staff growth.

While the report cited positive values and called for cooperation in a major missions emphasis, its negative implications were stinging.

It was obvious to his staff that Cauthen was distressed over the report and frustrated that the subcommittee should recommend that the Convention's Executive Committee assume tasks that he felt had been traditionally entrusted to the agency itself and its elected board.

Cauthen called the Administrative Committee of the board to Richmond for an initial study. Together they called an extraordinary meeting of the Foreign Mission Board in February to study the document and to prepare a response to be brought to the Executive Committee meeting in Nashville in late February.

Cauthen and Douglas Hudgins, president of the board at that

time, were to bring the board's position before the Executive Committee and urge that the recommendations be recast.

Meanwhile, Cauthen took steps within his administrative staff itself. "No more hiring" was his order. In a growing missionary enterprise constantly expanding its efforts, this wasn't an easy order to receive or to effect.

"The old man's overreacting" was the word in the coffee shop. "He sees his whole administration as being up for judgment in this thing" was the reply. But nobody questioned the order.

Cauthen kept a weather eye on a number of indicators in his administrative reports each year. One was the number of staff members based in Richmond in relationship to the missionary staff and financial growth. A second was the percentage of dollars that went into the overseas section as over against the homeside section. For many years the amount had been 6 percent. Gradually, as officers were increasingly located in Richmond because their work dealt with many countries, the amount of money involved in the homeside budget had increased to 10 percent. Cauthen desperately wanted to hold the line at that point.

It was pointed out to him that 10 percent of the dollar being kept in administrative, informational, and support levels was almost unheard of. Similar agencies went as high as 25 percent and 30 percent. Others reasoned that part of that 10 percent was for overseas administration. But Cauthen was adamant, and the budget was pared back toward that goal year after year.

As the Executive Committee meeting in Nashville commenced on February 18, 1974, the agenda revealed that the discussion on the Committee of Fifteen report would come the next day. The Foreign Mission Board's posture was to answer the individual questions raised, to point out the danger of turning over to the Executive Committee matters that had been historically entrusted to the Foreign Mission Board itself, and to call the committee's attention anew to facts that Cauthen had voiced in his January report to the board:

"Remarkable progress has been made in foreign missions, not only since 1948 when the Advance Program was adopted, but as far back as 1933 when the recovery from debt and discouragement began. We have had forty years of steady progress and growth in the missionary enterprise. What has come about is actually a

266

phenomenon and stands as an example of what God can do in leading a people to concern, prayer, giving, and life dedication."

In part, the silent message was, "Let's not mess with something that's been so successful." Cauthen, ever constructive, was working toward another solution. Ask the committee to recast the recommendation, entrusting a strategy study to a special committee. Return that to the boards. Ask them to develop a strategy for the next twenty-five years that would truly challenge Southern Baptists. And then put together a Challenge Committee that would develop the dimensions of support that Southern Baptists must mobilize for such a dramatic task.

Late into the night on the eighteenth, Baker James Cauthen, Jesse Fletcher, and Winston Crawley discussed the matter with Owen Cooper, a Mississippi businessman with a deep love for missions who had served ably as president of the Southern Baptist Convention. Would Cooper sponsor such a substitute motion? Could he not see some of the dangers in his sharp change in polity?

But Cooper was persistent. The board had nothing to fear. The matter could only result in constructive recommendations. It would be much more effective coming from a group outside and able to begin without the burden of agency defensiveness. It seemed like a standoff. Late in the evening, Cauthen asked Cooper if he would be open to a substitute recommendation that Fletcher might draft and put in his hands early the next morning. Cooper said he would consider such.

With the goodwill and genuine affection that existed between Cooper and Cauthen very obvious, they parted. Cauthen instructed Fletcher on the dimensions such a recommendation should take. Fletcher completed it and put it in Cauthen's hands at breakfast the next morning, and Cauthen gave it to Cooper. That recommendation didn't make it to the floor; but neither did Cooper object when a substitute motion with the same implications carried the day.

The Foreign Mission Board's position was actually voiced by Douglas Hudgins. He spoke adroitly and, most felt, carried his point overwhelmingly. Then Cauthen stood up to speak. Several of his supporters felt that he needed to be very careful, that he could easily overstate the case. Many of them judged what resulted—an impassioned plea for the right of the Foreign Mission Board to continue the task that it had done under God's leadership and by God's grace so remarkably in the years that had preceded—as exactly that, an overstatement or an overkill.

There were some strong replies. One Executive Committee member suggested that Cauthen had impugned the motives of the Committee of Fifteen. Cauthen didn't reply but took several other verbal shots to the jaw before the discussion was finished.

John Hurt had predicted the night before, "Cauthen will get exactly what he wants." In fact, the motion was referred back to a subcommittee who would meet and draft a recommendation to be brought to the Convention. That recommendation would, in essence, commit the study of strategy to the boards themselves and the missions support matter to a blue-ribbon committee. The group who subsequently wrote the recommendations that went to the convention worked in an atmosphere of complete harmony. The matter had been resolved.

Several agency heads congratulated Cauthen and the Foreign Mission Board and suggested that they had carried the day on behalf of all the agencies. Others felt they had almost lost it by overkill. Actually, the whole emotional furor died down rapidly. In retrospect, the feelings that were present at that time are hard to reconstruct.

But they were there. The *Baptist Standard* editor, John Jeter Hurt, sensed Cauthen's feelings and wrote him two days later:

> "Dear Baker,
> I think I know you well enought to know you are suffering tremendously today for having been forced into a verbal battle, and it's entirely possible your suffering is even greater because you were victorious."

This paragraph reveals how well Hurt understood Cauthen. Again and again, he was accused of winning his battle but of feeling so distressed about it that he gave away the spoils. But layman Hurt felt the need to minister to the missionary statesman he admired so much. He went on:

> "The penalty of leadership is conflict. Some of the conflict must be with those outside of immediate administrative responsibility. And some of it, of course, is within the official

family. You would not be true to your own stewardship of the Foreign Mission Board if you had failed to express an opinion. So find your comfort in your integrity of expression."

Voicing his opinion that ultimately the report would be healthy and would cause people to do some needed study, Hurt closed with another bit of wisdom and incredible insight into Cauthen's makeup:

"Conflict should concern many of us more than it does. Conflict should concern you much less than it does. I write only because I thought you might be interested in the observation of one who was sitting on the sidelines."

But Cauthen never winced from the implications of what did result. He set about to mobilize his staff and the missionary enterprise throughout the world and to enlist national colleagues in developing "Bold New Plans."

Thirteen committees made up of staff and board members were called together. A consultation was hastily set up for the summer of 1975 in Miami Beach, where the earlier one that had been a part of the new Advance Program in 1965 had been held.

In the next months, as he worked day and night to move his staff resolutely toward the development of the Bold New Plans, Cauthen looked like anything but a man ready to retire. He accepted the challenge for his final years in leadership at the Foreign Mission Board in terms of stating the plans and beginning their implementation. At the Convention in 1976 he presented them. They were, as he later summarized them in a special communication with the nearly 2,700 missionaries deployed by that year in eighty-four countries, as follows:

1. The great overarching objective is to preach the gospel to all the people in the world.

2. A 100 percent increase in missionary staff—more than five thousand by A.D. 2000.

3. Missionaries at work in at least 125 countries as God may lead.

4. Accelerated tempo of volunteer lay involvement—up to three thousand persons per year needed now and up to ten thousand per year by A.D. 2000.

5. Greatly expanded efforts in evangelism—major thrusts in urban areas and among students and other young people.

6. Tenfold multiplication of overseas churches—with parallel increases in baptism and church membership.

7. Extraordinary efforts in leadership training through strengthened seminaries, theological education by extension, and lay leadership training.

8. Vastly increased use of radio, television, and publications on mission fields and penetration by means of mass media of areas not presently open to missionary activities.

9. Accentuated attention to human need—through health care, disease prevention, benevolent and social ministries.

10. Vigorous, appropriate, and prompt response to world hunger and disasters.

It seemed that the closer Cauthen came to retirement, the more intense the work became. These new dimensions would have to be implemented with a whole new round of staff growth. The Mission Support Division head, Fletcher, feeling a strong mandate from his Lord, departed to take a pastorate. Reorganization in that division on one hand and a sharply escalated expansion of the Overseas Division staff on the other was demanding. A former area secretary, Keith Parks, succeeded Fletcher.

There were new challenges. "The Foreign Mission Board wasn't doing enought to respond to human tragedy." So-called "slow responses" to hurricane devastation in Honduras, to earthquake devastation in Guatemala, to a typhoon in Bangladesh, and to famine in West Africa took their turn on the stage as documentation for charges against the board. John Jeter Hurt was among those leading the criticism.

Once again, as the board had witnessed in earlier years in evangelism, unilateral efforts began to flourish. Cauthen spoke out again and again, pointing out that Southern Baptists looked to the Foreign Mission Board to be their channel for relief and that Baptists could use this channel to their fullest desire to respond to world suffering. This was a response to the growing numbers of organizations that began asking for the Southern Baptist relief dollar and also a response to the unilateral relief efforts being mounted in some quarters.

Baker James Cauthen addressing a group of Southwestern Baptist Theological Seminary graduates

Once again, as he had done with world evangelism, Cauthen put a special staff member on this task. Eugene Grubbs, a former state executive secretary, had been brought on the staff to effect a utilization of laymen in the overseas program. But he found that the emergency relief program was a more demanding issue.

In late 1976 Cauthen found interest within his own board regarding his retirement plans. At the October board meeting, members discussed the best way to approach his replacement when that time would inevitably come. No action was taken, however. He submitted humbly to the annual call, which was based on a physical examination and a report of a special committee, and moved on to effect the new "final quarter of this century's plans."

His surgery slowed him down some. Cauthen watchers said, "He didn't bounce back as he used to." Others more knowledgeable of the constitution of sixty-seven-year-old men said, "Look how he's come back. It's remarkable."

In the spring of 1977 the Foreign Mission Board held its annual meeting in Atlanta, Georgia, at the Omni, the city's huge convention center. Baptists came from all over the state and surrounding states. Over fourteen thousand of them gathered in the Omni to watch the missionary appointment service. At the board's urging, Cauthen preached. His finger thrust toward the heavens. His voice rose and fell and built and grew hushed and exploded with the excitement he felt about what God had called his people to do and with the imperative he continued to feel to go into all the world. Southern Baptists, who had grown used to his voice, never seemed to respond to it more. Over two hundred responded to an invitation to mission service extended at the end of his message.

As they filed down the aisles he stood waiting, his forehead glistening from the sweat of his efforts and his eyes alight with the pure joy he felt in preaching "the unsearchable riches" of the Lord Jesus Christ. He was, as so many people had come to see him and as in the providence of God he had become,

A MAN FOR ALL NATIONS.